P9-CLV-553

GOOD FRIDAY ON THE REZ

GOOD FRIDAY ON THE REZ

A PINE RIDGE ODYSSEY

DAVID HUGH BUNNELL

ST. MARTIN'S PRESS NEW YORK

Printed in the United States of America. For information, address St. Martin's Press, 175 Fifth Avenue, New York, N.Y. 10010.

www.stmartins.com

Designed by Anna Gorovoy

Photographs by David Bunnell unless noted otherwise

Map by Ken Kalman

The Library of Congress Cataloging-in-Publication Data is available upon request.

ISBN 978-1-250-11253-8 (hardcover)
ISBN 978-1-250-11254-5 (e-book)

First Edition: April 2017

10 9 8 7 6 5 4 3 2 1

Hoka hey!

Dedicated to Vernell White Thunder

and the Oglala Lakota Nation

CONTENTS

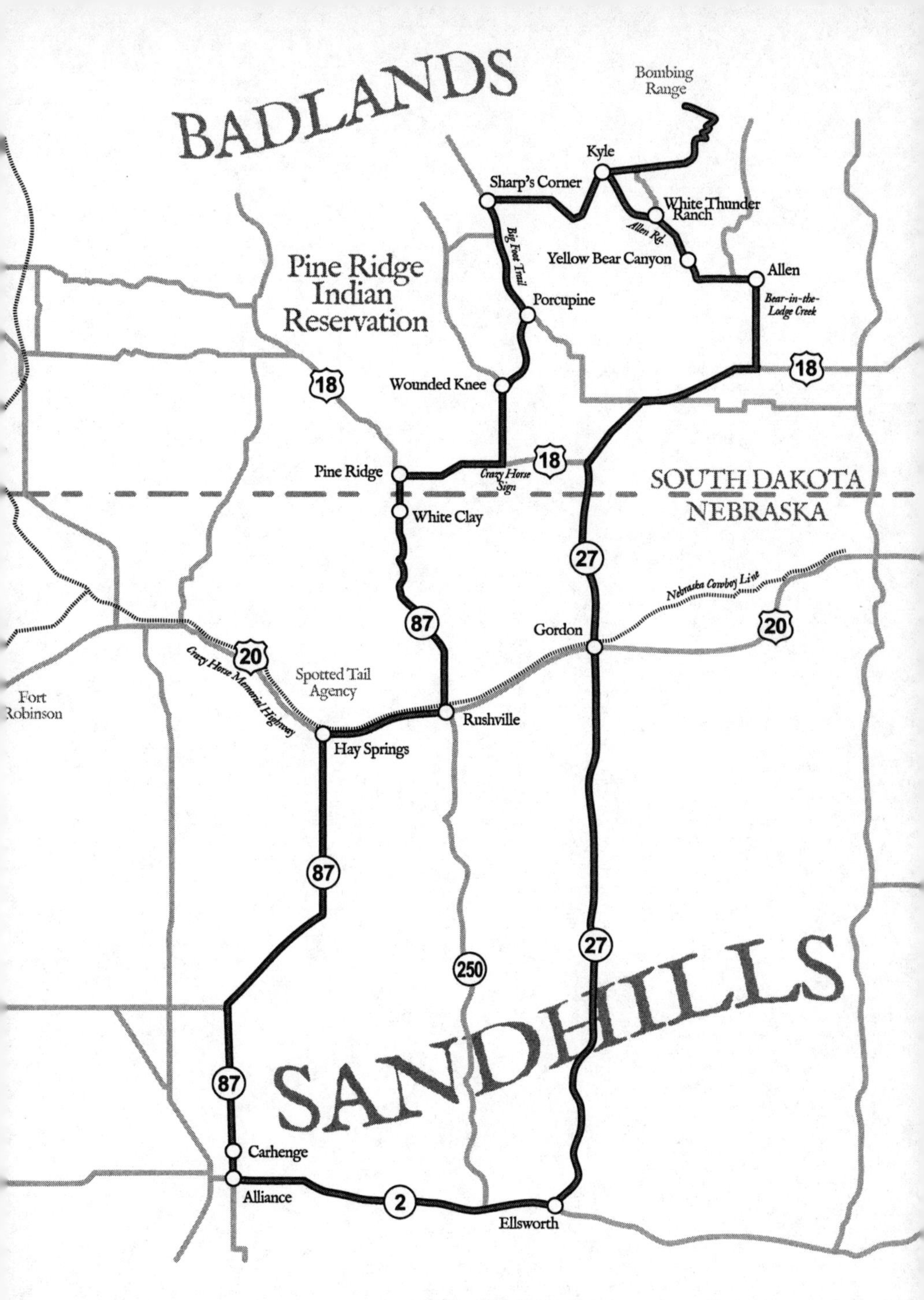

Moon of the Birth Calves
Good Friday, 2014

We had buffalo for food, and their hides for clothing and our tipis. We preferred hunting to a life of idleness on the reservations, where we were driven against our will. . . . We preferred our own way of living. We were no expense to the government then. All we wanted was peace and to be left alone.

—CRAZY HORSE, "I HAVE SPOKEN"

OVERTURE

Sandhills Sandwich Town

I can still feel my wet bare feet
slippin' on the hot summer concrete
coming home from your old swimming pool
Alliance, you are the Sandhills' sandwich town
with country-fried-chicken hospitality
so proud to be white-skinned
churchgoing and somewhat dim
Bible school, Boy Scouts, and bigotry
the mighty Lakota Sioux falling-down drunk
in your gutters
unending arrests, subsequent suicides
four dead in the time it takes a life to begin
AND I WON'T LET YOU FORGET
Jo No Leaf
Chillo Whirlwind
Arthur Gene Black Horse
Irene Blackfeather

not even Clarence Pumpkin Seed
the 250 times you locked him up
before they found him frozen stiff
in Whiteclay
so picture Chillo, at eighteen he's kicking
the wastebasket he's standing on
picture his bath-towel necktie
picture Gene's thin leather belt
and Jo's wine-stained sweatshirt
picture them dangling
in your jail cells
after they cut the bodies down
picture poor Irene coughing her lungs out
your chief cop who thought
she was just inebriated
and your doctor whose sleep
was more important than her life
then picture
the agony of nails pounded through the hands
of Jesus Christ

—David Hugh Bunnell
Published in the *Alliance Times-Herald*
October 15, 1971

ACT ONE

Memory is like riding a trail at night with a lighted torch. The torch casts its light only so far, and beyond that is the darkness.

—OLD LAKOTA SAYING

ALLIANCE

NO DOGS OR INDIANS ALLOWED

What luxury to wake up naked, a crisp morning breeze coming through the open window, my legs curled together to keep myself warm, clean sheets, cheap but adequate pillows on a king-size bed in a motel room alone, peacefully listening to the *chirp-chirp, chirp-chirp-chirp* of a western meadowlark, the buzz of a single-prop plane high overhead, the deep crunch of train cars coupling in the nearby railroad yard. I have much to look forward to today. Good Friday. Today I take my little yellow Volkswagen rental on a 280-mile round-trip from my hometown, Alliance, Nebraska, to the poorest community in America, the Pine Ridge Indian Reservation in South Dakota, to hang out with my blood brother Vernell White Thunder, whom I've talked hours to but haven't seen in a long time; I just want to sit in his living room, drink copious amounts of Susie's "cowboy coffee," and relive the many profound and sometimes funny moments we've had over many years in many places—Kyle and Wanblee on the rez; me trying to teach him to spell, him trying to teach me how to ride horse bareback; our silly idea about drinking Navajo girls under the bar in downtown Albuquerque; our Indian horse ranch in Boulder, Colorado, which we named Tiyospaya;

the little matter of the Buffalo Ranch; and the unresolved dispute over which of us danced with Jane Fonda. But first I must go for a swim.

Now residing in California, with my parents long gone and very few friends in the area, I don't visit often. My Lebanese former in-laws still live here, and I love seeing them, but not staying in Alliance, which might well be the most boring town in America; people drive five miles an hour down the middle of main street, park on the wrong side of the road, smoke inside the stores. I try hard to stay healthy at the only motel with a swimming pool, but this is hardly a Ritz-Carlton or Four Seasons. Perhaps it is a cut above the other motels here because it has an indoor swimming pool, but the pool is not long enough for lap swimming, and you can hardly get your heart pumping by splashing around. The best news is that they have a hot tub. I slip out of bed directly into my suit, grab the room key, head out, and amble down the hallway, only to discover a hand-scrawled sign on the door to the pool: CLOSED FOR MAINTENANCE. So I march to the front desk to inquire how long the pool will be closed.

The twentysomething clerk, a local girl with orange-and-blue hair and numerous piercings, says, "All weekend."

This is clearly wrong. I am on the verge of demanding a refund and moving across the road to the American Inn, which, by the way, is half the price. But before I start shouting, the older, mellow me emerges; obviously, this poor girl is powerless—she knows nothing about the pool, why it is closed, or why it will take all weekend to clean the scum off the surface.

I say, "Okay; thanks."

I skulk back to my room next to the noisy soft drink vending machine to work out with the latex stretch bands I fortuitously stashed in my carry-on bag yesterday before taking an Uber to the Oakland Airport. Exercise is my elixir, my antidote to premature aging.

During the 1950s and '60s, before America was thoroughly homogenized, when I still liked it here, Alliance had no Holiday Inn Express, Motel 6, McDonald's, Kmart, Pizza Hut, 7-Eleven, or Dunkin'

Donuts. Hard to imagine, but we had two proper hotels: the downtown Drake Hotel and the Alliance Hotel across from the train station, both locally owned with real lobbies, bellhops, public dining rooms, full bars, and banquet halls. When my parents could afford it, I loved eating in these hotels—chicken-fried steak on mashed potatoes smothered with onion gravy was my go-to favorite. Alliance also had two drugstores with classic '50s-style lunch counters, soda fountains, and jukeboxes. My mom worked at a shoe store called Howard's—Howard and his wife were family friends—and my dad was the editor of the local paper. My best friend Nace's dad worked at the Maytag appliance store, one of the few national businesses. There were three ice cream stands, one of which stayed open all year round even when the temperature dipped below zero, and two family hamburger places, the better of which was Rex's Hamburgers, where they sold fifteen-cent miniature burgers fried in three inches of grease on a smoky-hot griddle, served in little square dinner rolls—juicy and delicious; my brother and I could eat dozens. The grocery stores were all family owned; no chains until a Safeway opened up in 1962. Hardware stores, auto shops, a lumberyard, the farm implement company, an honest-to-Jesus smoke-filled pool hall with eight-ball and snooker tables, a drive-in movie theater where you could eat popcorn and lose your virginity while watching Jerry Lewis in *The Bellboy*, and a downtown movie theater that sponsored Saturday morning kiddie shows where during intermission Pepe the Clown (local sign painter Leonard Glarum) would drive his toy clown car out on the stage, make silly jokes, and hand out dorky prizes. Strategically located next to the movie theater was a candy store, and not far away were an all-night bakery *and* a doughnut shop.

Unlike with today's big-box stores in small-town franchise-dominated economies, most of the money made in Alliance stayed in Alliance; it was not siphoned off to some distant corporate headquarters in the Cayman Islands. People in Alliance felt prosperous and safe; they seldom bothered to lock their houses or car doors. On my tenth birthday, my parents gave me a Black Phantom Schwinn bicycle that elevated my status among my friends and brought me freedom and great joy. I could pedal anywhere—to the swimming pool, school, the movies, friends' houses, the soda fountain—and park without worry. My bike would be there when I needed it. I wasn't even aware that there was such a thing as a bicycle lock, much less a bicycle thief.

We lived in a Norman Rockwell painting during the 1950s, then moved on to *American Graffiti* in the '60s. Lily-white Alliance had one poor black family, the Chandlers. An iconic sight was Old Man Hayes Chandler driving his horse and wagon through the alleyways to haul away discarded things for housewives. When I was a small boy, like many local children when I saw Mr. Chandler, I waved and hollered, and he always stopped to give me a ride on the back of the wagon, all the way to the end of the block. His grandson Ernie was the star center on our high school basketball team, and his younger grandson, Leroy, was the star running back on the football team. He also had two granddaughters, and there was a grandmother, Florence, but no parents in the Chandler household, as the grandchildren's mother, Myrtle—Hayes's daughter—died giving birth to her last child.

Alliance had a handful of Mexicans, mostly seasonal farm laborers who lived outside of town in field-side shanties provided by the farmers who hired them to pick sugar beets and potatoes. The few other Mexicans were "true" Mexican-Americans, people whose families preceded Europeans in settling in the Southwest from Texas to California, and also next-door Colorado—a vast swath of North America, which before the 1848 Treaty of Guadalupe Hidalgo was part of Mexico. One of these was my classmate and friend Tom Flores, a handsomely chiseled brown-skinned boy with a magnetic smile who was a track and wrestling star yet couldn't get a date to the prom.

The only significant minority in Alliance was the indigenous population—four hundred or five hundred tortured souls—Native Americans, mostly Lakota, whom white people, when they weren't using pejoratives such as "Injun," "redskin," or "savage," referred to as Sioux, slang for "snake," a nickname given to them by early French trappers. Some had families who had lived in Alliance for generations; others had been recruited from the reservations in South Dakota during World War II to help build the Alliance Army Airfield, which served as a training center for paratroopers and military police attack dogs. Some had arrived more recently for part-time work in the beet and potato fields, to break horses on nearby ranches, or to sweep sidewalks and shovel snow for local businesses. Many traveled back and forth from the reservations; others became permanent residents. Vernell White Thunder's mom and dad met in Alliance during the summer of 1952, when they were picking potatoes. They got married, moved to Kyle, and never returned. Had they stayed, Vernell and I likely would have grown up in the same small town, but it is unlikely we would have met because I am seven years his senior. Or perhaps not. Vernell's outgoing personality has led him to become acquainted with many people of all ages, native and white. My first wife, Linda, and I got to know Vernell when he started hanging out in our Bureau of Indian Affairs (BIA) teacher housing unit in Kyle at age twelve, and other than him and his younger brother, Anthony, we got to know very few students, as fraternization with teachers was frowned upon. Had Vernell been born in Alliance, like most Lakota he would have lived in a squalid tent city on the other side of the railroad tracks that looked like a Middle East refugee camp. I can remember peering out the back window of our car when my dad drove by "Indian Town," wondering why the Indians didn't live in tepees. When the snow melted or when it rained, the area around the tents and the dirt roads turned into gooey mud intertwined with puddles of burnt umber. It was impossible for children or adults to keep the muck off their shoes, much less keep it out of the tents. During severe blizzards or thunderstorms, people were forced to use galvanized buckets for going to the bathroom, later disposing of the waste in one of the outdoor johns. There were no baths or showers. When people got sick, a frequent occurrence among children and elders, the local doctors refused to see them unless they paid an office visit fee of seven dollars ahead of time. Otherwise they had to brave out their illnesses or somehow travel to the Indian clinic in Pine Ridge.

As a young boy, I wasn't conscious of all these indignities and many others, but I do remember the ubiquitous NO DOGS OR INDIANS ALLOWED signs. They were displayed in the hotels and café windows, above cash registers, and even used as neon signs outside the bars. Most folks in Alliance said you should ignore the ugliness, but thanks to working on my dad's newspaper, I knew what racism was. I had seen photographs of the fire hoses, read the racists' insults and found them offensive, and never believed you should "turn the other cheek." If the intention of these local bigots was to denigrate the local natives, for me, it only elevated the natives. The Native Americans I got to know were exuberant, expressive, creative, and fun. Perhaps this explains why two of my best grade school friends, Timothy Good Shot and Elgin Bad Wound, were Indian boys. I was attracted to their craziness; they were wolf cubs who came right out of *National Geographic*, determined to live large no matter which direction they were pointed in. These Indian boys were different from my white friends. We bonded instantly. Beginning in the sixth grade, we met after school at the public basketball court in the park behind my house to scrimmage and play an endless shooting-skills game they appropriately called "Crazy Horse." But then one day after spring break, Timothy failed to show up and, sadly, I never saw him again. I worried. Elgin said the Good Shots had moved back to the reservation so Timothy's parents could enroll him in a government school, but I often wondered what became of him. When Elgin Wound disappeared too, I really started to worry, but eight years later I unexpectedly met up with him in the parking lot of the big shopping center in Pine Ridge during a Columbus Day protest demonstration, and I was amazed to learn that he had a PhD, was superintendent of the nearby Oglala Lakota College, wasn't diabetic, and seemed to have a happy family with many children, each of them enjoying the powwow part of the protest, all into Indian Pride. But Elgin still knew nothing about the whereabouts of the Good Shots.

Because Indians in Alliance weren't allowed in the bars, they drank in the streets and alleyways, and because public drunkenness was a crime, many were arrested, some frequently. Too poor to pay their fines, they languished in jail. To get out early, they worked on the street-sweeping and trash-hauling crews, and when the crews were short-handed, the cops simply rounded up a few more Indians. How funny we thought their names were when we read about their arrests and court appearances in the newspaper—Arthur Big Mouth, Jesse Kicking Bear, Martha Lame Deer, and, in particular, Clarence Pumpkin Seed, because he was arrested and convicted 250 times. This absurdity ceased to be funny long before it ceased to be funny, when during a nine-month Hell span from October 1970 to June 1971, four Indian prisoners on four different occasions died or were murdered in the Alliance City Jail. As we liked to say back then, "The shit really hit the fan this time!"

Arthur Gene Black Horse, age twenty-seven, was the first to go. Busted for prowling and intoxication late on Friday night, October 30, Black Horse allegedly wrapped a thin leather belt around his neck and tied the end of it to a cell bar. Twice, they say, the leather broke; twice he tied it back together. When it finally held long enough, Black Horse fell dead to the concrete floor, the belt dangling from the cell bar. Frequently arrested, mostly for drunkenness but once for removing a screen window from a house in the better part of town, Black Horse lived in a two-room shack with thirty-four other Indians, adults and children. Assuming the circumstances of his death as reported by the burly Alliance police chief Verlin Hutton are true, the obvious question is why did he have a belt? Was he properly searched? When *Kansas City Star* reporter Robert Dye asked Hutton about this, the police chief, staring at the belt in question curled into a tiny ball in his massive hand, said he didn't know how Black Horse got it. "He may have hidden it inside his trousers."

Hutton recalled that on the same day years ago, when he was a rookie cop, Black Horse's father hanged himself from the family tent pole by tying a rope around his neck and simply sitting down. "Arthur Gene Black Horse," he claimed, "told another inmate it was the anniversary of his father's death." Hutton speculated that grief had driven him to do it, and then added, "You know, the relatives who watched his father kill himself made no attempt to pick up a nearby ax to cut him down."

Jo No Leaf, thirty-four, was next. A few weeks after Black Horse's reported suicide, No Leaf allegedly used a water hose to hang himself in a shower stall in the drunk tank. Picked up for drinking in public and disturbing the peace, No Leaf had been in many drunken brawls; his jaw was wired shut from a recent fight. Refused admittance into the Alliance hospital, he somehow got to the hospital in Pine Ridge, was treated, and came back. Unable to eat, No Leaf sustained himself mostly on cheap wine that he sucked through a straw. No Leaf had no home; he usually slept in a dilapidated car in the city junkyard.

When asked why Alliance cops arrested drunken Indians while they never arrested intoxicated whites, Hutton remarked, "The Elks Club has a tendency to take care of their own."

The third Alliance City Jail victim was an eighteen-year-old named Chillo Whirlwind. In the wee hours of an early June morning, on the thirty-fourth day of his imprisonment, he allegedly stood on a wastebasket with a towel around his neck. After tying the towel to a cell bar, he kicked the wastebasket across the floor, which had to have made a loud, banging sound. Police Chief Hutton complained that Whirlwind's dozing cellmates failed to wake up. Two years earlier, Chillo had been sent to the Nebraska State Reform School for Juvenile Offenders in Kearney, Nebraska, where he got into frequent fights with other kids and was often placed in solitary confinement. Back in Alliance only a couple of months, Chillo was arrested for breaking into a gas station. It is said that when he was two years old, his mother gave him up for adoption to the Swalley family, whose immigrant forefather came to

Nebraska from Lancashire, England, and married a Lakota woman who may have been Chillo's great-aunt. When a city councilman suggested the police install a closed-circuit TV system in the city jail to better monitor the prisoners, Police Chief Hutton huffed, "Some of our jail guards are women, and I can't have women watching the sex acts that go on in the drunk tank."

And finally there was Irene Blackfeather, forty-three, whose death later that same month may have been the most disturbing of all. Sick and lying in a pool of blood and vomit, she moaned and cried in agony while her sister Betty, in the next jail cell, yelled out for the cops to call a doctor. Police Chief Hutton, on duty at the time, ignored Irene's cries and Betty's pleas until they became unbearable. When he finally came up the stairs to the cellblock to tell "those noisy squaw bitches to shut up," Irene had passed out and was barely breathing. Hutton called for an ambulance, but it was too late; Irene was DOA at the emergency room.

Bad press and the fact that Irene was the fourth to die in a short period prompted the governor of Nebraska, J. James Exon, to call for a grand jury investigation. As part of the investigation, an autopsy on Irene's body was ordered, and when confronted with the news that she had died from pneumonia complicated by cirrhosis, Hutton complained, "God, we're not doctors!"

Sadly but predictably, the investigation turned out to be a whitewash—Chief Hutton and his merry band of bigots were exonerated. Reports that the Alliance cops arbitrarily arrested Indians to work on the street-cleaning crew, beat them in jail and allowed them to fight among themselves until bloody handprints could be seen on the cell walls, sexually abused women prisoners, and staged suicides were found by the grand jury to be based on rumor and hearsay. The suicides in Alliance, the jurors concluded, were not attributable to criminal negligence by the police but were the "tragic consequence of the socio-economic conditions under which the Indians live."

Outraged, I wrote the protest poem that serves as the overture of this libretto, and submitted it to the *Alliance Times-Herald* for the annual "Poetry Day" edition. Of course, my father, who was the editor, published it, but I rather wish he hadn't positioned it as the lead poem in the two-page section. My words ignited a firestorm—subscriptions were canceled and advertising pulled, and letters to the editor flooded the newsroom; at home my dad received anonymous threatening phone calls and my mom was embarrassed. I became a persona non grata.

Thinking about good old Alliance, how wonderful and yet how monstrous it was, makes me super hungry. Holiday Inn Express prides itself on the "free" breakfast brunch it serves every morning, and I know people who say it is delicious, but what do they know? OK, I admit that living on the West Coast has spoiled me food-wise forever. I refuse to eat microwaved biscuits, yogurt infused with high-fructose corn syrup, powdered eggs, chewy toast with fake butter, sugar-laden cereals—at least the Holiday Inn has real bananas picked from real banana trees (I presume), and the coffee, while it looks and tastes like it was brewed during the Eisenhower administration, does the trick as long as I drink a lot of it and drink it black, without the complementary powdered cream. Banana, black coffee, plus a tangerine and a few almonds from my travel bag, and I am good to go.

Alliance is a small town in an area of Nebraska called the "Panhandle," because if you look at a Nebraska map, the state is shaped like a pan and Alliance is in the middle of the handle. Founded by land speculators in 1888 at the north-south, east-west junction of the Burlington and Missouri River Railroad, the town grew quickly, populated by Civil War veterans and European immigrants drawn by the promise of "free" land courtesy of the Homestead Act, the claim size having recently been increased from 160 acres to 640 acres (equivalent to one square mile). Never mind that in 1868 this land had been ceded by treaty to the Lakota Sioux Nation.

Due to the lack of law enforcement, Alliance also attracted a subculture of thieves, prostitutes, and escaped convicts. Within a few years, the population grew to five thousand as churches, hotels, schools, and farm and ranch supply businesses sprang up alongside the saloons and whorehouses. Ranchers and homesteaders traveled to Alliance by horseback and wagon from as far away as Torrence, Wyoming, to trade and buy goods, gamble, get drunk, and get laid.

The terrain north and west of Alliance has always been much the same—boring patches of flat farmland where farmers mostly grow wheat, potatoes, barley, and sugar beets. South and east of Alliance is dramatically different, breathtakingly beautiful—the Nebraska Sandhills, twenty thousand square miles of semi-arid sand dunes pockmarked by hundreds of spring-fed ponds and lakes, with a thin coating of prairie grass, a frozen ocean of green-gold-brown colors stretching out to faraway horizons, and a vast metallic-blue sky arching overhead.

In more recent times, the consolidation of farms and ranches and the flight of young people to bigger cities have depopulated most of the surrounding Nebraska towns, but Alliance keeps on growing thanks to the little railway company Nebraska mogul Warren Buffett purchased in 2007 for the bargain price of $44 billion. Every day, hundreds of 120-car Burlington Northern Santa Fe trains slowly rumble through Alliance. They haul coal from the Powder River Basin in Wyoming or crude oil from the fracking operations in North Dakota—and Alliance is not just a point on the map that these sooty trains pass through, it is also the location of a huge locomotive repair shop, by far the city's largest employer.

But now it is time to let my adventure begin. Back in my room I grab my camera and head outside to my yellow Mexican VW rental car, which I have decided to christen *Villa VW* in honor of the great revolutionary hero Pancho Villa, because building Volkswagens in Mexico is definitely revolutionary, isn't it? There's a cold, bright sun peeking over the horizon, but my iPhone tells me it's going to be an unusually warm

Good Friday, with temperatures in the mid to high seventies. Already, cars are parked at the Arby's drive-through across the highway from the Holiday Inn Express, and there are more at McDonald's. I notice that the Kmart opposite McDonald's is also open and can't help recall a recent book I read called *The Magician's Assistant*, by Ann Patchett, which takes place in Alliance some year during the freezing days of February, a time when according to Ms. Patchett, many locals, including teachers and students, meet up with each other and find refuge from the cold in Kmart. I'm wondering if they are doing that now. Driving out from my designated Holiday Inn courtesy parking onto East Third, a brick-paved road, *Villa VW* and I cruise past the Wonderful Kitchen Chinese takeout and head directly under the railroad underpass where as a high school sophomore my brother, Roger, tried to outrun the local cops. His souped-up Chevy Impala was definitely up to the task, but unluckily, Roger spun out across the highway into a pillar and ended up spending his next six weekends in the county jail. There are so many things to remember driving down the streets of Alliance. There's Ken and Dales Restaurant, where I should have had breakfast, but there is no time for that now. Vernell is waiting and I can't wait to see him.

A few minutes later I'm outside the Alliance city limits, driving past my old classmate Jim Furman's sprawling ranch house, his veterinary center and horse corrals and the prefab metal barn where in the summer of 1995 we had our thirtieth high school reunion dance in ridiculous ninety-degree heat, an overflowing beer keg on the straw floor and a tape player barking out country tunes. I could see right away which of my classmates had moved to Colorado or California and which ones had stayed in Nebraska—the exiles looked trim and healthy in their Polo outfits; the left-behinds were much heavier, and decidedly less stylish. I smile thinking of the impression my wife and I must have made with our in-your-face interracial family: my dark, large-framed stepdaughter, Jazz, her massive dreadlocks piled on her head like a coiled boa constrictor; my toddler granddaughter, Jamaica, so precious with designer wire-rim glasses magnifying her sparkling brown eyes; and especially Darrell, Jazz's latest boyfriend, fresh out of San Quentin, licorice-black, pick comb sticking straight up from his head, a true pioneer of the sagging-pants look. At all times, Darrell was on DEFCON 1 alert for racial slights—poised to confront local cowboys who happened to look at him in the wrong way.

News that my crew and I were going up to the reservation over the coming Fourth of July weekend for a powwow at Vernell White Thunder's ranch along with my friends Dennis and Connie McCullah; Don Nace and his wife, Linda; and their unsuspecting children only added to the shock value. One of my ex-girlfriends warned Linda to stay in the car. "White women who venture onto the reservation," she said, "get killed *or worse*," which would have made me laugh if it hadn't been so stupid.

So little traffic. Windows down, I can take in the clean country air, hear my tires humming on recently repaved blacktop. I'm only seven miles down the road, but already I need to make a pit stop because I drank so much weak coffee. So I stop at Carhenge—an odd replica of Stonehenge formed by thirty-eight classic cars from the 1950s and '60s, uniformly coated with gray spray paint. Without seeking the advice or consent of the locals, farmer Jim Reinders buried some of these cars upright in five-foot pits and welded others on top to form Stonehenge-like arches—on his own land, mind you, but within clear sight of the highway. The citizens were scandalized; they insisted Reinders dismantle his atrocity, which surely would turn Alliance into the laughingstock of the nation.

And then, as Reinders was wrangling with the city council over a business permit, an online travel Web site, TripAdvisor, named Carhenge one of "America's Top Roadside Attractions," and the tourists started coming. Carhenge was featured in a network TV commercial.

More tourists came. Some stayed overnight, gassed up and ate in Alliance, even wrote appreciative letters to the *Alliance Times-Herald*. Reinders suddenly became a local hero. These days people from Alliance love Carhenge; if you happen to run into one of them, say in Pocatello, Idaho, they will invariably ask, "Have you been to Carhenge?"

HAY SPRINGS

WHY CROW DOG WAS SET FREE

How many years has it been since I've had to slow to a crawl for some crazy-ass farmer driving a tractor right down the middle of the goddamn highway? I wonder as I patiently wait for my opportunity to zoom by. The odds that I can safely go around him are ten thousand to one in my favor, no need to worry, these roads are deserted, but then I think of my boyhood friend, twelve-year-old Buddy Oswald, riding his bicycle not far from here, probably daydreaming when he crossed the road right in front of a semitruck. They say he was decapitated. Buddy's death was my earliest experience with traumatic death. So many people came to Buddy's funeral that they couldn't cram them all into the church, so they piped the sound outside. I was one of those outside. His mom was crying and carrying on so much it was hard to hear the pastor, but I do distinctly remember him saying it was part of God's plan for Buddy to die, to be snatched away from his family, and as hard as it was to understand, we must accept this. "Buddy is in Heaven now," the pastor said. "He's playing with other prematurely dead children, waiting for the rest of us."

Now that I have at last passed the tractor, I can see for miles and miles ahead as I enter what locals call the "Box Butte Tableland"—flat and nearly featureless endless brown-yellow stubble on my left side, field of pale green on my right, most likely cover crop, ryegrass or buckwheat. Cloudless, the sky looks two-dimensional, a muddy canvas of splotchy blues.

This small tip of the North American prairie was once part of the Great Sioux Reservation, an immense twenty-five-million-acre expanse stretching from the Yellowstone River in Montana across eastern Wyoming, including a slice of North Dakota, the western half of South Dakota, most of western Nebraska, and parts of northeastern Colorado, blanketed with mixed short and long grasses—buffalo, porcupine grass, switch grass, and Indian grass—interspersed with a kaleidoscope of colors impossible to duplicate in man-made gardens: violet and indigo flowers, white and purple prairie clover, black-eyed Susans, wild licorice and strawberries, goldenrods, prickly pear, sage, purple coneflowers, wild onions, prairie turnips, gooseberry and chokecherry bushes. An inland sea of nutrition teeming with fat prairie chickens, grouse, and quail, great herds of elk, mule deer, pronghorn antelopes, and tens of millions of buffalo. There were also wolves and grizzlies, but no fences, no farms, no roads, no telegraph poles or railroad tracks.

The Fort Laramie Treaty of 1868, ratified by the U.S. Senate, granted the Great Sioux Reservation to the Lakota people in perpetuity. The "country north of the North Platte river and east of the summits of the Bighorn mountains" was to remain unceded, meaning no white person or persons would "be permitted to pass over, settle upon, or reside in the territory." Included was an isolated mountain range in present-day northwest South Dakota, the Black Hills (Paha Sapa), sacred to the Lakota and the Cheyenne—thusly named because the pine-covered slopes appear to be black when viewed from a distance.

A mere six years after the treaty was signed, Civil War hero "Boy General" George Armstrong Custer embarked on a "scientific mapping expedition" through the Black Hills. You might think such a mission would require a dozen men on horseback and perhaps another dozen pack horses, but sensing an opportunity to advance his growing public profile and his ambitions for the White House, Custer turned his little treaty-violating adventure into a virtual invasion of Indian lands by hauling along more than a hundred wagons and nearly a thousand men—soldiers, bandits, prospectors, thugs, Indian scouts, newspaper writers, and, for cover, one paleontologist, one geologist, one topologist, and one botanist. He did not bother to notify or seek permission from the Indians. Thus, August 2, 1874, became a very sad day in the history of the Lakota people when the prospectors accompanying Custer's outing found traces of gold in the gravel bed of an intermittent stream called French Creek, near where it empties into the Cheyenne River. One of the scouts who witnessed this historic moment of discovery, a Yankton Lakota known as Goose, reportedly said, "The whites threw their hats in the air, jumped up and down, and ran in circles like headless prairie chickens. Laughing, screaming—I could not understand. A few specks of yellow dust made them crazy."

Embedded correspondent William Curtis understood well enough. The *Chicago Inter Ocean* newspaper published his sensationalized version of the discovery on August 17 under a one-word banner headline:

GOLD!

> From the grassroots down, it was pay dirt; all the camp was aglow with gold fever. Shovels and spades, picks, axes, tent-pins, pot hooks, bowie knives, mess pans, kettles, plates, platters, tin cups, and everything within reach that could either lift dirt or hold it was put into service by the worshipers of that god, gold. . . . The expedition has solved the mystery of the Black Hills, and

> will carry back the news that there is gold here, in quantities as rich as were ever dreamed of.

Curtis's article—reprinted in papers around the world—inspired thousands of prospectors, speculators, dreamers, and the merely out of work to pour like the spring floods into the Black Hills.

At first the U.S. Army vigorously turned back these greedy-eyed whites from entering the Black Hills, expelling those who slipped through, destroying their wagons, burning equipment and supplies. As more and more kept coming, however, it became politically unpopular to hold them back. Millions of discharged Civil War veterans were out of work, and the Union army was standing in the way of economic expansion; standing in the way, in fact, of Manifest Destiny! Within two years of Custer's discovery, the generals caved and began protecting the prospectors. And in another violation of the Fort Laramie treaty, a new railroad called the Cowboy Line was hastily built across northern Nebraska. It brought in thousands more, including recent Irish and German immigrants. Many of those who didn't travel on by wagon or horseback to the Black Hills settled in the small towns that sprang up alongside its tracks.

One of these small towns, Hay Springs, is ahead of me. Mari Sandoz, chronicler of pioneer life, biographer of Crazy Horse, was born on a homestead near here in 1896. Her father, the "Jules" of her book *Old Jules*, unlike most of his European neighbors, liked the Indians living nearby, enjoyed visiting with them, befriended many. Elder warriors from the Lakota, Brulé, and Cheyenne tribes spent hours around his kitchen table, drinking coffee, telling colorful tales from the old life about hunting buffalo, raiding Pawnee, dancing the Sun Dance, and battling Custer. Sometimes they even camped across the road from the house. As a little girl, Mari often sat on the floor, sometimes under the table, and around the campfire listening to their stories. She learned many Lakota phrases, became familiar with their ways. Later she would beautifully transcribe firsthand accounts from Indians who survived the Sand Creek and Powder River massacres, who participated in the Battle of Platte Bridge, Roman Nose's Fight, Red Cloud's War, the Fetterman Fight, the Battle of the Greasy Grass (Little Bighorn), and many others. When writing what many consider her masterpiece, *Crazy Horse: The Strange Man of the Oglalas* (published in 1942), she made a three-thousand-mile trip through Indian country, spending weeks interviewing Crazy Horse's friends and relatives, including Red Feather, Little Killer, Short Bull, and his closest friend, He Dog, then a blind old man who ultimately lived to be ninety-nine.

The view out the window of *Villa VW* is no longer defined by a horizon line of tableland and sky, but by skeletal maple trees, ramshackle buildings, a looming off-white grain elevator, and a dull-gray steel cone-shaped storage tank. The elevator with its fading CO-OP sign, situated alongside the defunct tracks of the Nebraska Cowboy Line, is how I remember Hay Springs. There's not much else here: a few crumbling streets, an ancient water tower, old wood-framed houses, a one-block-long main street called Main Street. Abandoned storefronts, a few existing businesses, a grocery store, a café, a corner bank, mostly dirt roads, trailer houses here and there, and a pretty little well-manicured park. A perfect rest spot; not only did I get up early this morning, but last night I stayed up much too late, sipping whiskey at Ken & Dale's, watching NBA basketball. Perhaps if I stop and close my eyes for a few minutes, I'll be alert enough to move on.

I turn into the park entrance, pull up to a blue Nebraska historical marker with raised white lead type. Over the years, I must have read this sign before—as you might suspect, I make it a habit to stop at all such signs—so I read it again. It is brief and to the point: a federal Indian agency, named for a Lakota chief named Spotted Tail (Sinte Gleska), was located near here to supply food to the Indians. The Spotted Tail Agency was generally peaceful—the only bit of historical excitement came in 1877, when Crazy Horse "surrendered" here . . . misleading because Crazy Horse actually surrendered weeks earlier at

Fort Robinson, forty miles to the west. Fearing for his life at Fort Robinson, Crazy Horse came to the Spotted Tail Agency to seek advice from Chief Spotted Tail, who was his uncle. A few days later, Spotted Tail convinced him to return to Fort Robinson, where his fears were tragically realized—on his first night back, he was murdered.

The Nebraska historical marker doesn't tell you a damn thing about Spotted Tail, a Brulé chief who was one of the greatest Lakota diplomats, a celebrated warrior who early on saw the inevitability of white domination and did his best to minimize its impact. Spotted Tail refused to join in Red Cloud's War and dedicated himself to both peace and defending the rights of his people. As an elder statesman, he was much revered by Indians and whites alike but often found himself entangled in a maze of competing interests, political pressures, and petty jealousies.

In 1877, Spotted Tail invited Indians from other reservations to come to his big summer Sun Dance. The whites who normally supported him, fearing trouble, urged him to cancel the event. He refused, but he made sure the dance was peaceful. Still, the government retaliated by banning all future Sun Dances, and although many were held secretly, it wasn't until Congress passed the American Indian Religious Freedom Act in 1978 that they were made legal again. Meanwhile, Spotted Tail had plenty of trouble with his own people; some said he was pocketing money by selling tribal lands to the railroad company, even though he sabotaged efforts to extend the railway across agency grounds by refusing tribal police protection to the railroad surveyors.

Some of Spotted Tail's Brulé rivals claimed he was an illegitimate chief. Among these were the resentful relatives of the previous chief, Conquering Bear, who in 1854 was murdered by U.S. soldiers near Fort Laramie when he tried to settle a dispute over a stray Mormon cow that had been shot and butchered by a Miniconjou Lakota warrior named High Forehead. After Spotted Tail proclaimed himself the new chief, Conquering Bear's family spread rumors about Spotted Tail, took every opportunity to oppose all his policies, and tried to get him impeached by the tribal council. And even today the bad blood lingers, as some believe Spotted Tail stole a young wife from a crippled elder named Medicine Bear. Her name, they say, was "Light-in-the-Lodge," implying that she was so beautiful, her presence lit the lodge she dwelled in. Trouble is, Light-in-the-Lodge is a ludicrous name, one of many stereotypes designed to make native women attractive as potential mates for white men.

Conquering Bear's nephew, Crow Dog, hated Spotted Tail the most. As tribal chief of police, Crow Dog tried to collect grazing fees from white ranchers who were running their herds on Indian land, only to discover that Spotted Tail was already collecting such fees. The ranchers had papers signed with Spotted Tail's X-mark, showing that the fees had been paid. Back at the agency, Crow Dog angrily railed at Spotted Tail for collecting money from cattlemen, keeping it for his personal use. Spotted Tail shrugged his shoulders; said Crow Dog intended to do the same thing. As head chief, Spotted Tail had to take care of many people who came to see him about tribal matters, thus the grazing fees were his perquisites; he kept them only to help defray his heavy expenses.

Crow Dog took sides against Spotted Tail whenever disputes arose, and for this he was fired from his chief of police position by the tribal council, reinstated, and fired again.

On the night of August 5, 1881, Crow Dog and his wife happened to deliver a load of wood to the agency while the tribal council was in session. Finished with the job, they were driving their team back to home camp when Crow Dog noticed four men coming up behind him. The meeting must have just broken up. The men were chiefs, three—Two Strike, He Dog, and Ring Thunder—on foot and one riding ahead: Spotted Tail; Crow Dog recognized him from his distinct upright posture. On impulse, Crow Dog stopped his team and handed the reins to his wife. He grabbed his rifle, jumped down from the wagon, and knelt down in the dust of the trail as if he were tying his moccasin strings. As Spotted Tail rode up, Crow Dog lifted the rifle and shot him through the chest. Spotted Tail fell off his horse, struggled to his feet, and took several steps toward Crow Dog while trying to draw his revolver out of its holster. Before he could do this, he fell backward and lay still. Crow Dog leaped up onto his wagon, whipped his horses, and went flying up the trail to the safety of his camp.

The Indian police, now headed by Eagle Hawk, dared not arrest Crow Dog because they feared it was too dangerous, so they called for an emergency meeting of the tribal council. As was tribal custom, the council sent peacekeepers to meet with Crow Dog's and Spotted Tail's families. These ambassadors successfully arranged for Crow Dog to pay six hundred dollars in blood money for the killing of Spotted Tail, plus a few ponies and blankets. Ordinarily, this would have settled the matter, but newspapers around the country published sensationalized details of Spotted Tail's killing, claiming that Crow Dog had gotten away with murder by paying off Spotted Tail's family. Even though most of the readers had never heard of Spotted Tail, they were outraged.

Responding to pleas from Rosebud Indian Reservation agent John Cook, the tribal council summoned Crow Dog and his son-in-law Black Crow to another meeting. After many hours of talk, smoking of the pipe, and assurances that no lasting harm could be done to them, Crow Dog and Black Crow agreed to be arrested. Early the next morning, they peacefully rode with Police Chief Eagle Hawk to Fort Niobrara, Nebraska, and turned themselves in to the army. As soon as Eagle Hawk left the fort to go home, the soldiers grabbed Crow Dog and pushed Black Crow to the floor. They chained the Indians' hands behind their backs, savagely beat them, and heaved them into a cold stone-walled cell. Crow Dog and Black Crow were charged with first-degree murder.

The case against Black Crow was dropped for lack of evidence, but Crow Dog was transported by wagon to stand trial in Deadwood, South Dakota. His appointed attorney defended him on the grounds of self-defense, saying that Crow Dog felt threatened by Spotted Tail, who was known to be armed. But the three chiefs who followed Spotted Tail the night he was killed testified that they saw Crow Dog crouch in the dust, concealing his rifle until Spotted Tail was close enough to make the perfect target. An all-white jury sentenced Crow Dog to hang for murder.

Crow Dog's case was appealed all the way to the U.S. Supreme Court. In a nod to tribal sovereignty, the justices ruled that the government did not have jurisdiction over a crime committed on a reservation by one Indian against another. Crow Dog was set free, and he lived to become a respected elder of his tribe. In 1885, Congress passed the Major Indian Crimes Act, making fifteen major crimes—among them murder, kidnapping, rape, maiming, incest, and arson—by one Indian against another Indian a federal crime, enforced by the FBI, tried by federal judges. The Hay Springs historical marker tells you none of these things.

A dirt road crosses through the park, so I pull in and drive up to an inviting bench, get out of *Villa VW.* Such a peaceful spot. There's a slight cool breeze, patches of early spring grass, a few buds on otherwise barren bushes, and no one else in the park. Directly across the street from the historical marker, however, I see a balding old man puttering around in the yard of his mobile home. Neither appears to have gone anywhere in years, as high weeds grow around the trailer, which rests on cinder blocks, and the man moves very slowly. Wearing a grease-stained sleeveless T-shirt, baggy shorts, and flip-flops, he looks up at me, stares. I wonder what he's thinking; is he suspicious of strangers? Does he think I am going to somehow defile his park, light up a joint, piss on the grass? But then he returns to whatever he's doing, doesn't look up again. Perhaps he wonders what I think of him. I try lying down on the bench, but the bench is too short, so I sit, close my eyes, let my mind wander. I listen to the wind; the sound of an occasional vehicle on the highway, chirping birds—the rapid-fire *tap, tap, tap*ping of what I think is a downy woodpecker. After a brief nap, I wake up groggy, in dire need of coffee.

There must be coffee somewhere in Hay Springs. Much too small for Starbucks, the town doesn't have a single fast-food restaurant or convenience store—no McDonald's, not even a 7-Eleven, where they might at least have some horrible caffeine facsimile. My best shot is probably the funky downtown café I remember from previous visits. So I drive back to the highway, turn past the grain elevator to the only stoplight, turn left on Main Street, and drive up a broad street, two blocks long, where most of the businesses on both sides have been shuttered. The bank, newspaper office, drugstore, grocery store, hair salon, Western clothing store . . . closed for a long time, and from the looks of them—boarded-up doors and windows, crumbling roofs, general disrepair—closed forever. The only open businesses I can see are a pawnshop and what looks like a hardware store. And oh, yes, there is the old funky café, but wouldn't you know it, it is open only for lunch. Utterly defeated, I turn *Villa VW* around, drive back to Highway 20.

I wonder what Mari Sandoz would say if she could see her hometown now?

RUSHVILLE

WAKAN TANKA SPEAKS TO SITTING BULL

Only fifteen miles east of Hay Springs, but ten miles past the turnoff to the rez, is a bigger town where they are bound to have coffee or I'm on a fool's errand. It would be damn embarrassing to find myself soundly snoozing in a ditch, so I turn up the radio and am pleasantly surprised to hear a Hank Williams Jr. song I know. This should keep me going. I sing along.

And before I know it, looming ahead is Rushville, Nebraska, county seat of Sheridan County, named for Civil War "hero" General Philip Sheridan. How vile to name anything other than an execution chamber after this five-foot-two maniacal exterminator, the Yankee strategist who invented the "scorched earth strategy." From May to October 1864, Sheridan's forty-thousand-man Union army obliterated the Shenandoah Valley—the vast "Granary of Virginia." They looted and destroyed all the buildings they could find, including homes and even slave cabins, destroyed the livestock they couldn't eat and burned the fields, killed civilians who got in the way and randomly raped women, including slaves. Sergeant William Patterson wrote in a letter to his sweetheart: "The whole country around is wrapped in flames, the heavens are aglow with the light thereof and such mournings, such lamentations, such crying and pleading for mercy by defenseless women I never want to see again."

Post–Civil War, Sheridan was appointed Commander of the Military Division of the Missouri; in this role, he advocated the wholesale extermination of Indians, their horses, and the buffalo they depended upon for food, clothing, and shelter. In 1868, he ordered then–Lieutenant Colonel Armstrong Custer to lead an expedition to traditional Cheyenne wintering grounds in present-day Oklahoma. Sheridan's instructions were unambiguous: "Find and destroy Indian villages and ponies, kill or hang all warriors, bring back all women and children." In a dawn attack on November 27, Custer's men charged a large Cheyenne village on the Washita River, killing more than one hundred Cheyenne warriors, including the peaceful chiefs Black Kettle and Little Rock, and capturing eight hundred ponies. To save ammunition, Custer ordered his men to cut the ponies' throats. Men who witnessed this slaughter are said to have remembered the flow of blood and the shrieks of horses for the rest of their lives.

When a Comanche named Tosawi told Sheridan, "Me Tosawi, me good Indian," Sheridan is said to have replied, "The only good Indians I ever saw were dead." Thus came the racist saying I remember from my boyhood days: "The only good Indian is a dead Indian."

Rushville looks much like Hay Springs—grain elevator along the defunct Nebraska Cowboy Line tracks, better-looking water tower, and no welcome signs, only a green highway sign:

RUSHVILLE
POP 890

Out the window to my right is a baseball park, Modisett Ball Park, a state-of-the-art field of dreams built by donations from rich ranchers, the Modisett brothers. Queerly enough, their fortune originated from the massive mounds of buffalo bones found on the land they bought in 1878. The clever boys shipped these bones to a refinery in Pennsylvania, where they were processed for the bone char used to make cane sugar. They lent the proceeds from the buffalo bone char to foolish homesteaders, waited a season or two, and bought back their land for cheap in subsequent foreclosures. By the early 1900s, the Brothers Modisett owned a substantial ranch and much of Rushville, including the local bank. When both died in a fiery car crash in 1944, it was discovered that they had willed some of their fortune for the construction of a baseball park. Rushville was free to operate Modisett Ball Park with only one restriction: they could never, under any circumstances, use it for "kitten-ball," by which the brothers meant girls' softball.

On the left side of the road sits a sprawling one-story Family Dollar store, freshly painted, white with red trim and bold signage; ten or twelve cars and pickup trucks are parked out front, and people are coming and going. It's the most life I've seen since leaving Alliance—you sure as hell aren't going to see a Macy's or J. C. Penney here. Ahead is a strange highway sign: NO DOWNSHIFTING TO BRAKE. I have no idea what it means. There's a shuttered Frontier gas station and a rusty old train caboose; strange that no one has turned either of these into a tourist shop or hamburger stand. Behind the odd sign sits an overturned combine harvester awkwardly positioned next to a genuine Mobil gas station with its familiar flying horse logo, the paint now chipped—they must have pumped its last tank of "tetraethyl lead" gasoline out of this baby in the mid-'50s. I turn off the highway onto the main downtown street, just as in Hay Springs named Main Street, only here you have North Main Street to the left and South Main Street to the right, and while half the stores are empty, at least half are still in business.

"Welcome to Rushville. It's half full, not half empty." I chuckle to myself driving up North Main Street looking for the grand two-story redbrick building I remember, the one with stylish circle-top entrances and windows, the old hotel I visited years ago.

My wife and I stopped there many times when we taught at Little

Wound Day School in nearby Kyle and at the Crazy Horse High School in Wanblee. There are crumbling structures on both sides, including a small grocery store with a vintage Pepsi sign and a box of produce outside the front window; a classic western saloon with a flashing neon Budweiser sign and what look to be actual hitching posts; the old *Sheridan County Journal Star* building; and at least one new establishment: the U.S. Department of Agriculture Service Center, with its freshly mowed lawn, American flag at full staff—a convenient place where ranch hands from nearby farms and ranches can stop in to shop for chewing tobacco and new boots. And at last I see it, the once proud Pfister Hotel, boarded up and sadly abandoned.

I drive past the hotel to where North Main abruptly ends at a small grove of evergreen bushes, turn around, and go back to the hotel, park out front. There's a padlock on the door, a sign with missing letters that reads, B E D WO K. Helen, the craggy-faced, chain-smoking lady with cheddar-colored hair who once ran the pawnshop located here long after the hotel business had run its course, is probably dead. I last saw her thirty-five years ago, and I don't see her spirit. Inside the lobby, several long glass display cases are crammed with a mind-boggling collection of Lakota porcupine quillwork, the oldest form of Indian embroidery—porcupine quills colorfully dyed with berry juice, dried and pulled through teeth until they are flat, folded, twisted, wrapped, plaited, worked into geometric diamonds and triangular shapes, or made to look like birds, flowers, animals, stars, the sun. Quillwork once used to decorate moccasins, medicine bags, headbands, war clubs, war shirts, and many other objects—an art form that flourished among the Lakota until the early nineteenth century, when French trappers brought their glass beads to trade for beaver belts. I never knew for sure if Helen understood the value of what she had, and I was reluctant to buy any of it, though now I wish I had. She acquired her collection cheaply only because people were desperate; perhaps desperate for a drink, true, or for food and gas money. When I bluntly asked her how she felt about this, Helen coughed and in a raspy smoker's voice said, "I have to make a living, and there's not much else to do around here." And then she added, "You should see the cavalry stuff I have in the basement."

I followed Helen down the creaky staircase to a large room that was probably once used by the Modisett brothers for banquets and meetings. How or why she had all those saddles, I'll never know. Dozens of for-real 7th Cavalry McClellan saddles nicely displayed on slickly varnished sawhorses next to several upright glass cases filled with uniforms, sabers, pistols, rifles, boots, spurs, canteens, and at least one short, triple-twist bugle, plus soldiers' personal effects—tintypes of sweethearts and family members, wallets, watches, medals, rings. "How did you get all this?" I asked, but I never got a straight answer. She just said she had been collecting things for years. And then one time, as an aside, she mentioned that she'd rented out "some of this stuff" to Kevin Costner when he was filming the movie *Dances with Wolves*.

"I made Kevin sign a nondisclosure," she said. "He's not allowed to tell anyone where it came from."

If this wasn't overwhelming enough, Helen also had a collection of Edward Curtis's large, portfolio-sized original copper photogravure printing plates from his *North American Indian* project, the most extensive (and expensive) photographic project ever undertaken. Over a thirty-year period beginning in 1906, supported by a $35 million grant from J. P. Morgan, the renowned photographer attempted to preserve the culture of American Indians by creating a twenty-volume documentation of 125 tribes, each of which included 1,172 hand-pressed photogravures (from the copper plates) and four thousand pages of written text. Curtis spent more time painstakingly perfecting the imagery of each copper plate than on any of his other photographic processes, working the plate to get an image that would equal or better the original negative. Today these plates sell for about $20,000 each, and I'd gladly wager that if Helen's collection were still intact, its value would be in the millions.

Sitting in my idling *Villa VW* with the air-conditioning running, as it is becoming a sizzling hot day, wondering anew about the origin of Helen's 7th Cavalry paraphernalia, I remember an old story about the great leader Sitting Bull (Tatanka Iyotake) that might explain the mystery of some of these objects.

At the end of a grueling daylong Sun Dance in which he was the only participant, Sitting Bull envisioned the upcoming Battle of Little Bighorn—Custer's Last Stand—known today by the Lakota as the Battle of the Greasy Grass. For hours and hours, Sitting Bull danced in circles, staring at the sun while singing holy songs, dragging a heavy buffalo skull tethered to two small bones pierced through the flesh on his back. As an additional sign of sacrifice, Sitting Bull had his brother Jumping Bull cut each of his arms fifty times—thus, blood flowed from his arms, from his back, and also from his feet as he was dancing on sharp gravel. Just before sunset, when Sitting Bull was totally exhausted and could move no more, he collapsed on the ground. Nearly unable to speak, Sitting Bull whispered to Jumping Bull, "Wakan Tanka told me to look just below the sun, where I saw many Long Knives falling into camp. These Long Knives looked like grasshoppers, they had no ears, and their feet were above their heads." The Long Knives in Sitting Bull's vision were the 7th Cavalry soldiers. Wakan Tanka warned Sitting Bull, however, that the people must not touch or steal any of the soldiers' belongings.

On June 25, 1876, the day his vision was fulfilled, Sitting Bull was too old to take part in the actual fighting, but afterward, he toured the battleground. Seeing Custer and all his men dead on the hillside should have been a proud moment for him, but their bodies were stripped and mutilated, and Sitting Bull was deeply angry. The people had not obeyed Wakan Tanka about not touching the fallen soldiers or taking things from them, and thus their descendants would be made to suffer by the revengeful families of these Long Knives.

Somehow a great deal of the loot they took that day ended up in an old hotel in Rushville, Nebraska.

Now craving coffee like a tweaking crackhead, I haltingly drive down Main Street, my eyes darting from one side to the other as I scan each building. Optimistically, I stop at the grocery store with the Pepsi sign. There's an old freezer chest out front, some discarded wooden boxes, hand-lettered signs, a few flyers and posters taped to the front window. As I walk in, I see a display of past-their-prime apples, moldy grapes, and surprisingly fresh-looking pears. I pick out a pear, walk up to the checkout stand. A teenage clerk who looks much too hip for a small-town Nebraska girl—pierced eyebrow, tasteful makeup, hair neatly tied back—looks into my eyes and cheerfully says, "Haven't seen you here before. Where you from?" When I tell her, "Berkeley, California," she says she is planning to go to college in Southern California, hopefully UCLA or USC, but this fall she will be a high school senior: "One more dreadful year." She's been working in the store since age ten. She lowers her voice and adds, "To be honest, I can't wait to get the hell out of this pissant town, but don't tell my dad." She motions with a turn of her head to a middle-aged man on his knees, wearing a white butcher's apron, carefully placing large pickle jars on a bottom shelf.

"He's a great dad, but there's nothing here for me, hope you don't mind me saying."

"I don't mind. Just tell me where a fellow can get a cup of coffee."

"Home Cafe, halfway down the block, 'cross the street."

As I walk out, I think that I would have liked to have met a girl just like her when I was a student at Alliance High School. None of the girls I knew would dare say "pissant" to a stranger.

The Home Cafe is an honest café, the kind of place you'd like to eat in every morning if you had to live in a small town. The molecular scent of brewing coffee, sizzling bacon, and fresh-baked bread hits the back of my nostrils as I walk in. I notice the scuffed but once-beautiful wooden floors, the spaciousness of the place. There are tables in the front, booths along the side, and a long counter in back, behind which is a retro kitchen. Local folks eating breakfast look up at me curiously. One man wears a grease-stained John Deere cap; an older woman is in a pretty flower-print dress that she must have gotten back in the '40s. No children. If these people have children, the children moved away a long time ago. The convivial hum of the place stops, but only for a moment as the customers quickly decide I am no threat or just not that interesting. A stout young man calls out to me from behind a large mechanical brass cash register that, if it were polished up, might be worth a few bucks on eBay.

The young man says, "Welcome to the Home Cafe. Are you having breakfast with us?" and before I answer that I just want some coffee to go, he tells me his name is Perry and he's been in town only a few months after serving six years in the U.S. Navy, where he traveled all over the world, most recently to the Persian Gulf. To be polite, I look over the menu he hands me, wonder if the sirloin steak special with homemade biscuits and gravy and green beans is as good as it looks. Maybe I'll stop in on my way back to Alliance later this evening.

Perry continues to tell me about his naval adventures. He's been to Qatar, Egypt, Greece, Italy, Japan, and Singapore, as well as San Diego and San Francisco. He's met all kinds of people and really likes people, although the best people live right here in good ol' Rushville, "especially that young lady in the back," he says, referring to the owner and cook he met by happenstance while she was visiting relatives in Reno, where he was spending his leave with some Navy buddies. "My good fortune it was early morning. We hadn't started drinking or Melissa wouldn't have given me the time of day," he laughs. "God, I'm loving it in Rushville."

I wonder whether one day he will break her heart and reenlist. I also wonder how long it will be before I can detach myself, get that coffee, get back on the road. So I lie. “Perry, I’ve got to meet some friends in Rapid City, need to get going.”

Snapping to attention, Perry turns and hollers, “Hey, Melissa, this here gentleman wants coffee to go.”

A middle-aged redhead with a pleasant demeanor and stereotypical green Irish eyes pops out from the kitchen, hands me a sixteen-ounce Styrofoam cup. “Help yourself,” she says. “Coffee is over there. We don’t have decaf; no one here drinks decaf.”

Turns out the hot black syrupy glop tastes like the peyote tea I once unsuccessfully tried to swallow during a Native American church ceremony in New Mexico . . . but, hey, after a couple of sips, I can feel my heart racing—Christ Almighty, I got my high-octane caffeine infusion!

WHITECLAY

TWELVE THOUSAND CANS OF BEER ON THE WALL

I'm on the road again, heading north on Highway 87, edging closer to the Pine Ridge Indian Reservation. The land is still flat—there are no other travelers in sight, just an abandoned schoolhouse not so dilapidated that it couldn't be restored if there happened to be any children around, a crumbling but still occupied farmhouse, hay rolls, cows, a few goats wandering dangerously near the blacktop . . . and nothing but static on *Villa VW*'s radio. As I round a forty-degree turn, the monotony ends; I see the beginning of the rugged, ponderosa-coated buttes and ridges that define most of the Pine Ridge Indian Reservation, an evergreen paradise formed millions of years ago as the result of a fault line between the Niobrara and White Rivers, dueling tributaries of the Missouri.

A beer truck whizzes by—the driver must be going ninety. No worries for him here about the Nebraska State Patrol. The beer truck is headed for Whiteclay; I'll be in Whiteclay soon enough. (I hate speeding beer trucks, and I especially hate Whiteclay.)

After ten more miles of glorious rock formations, tall grasses, chokecherry bushes, towering pine trees, I find myself in the armpit of Nebraska, skid row of the plains, an unincorporated border town of fourteen people with a post office, a gas station, a house or two, abandoned buildings. Charred foundations. Smoldering trash pits. Dirt sidewalks. And four liquor stores that sell twelve thousand cans of beer a day to Indians who walk or drive from the nearby community of Pine Ridge, the most populous town on the reservation, where the sale and even the possession of alcohol is illegal. There are no cops in Whiteclay, no mayor, no officials of any kind. Small wonder that beer is sold to minors, to the obviously intoxicated; traded for sex, for leaning on some poor fool who hasn't paid his tab.

I slow *Villa VW* to a sputter, wondering if Whiteclay is still as bad as I remember it. It doesn't take long to see that it is the same, if not worse. Two disheveled Indian men sit drinking on the steps of an abandoned building next to a man and woman who are passed out, lovingly curled up together. I watch cars and pickup trucks coming and going from the four liquor stores: Jumping Eagle Inn, Arrowhead Foods, Mike's Pioneer Service, and the unimaginatively named Stateline Liquor. In addition to alcohol, these stores sell cigarettes, soda, and junk food. I remember when they sold cheap wino wine and rotgut whiskey; today it's only malt liquor, lots of bottom-shelf shitbrew, Steel Reserve (8.1% alcohol), Earthquake High Gravity (12%), and Joose (9%)—brands you'll never see at your local Safeway. Drunks outside one of the liquor stores lean on each other, laughing, some of their brew spilling out of tall cans. An older woman, seemingly lost, staggers across the highway.

In Nebraska, it is illegal to drink in the vicinity of a liquor store—liquor store owners could lose their license—but these violations have been going on for many years. I know of at least one protest group that meticulously documented the sad fact of Whiteclay on-premises drinking. Volunteer students from nearby Chadron State College and the University of Nebraska–Lincoln spent a couple of weeks in Whiteclay taking hundreds of damning photos, which they forwarded to the Nebraska Liquor Control Commission. There was a hearing, but nothing was done—nothing will be done.

Sheridan County sheriff's deputies and Nebraska patrol cars come to Whiteclay only when a fatal accident is reported or when the Indians mount a protest, such as the Lakota Women's Day of Peace March in August 2013. Several hundred Indian women and supporters walked to Whiteclay from Pine Ridge in hundred-degree heat and stood in a circle in the middle of the highway blocking traffic. Chanting "As long as it takes," five of the protesters locked their arms together with makeshift handcuffs and sat down across the highway, effectively shutting down the town and beer sales for the rest of the day and into the night. Notified ahead of time but not expecting such a large group, the few overwhelmed lawmen were afraid to get out of their cars, so they rolled down the windows, drove around the edges of the protest, and "indiscriminately pepper-sprayed the crowd."

Three drunkards yelled at the protesters, calling the women "white bitches." When one of the drunkards tried to hit a fourteen-year-old Lakota boy, a patrolman grabbed the kid, cuffed him, and shoved him in the backseat of a patrol car. Another young Lakota peeked into the car, demanded to know why the fourteen-year-old was being held. He too was pepper-sprayed. Tensions mounted. A riot was in the making when Pine Ridge tribal police, parked on the other side of the border, entered Whiteclay even though they were out of their jurisdiction. The tribal police chief demanded the highway patrolman release the boy and instead arrest the drunkards who had started it all. Looking relieved, the patrolman complied.

By sunset, most of the protesters had drifted off except for the five hard-core activists who remained locked down across the road. In spite of the danger of an unlit highway, they were determined to stay the night. After dark, a pickup truck pulling a horse trailer arrived in Whiteclay and backed up to within a few feet of where they were sitting. According to press accounts, police officers arrested the "White Clay Five," removed their handcuffs with bolt cutters, and, picking them up one by one, tossed them into the back of the trailer. As it was impossible for the protesters to stand during the bumpy ride to

Rushville's Sheridan County Jail, they had no choice but to sit on the horse dung that littered the horse trailer floor.

I stop at a stone monument on the edge of Whiteclay that honors the memory of Wilson "Wally" Black Elk Jr. and Ronald Hard Heart, who were found shot to death here on June 8, 1999, some suspect by law enforcement officers. A march protesting these killings disintegrated into rock throwing and looting; one liquor store was set on fire, and nearly burned down. This time fifty Nebraska State Patrol officers wearing Plexiglas face shields and carrying tear gas met up with the protesters. There was much mayhem, many arrests that day; fortunately, no one was killed. The words on the polished stone monument in all caps reads:

IN MEMORY OF
WILSON WALLY BLACK ELK JR
& RON HARD HEART
TWO LAKOTA BROTHERS WHO GAVE
THE ULTIMATE SACRIFICE FOR THEIR PEOPLE
SO THE PEOPLE WILL ALWAYS SEEK JUSTICE
FOR THE FUTURE GENERATIONS

Four drunks sit on the ground across the highway from the stone monument, looking at me with bemused expressions, their backs resting against the metal door of what looks to be a beer-storage warehouse. All wear coats even though it is getting to be a hot day. One shouts out, "Come over here and talk to us." Another staggers to his feet and hobbles my way, his bulbous nose so misshapen (it must have been busted on more than one occasion), so huge, I nearly fail to see his moon-cratered cheeks, bloodshot eyes, faded blue bandana. He walks right up to me, so close I can smell the stale beer, urine, and sweat of his sad life, and says, "Can I have a loan?"

"What you need a loan for?" I ask him.

"Need to buy beer."

"I don't think I should give you money to buy beer."

He grumbles, "You white people come here all the time and say, 'Oh, we are going to help you, we are going to fix up your house.' What the fuck is that going to do? I was a Marine in Vietnam, but I don't consider myself a goddamn Marine no more."

Sheepishly, I reach into my pocket and hand him a five-dollar bill. His Indian friends across the road laugh. He says, "Thank you, bro. When you goin' back to New York?" He walks away before I can answer.

When I lived on the reservation in the turbulent 1970s, there were bars in Whiteclay, not just liquor stores. One was Toad's Lounge, owned by Toad Frohman, a solid Irish Catholic citizen from Alliance who also owned a bar in Alliance with the same name and a Schlitz beer wholesale distributorship. In 2011, when he died at age eighty-three, people remembered him for his kindness. They said Toad was always lending strangers a helping hand. In the winter, he plowed the snow for the entire neighborhood, he was very active in the Chamber of Commerce, and he could be counted on every summer to help out with the annual Little Britches Rodeo. People were not aware or didn't care that Toad's success was based on selling liquor to vulnerable Native Americans. His little bar in Whiteclay, now long closed, was his first business; it provided the cash flow for his beer distributorship and his bar in Alliance.

Out of curiosity, I once went into Toad's Whiteclay tavern; I was surprised at how ordinary it was—there was a barrel-chested white bartender who must have played defensive lineman on his high school football team standing behind a long wooden bar fully stocked with beer, cheap whiskey, cheap vodka, and Schlitz on tap. Decorations included old beer posters, license plates from neighboring states, the ubiquitous bikini girl calendar, and an up-to-date Nebraska football schedule. There was no indication that nearly all the customers in this establishment were Native American, except, of course, for their presence: two Indian men and an Indian woman sitting on barstools, smoking, drinking, loudly talking; three or four more at tables opposite the bar; and an intoxicated man, passed out, slumped down in an old-fashioned barber chair in the far back corner near the bathroom.

A few years earlier this very barber chair had allegedly been the site of a depraved episode where an Indian woman was hog-tied, a balled-up napkin stuck in her mouth, and gang-raped by several men, Indian and white. Finished, the men gleefully dumped her battered body outside in the subzero snow, where she would surely have frozen to death if a Lakota rancher driving there hadn't stopped, put her in the back of his pickup, and driven her to the Indian hospital in Pine Ridge.

Some of the bar's admirers, no surprise, told a different story. "Old squaw bitch was giving head for drinks until she got so plastered she plumb fell off the barber chair, banged her face on the edge of a table. Crawled out of here, said she was going home. It was all her own damn fault."

You might think there are no bars in Whiteclay these days because Indian activists finally succeeded in shutting them down, but this is not the case. Whiteclay bartenders had to be extremely good negotiators and tough; if serving drinks was the number one task in their job description, breaking up fights was number two. When persuasion failed, bartenders resorted to ax handles or baseball bats. Most carried a pistol or kept a shotgun behind the bar. Calling the police wasn't an option. After decades of barroom fistfights, stabbings, shootings, barstools smashed over people's heads, windows shattered, bathrooms torched, it became so difficult to hire and keep bartenders that the white creeps who owned these places gave up. They met, decided to close down the bars.

"Shoot, if Injuns need to drink in Whiteclay, they can drink outside. When it's too cold, plenty of abandoned buildings where they can crash."

Whiteclay is an extreme example of do-gooding gone bad. In 1882, Pine Ridge reservation agent Valentine McGillycuddy asked President Chester Arthur to issue an executive order that would establish a ten-mile-wide buffer zone extending five miles south of Pine Ridge. In this zone, white peddlers would not be allowed to sell guns or alcohol to Indians. Valentine adroitly explained to our not-so-swift twenty-first president that Indians "just can't hold their liquor. Something in their makeup. When an Indian drinks, he can't function. The only thing we can do, Mr. President, is keep liquor away from him."

Originally known as the White Clay Extension, the buffer zone served its purpose until 1904. Intensively lobbied by the Joseph Schlitz Brewing Company, Theodore Roosevelt rescinded the order and returned the land to Sheridan County. Nearby tavern keepers and liquor store owners, men like Toad Frohman, leaped into action. They established the town of Whiteclay, and in so doing turned the White Clay Extension into the exact opposite of what it was intended to be.

As I drive off, I wonder if I'll ever be in Whiteclay again. If I do come back, what will be left? A few rotting buildings, cement foundations, the whole stinking place finally burned down? Perhaps the memorial to Black Elk and Hard Heart will be all that remains. Now, however, I am off to Pine Ridge, only three miles up the road.

I need to stop at Big Bat's. I need to buy Vernell White Thunder a case of Perrier sparkling water and a case of Dinty Moore beef stew, his favorites.

PINE RIDGE

LAKOTA TACO TRUCK

Over a slight rise a few minutes from Whiteclay and I'm already on the outskirts of the village of Pine Ridge, population four thousand, de facto capital of the Pine Ridge Indian Reservation. Off to my right is a BIA housing project: signature wood-frame dwellings depressingly painted in subdued pastels—pale peach, chalky blue, toxic green, fading marigold—with much too much bright white trim. The windowless doors, front and back, open onto dirt yards. There are no windows on the sides of these houses; only a small window or two in the front and one in the back. Some of the yards have a few shrubs and small patches of grass or gardens, and most are filled up with old, parked cars and trucks, two or three or up to a dozen or more, as I've been told rez folks like to keep old clunkers around for spare parts. Believe it or not, these BIA houses are new—freshly painted, no broken glass, no apparent fire damage—and they are nicely positioned near a stand of evergreen spruce trees. By Pine Ridge standards, this neighborhood is upscale; I imagine that the people living here work for the tribal government.

Straight ahead is the "Pine Ridge 4-way," the only four-way traffic light on the rez. Here highway SD-407 intersects with Pine Ridge's main street, which is actually another highway, U.S. 18, one of the

Midwest's first paved roads. Lightly traveled these days, U.S. 18 was an important route before they built the Interstate System. It was opened in 1926 to connect the breweries in Milwaukee with all the thirsty people out West in South Dakota, Wyoming, Idaho, Nevada, and Northern California. And looming to my left is an enormous, bright-red-and-white Conoco gas station, home of Big Bat's, one of the weirdest combination café–convenience store–tourist stop–local hangouts ever conceived. As I turn at the intersection and into the station, past the gas pumps, my eyes are drawn above the front entrance to an avant-garde metal sculpture of three fierce warriors on horseback charging forward—feathers and horsetails flying behind—looking as if they are about to overrun the 7th Cavalry. Next to this "corporate trademark" is a bigger, even bolder Big Bat logo. And just below these images, nearly as conspicuous, a message in sun-bright yellow type on a blue background reads:

Waves of Change

There are at least a dozen parked cars and trucks around the place; some obviously clean tourist rentals, others unwashed forever, belonging to the locals. Extracting myself from *Villa VW,* I am greeted by extremely loud country music coming from outdoor speakers, which must originate from KILI Radio, the Voice of the Lakota Nation, an FM station perched on a nearby bluff overlooking the little village of Porcupine. Everybody on the rez listens to KILI. When it isn't broadcasting local news and gossip alternatively in English and Lakota, indigenous music, or born-again religious banter, it plays country music. I can't believe my ears—Charlie Daniels belting out "The South's Gonna Do It (Again)"! I don't know why Indians like this shit, but the lyrics "Well you can be proud" follow me into Big Bat's cavernous dining area with its sloppy mix of round wood, square wood, and rectangular Formica tables, and a long horseshoe-shaped counter in front of the food preparation area where you can order from an immense menu of hamburgers, sandwiches, onion rings, hot plates, bean soup, ice cream, sodas, and Indian fry bread. The shelves are neatly stocked with junk food and souvenirs, but what most catches my attention inside Big Bat's are the story murals that wrap their way along the top half of the walls and ceiling; murals that illustrate for anyone who cares to know the complexity and beauty of Lakota spiritual mythology, mythology every bit as meaningful and poignant as that which has stirred human imagination since the dawning of civilization and probably for many millennia before. Beings from all cultures, forever curious, seek answers to probing questions about their world, beginning with questions about human origin and the origin of the stars, the oceans, the land, and the myriad other creatures with which we share this universe. The result is creation stories, stories difficult to understand without science and the scientific method, and even then. Using visual literacy and oral tradition to teach Lakota mythology to Lakota children is a powerful way to counterbalance the absurd colonial notion that white people, and particularly Christian white people, have a lock on religion and thereby cultural correctness and knowledge. Among the Brulé, who are related to the Lakota, origin starts with a great flood, when the first people were attacked by Unktehi, the Big Water Monster, who sent the waters to kill them. The people climbed a steep hill to escape, but still the water immersed them and they drowned. The remaining pool of water turned to blood, which became a quarry from which the surviving people made sacred red stone pipes. These pipes had great power because their smoke represented the breath of the ancestors. After the flood, Unktehi turned into stone and became the Badlands. Only one person—a young girl—survived the flood, having been picked up by Wanblee, the eagle, and flown to Wanblee's home in a tall tree. The girl became Wanblee's wife, and from their union came two pairs of twins, one set male and the other female. These were the parents of the Brulé people, who take pride in being known as the "Eagle People."

When I was fired after my first year in Kyle, Linda landed a position teaching high school sophomore English in Wanblee, thirty-three miles west of Kyle, where we lived in a leaky two-room trailer with our infant daughter, Mara. Strangely enough, Vernell too moved to Wanblee, starred on the Crazy Horse basketball team, and continued to be our best Indian friend. The Wanblee creation story is the first of many on the walls of Big Bat's; another tells how a young Lakota warrior captured and tamed the first horse, how people acquired the flute, and, most important to the Lakota and many related tribes, of White Buffalo Calf Woman's gift of the peace pipe—my favorite of all Lakota legends, and in my opinion the most beautiful. When I was teaching in Kyle, I memorized and recited this tale to all my classes, and I still can recall much of it.

During a time of winter hardships and starvation, two young warriors leave the camp in search of buffalo. They wander for many days not even seeing hoofprints, and are about to give up when they see the ghost of a beautiful young woman dressed in white buckskin walking toward them. She carries what looks like a stick wrapped in a bundle of sage. So struck by her, one of the men declares he is going to make her his wife, but the other man objects, saying that she is holy, that it would be wrong to claim her.

But his friend does not listen. He runs up to the beautiful woman and tries to hug her. At that very moment, he disappears with her in a violent whirlwind reaching high into the sky. When the whirlwind stops, the woman is still standing as before with the bundle in her arm. The man, however, is now a pile of bones.

Too afraid to run away, the surviving warrior stares at her. She speaks to him: "Go back to your camp and tell your people I will soon be there to meet with a good man who lives among you. His name is Bull Walking Upright. Tell your people to pitch their tepees in a circle, leave an opening that faces north. In the center of this circle, place a large tepee, also facing north. This is where I will meet with Bull Walking Upright."

Relieved that he too is not going to be turned into a pile of bones, the man runs as fast as he can back to the camp. The people listen to him and follow all the instructions. When White Buffalo Calf Woman meets with Bull Walking Upright in the center tepee, she unwraps her bundle and gives him the gift of a small pipe made of red stone upon which is carved the tiny outline of a buffalo calf. This is the sacred pipe. She teaches him the prayers he should recite to the Strong One Above. "When you pray to the Strong One Above," she says, "you must also use the pipe. If the people are hungry, unwrap it and lay it bare in the air. The buffalo will then come where your warriors can easily hunt and kill them."

White Buffalo Calf Woman slowly turns and walks out of the tepee. With all the people watching her in awe, she lies down on the ground and rolls over and over. When she stands up, she is a black buffalo. Again she lies down, rolls over and over. This time she rises as a red buffalo. The third time, she is a brown buffalo. The fourth and final time, she takes the form of a spotless white buffalo. In this form she walks into the distance and disappears.

There are all kinds of people inside Big Bat's—three or four chunky truck drivers from faraway places devour cheeseburgers; a bald tourist stands at the deli counter and orders a submarine sandwich with the works, and I can't help but notice his open Hawaiian shirt, his camera with a much too conspicuous zoom lens *and* high-powered binoculars awkwardly suspended from his neck. A group of Lakota teenage boys wearing Oakland Raiders jerseys and backward caps sit sloppily at a far corner table swearing and laughing. They toss French fries at each other, make loud squeaks scooting their chairs, and dare anyone to object. Nearby sit two young women, towheaded Germans, much too stylish for this place, oblivious to stares. Opposite the unruly boys in the other far corner is a drunken man who must have popped in from Whiteclay. He stares into his coffee, and I have a feeling he is going to be here for a very long time. Most striking, though, is a table of old Lakota men; one in particular catches my fancy, the one with a large-brim cowboy hat wearing two worn but classic polo shirts, with suspenders holding up his blue jeans—a good thing because they sag below his portly belly. His raccoon eyebrows rise above the upper rim of his glasses as he skeptically looks over at me to convey the message *You definitely not fooling anyone, white man*. The other two glance my way as well, so I meekly wave and say, "Hi, there." Poker-faced, they go back to their conversation. Only then do I realize that they must have thought I was trying to listen in to their subversive talk, as I hear one of them say "Keystone Pipeline." Naturally, I look downward and focus as hard as I can on what they are saying. One phrase is crystal clear, and it warms my greedy little green heart: "The people will never allow the pipeline; they will block the bulldozers." Once I dare to look up again, I notice that there is no coffee or food on their table; they are simply having a strategic meeting. I wonder, do they come to Big Bat's every day to plot counterrevolution?

In the midst of the junk food I spot a rack of so-called "healthy choices": peanuts, sunflower seeds, gluten-free cookies, cheese sticks, and something called Tanka nutrition bars, which look similar to granola bars. Picking one up and reading the label, I learn that Tanka bars are made on the reservation, that they are a combination of smoked buffalo meat and flavor additives including apple, orange peel, and spicy pepper. And I see that they also have Tanka jerky and Tanka trail mix. Unfortunately, Big Bat's does not carry Perrier or Dinty Moore—for that I'll have to try the nearby Sioux Nation Shopping Center. So I select a few Tanka bars and walk up to the counter, where on impulse I ask the cute girl behind the cash machine, "Why is this place called Big Bat's?" She shrugs, turns, and points her finger at a giant middle-aged man wearing an elegantly embroidered yet dog-eared cowboy shirt and chatting with the cook, and says, "That's Big Bat. He's the owner."

"Can you tell him I would like to introduce myself and ask him about this place?"

"You're not the FBI, are you?" she jokes.

"Hell no. You kidding? I lived near here. I'm on my way to Kyle to visit my friend Vernell White Thunder. Do you know him?"

"I don't know no Vernell."

Much louder than the occasion requires, she shouts out, "Hey, Big Bat. This white dude wants to talk to you!"

When Big Bat looks at me, I notice his facial features—green eyes and cocoa complexion, pointed nose, narrow chin, and thin eyebrows. More European than native. He smiles, motions me to sit at an empty table, and ambles over to join me. Extending a bear paw hand, he says, "People call me Big Bat; my real name is Tye, Tye Pourier. Suppose you want to know about this place, right?"

"Good guess," I answer. "I lived in Kyle long ago, was in Pine Ridge many times, but back then there was nothing like Big Bat's. I love this place, but how did it come about?"

Proud and convivial, Big Bat tells me the business was started in 1990 by his parents, who wanted a place for people to gather; in Lakota, a "*tiyospaye*," an extended family place where anyone can come to eat decent food and talk, stay as long as they want, a place that reflects the generosity and beauty of Lakota culture. They named it "Big Bat" after his great-grandfather, a famous French trader originally from St. Louis who married the sister of Oglala chief Smoke and became a trusted member of the tribe. The original Big Bat could speak fluent Lakota and was friends with Chief Red Cloud. He also knew all the other chiefs and went on many hunting trips and even on pony raids against the Crow. Big Bat was present when Crazy Horse was stabbed to death at Fort Robinson. When Big Bat wasn't riding with his warrior friends, he traded beads, cooking pots, hunting rifles, and bullets for beaver pelts and buffalo hides. To get more inventory for his trading post, and to sell the pelts and hides, Big Bat routinely rafted down the Missouri River all the way to St. Louis—an arduous twelve-hundred-mile journey—and returned by pack mule.

"My great-grandfather never sold alcohol," the younger Big Bat says. "In 1996 a terrible kitchen fire, never should have happened, burned down this whole frickin' place, right to the ground. We rebuilt it, made it bigger and better. Big Bat is no joke; for us it is a road map to the future. We come from a warrior culture; my grandfather and father were warriors, and I too am a warrior. Business is today's battlefield."

"And when did you become 'Big Bat'?"

"When my dad opened Big Bat's, people thought he must be Big Bat, so they started calling him Big Bat, and he accepted this. When I took over, I became Big Bat, and when my son takes over, he too will be Big Bat." He paused and nodded slowly.

"I guess there will always be a Big Bat."

Before leaving Big Bat's, I pause to look across the highway in utter disgust at the Pine Ridge Agency, official BIA headquarters housed in an anemic redbrick building, once occupied by imperial-minded bureaucrats who thought God had put them on earth to annihilate Indian culture. Something must be going right, because these days the agency is just a stopover for unhappy government employees who spend most of their time filling out transfer forms to better places—say, the Great Plains Regional Office in Aberdeen or, better yet, the Northwest Regional Office in Portland. I imagine how worthless they must feel as they try to maintain the fiction that they are in charge of something, that they still matter. To many, the agency is a symbol of past oppression and failed policies such as the Indian Removal Act, which forced people onto reservations; the Dawes Act, which reduced the size of these reservations by more than half; and the 1956 Indian Relocation Act, which moved people back off the reservation into cities, where they found only more poverty and despair.

The agency itself is an unsightly structure except for one thing—positioned near the front entrance is a sweet memorial to thirty-one Lakota soldiers from the Pine Ridge Indian Reservation who died during World War II, their names etched in marble next to the date of their deaths: Albert Chief Eagle, Mar. 14, 1943; Floyd Bear Saves Life, June 6, 1944; Lester Red Boy, Nov. 17, 1944; Clement Crazy Thunder, Mar. 11, 1945; Chester Afraid of Bear, April 8, 1945; Earl

Two Bulls, Nov. 30, 1944; and so on. Like all Indians, the Lakota are tremendously proud of their soldiers. As a proportion of their population, by far more Native Americans serve in the armed forces than any other ethnic group, remarkable considering that the U.S. Army exterminated so many. More than ten thousand native men volunteered to serve during World War I despite the fact that most were not U.S. "citizens" at the time and were unprotected under the Constitution. In fact, it was not until after World War II with the 1965 passage of the Voting Rights Act that all states were required to allow Native Americans to vote on the same basis as any other American. Despite decades of persecution and broken promises, despite being dispossessed of, and often forcibly removed from, their ancestral homelands, American Indians served and continue to serve in our nation's armed forces in numbers that belie their small percentage of the American population.

To get to the Sioux Nation Shopping Center, I have to drive only a short distance past Billy Mills Hall, where funerals, powwows, and important community meetings are held. I once met Billy Mills, years ago when he came here for the dedication of this building. In 1964, when he pulled off one of the greatest upsets in Olympic history, I was a junior in high school, glued to my TV set. I already knew quite a bit about him because he twice led the Kansas University cross-country team to a national championship, and because he was from Pine Ridge. Mills was the Jim Thorpe of his day, but there was no way he was going to win the ten-thousand-meter run. World record holder Ron Clarke, who had the advantageous inside lane, was figured to win going away. Billy's best time in the ten thousand was ten seconds slower than Clarke's—if anyone was to give Clarke a race, it wouldn't be Mills but Kōkichi Tsuburaya from Japan or Tunisia's Mohammed Gammoudi.

Yet, in fourth place with three laps to go, Mills was within striking distance. Tsuburaya took the lead, and the home crowd went wild; Clarke was boxed in—Gammoudi in front, Mills to his right. When

Clarke tried to elbow Billy out of the way, it looked for a moment like Billy would stumble, but just then Gammoudi charged between Clarke and Mills and into the lead. Tsuburaya began to fade. Clarke passed Gammoudi—things were just as they were supposed to be; Clarke would win for sure. But then came Mills. Swinging wide to the outside, he put on a burst of speed the likes of which had never been seen before in distance running. When he surged past Gammoudi and Clarke, I could not believe it, nor could the announcer, who famously yelled, "Look at Mills! Look at Mills! Look at Mills!" The whole country was transfixed, and at that moment, Mills became a genuine American hero.

When I heard Billy Mills speak, an inebriated heckler interrupted him, yelled out, "I'm going to burn this place down because it is named after you."

"Please don't burn it down," Mills said. "Just change the name."

A few feet past Billy Mills Hall, I pull into a parking lot in front of the biggest, ugliest building on the rez, a mass of cinder blocks painted vomit yellow. The sign

Sioux Nation
Shopping Center
Hardware Meat Produce

is matter-of-factly painted in garish fluorescent-orange letters on one end of the building next to an amateurish mural painting of an eagle, peace pipe in its claws, swooping down on a green valley where there are two or three tepees. Similar to many prisons, the Sioux Nation Shopping Center has no windows. You can't see the entrance because it is around the corner of a false brick wall, making it awkward to get in and out of the place; a deterrent, I suppose, to shoplifting. I park on the far side of the lot, move my camera from the seat to the floor, get out, and saunter across the gravel surface. Several local people are around, but no one seems to take note of me, not even the stray dogs hoping for handouts.

Inside, the Sioux Nation Shopping Center looks like any urban grocery store: shopping carts, checkout stands, aisles of packaged food, and shoppers scurrying about. Everything is neat, tidy, clean, and well lighted, and I think, *Why shouldn't it be?* Ahead is the drink aisle, more than half its length occupied by every brand of oversized soda you can imagine, but sadly no Perrier; they used to carry Perrier, and Vernell won't settle for less. Perrier is sort of a running joke between us. At least they have Dinty Moore beef stew, so I stash a dozen cans in my cart and look for other things he might like. I'm so focused on reading labels, I nearly run my cart into an elderly Indian woman, a weathered grandmother, rock of the Lakota world, who has surely seen more than anyone's share of hard times. Two small children, a boy and a girl, stand in her grocery cart eating Oreo cookies from a package. The children don't object when she gently takes the package from the little girl's hands and puts it back on the shelf—they've had their treat. No need for Grandmother to buy this, and I certainly don't blame her; Lakota grandmothers are the primary caregivers of many children, a tradition in a culture where many teenage girls have babies, where many parents drink away their miseries and are too incapacitated to raise kids. They say over half the children on the rez live with their grandparents, and it is a good thing, or more would be snatched away to the do-gooder orphanages and foster care agencies, and in some cases adopted overseas.

Six aisles of canned food seems out of proportion to the tiny frozen food, produce, and fresh meat sections. You might get the impression that Indians just like eating stuff out of cans, but there is a more insidious reason; nearly a third of their homes don't have electricity, and people have long forgotten the old ways of smoking meat, storing dairy food in cold streams, and burying root vegetables under the earth. Produce at Sioux Nation is limited—iceberg lettuce, a few wrinkled tomatoes, strawberries on the edge, moldy spinach, limp carrots, old corn—nearly all would have been tossed in the Dumpster where I shop back home, but here it stays on the shelf until it is so green no one even looks at it. I spot a FRESH MEAT sign above a refrigerated display case stocked with packaged steaks and hamburger in front of the in-store butcher shop. The meat seems fresh enough, but there is a disturbing bulletin posted nearby, alerting customers to something I didn't know about; it explains why hamburger is sometimes grayish brown on the inside even if it is red on the outside. "Oxygen from the air," it reads, "triggers a pigment in hamburger called 'oxymyoglobin,' which gives it its red color. Because the meat beneath the surface is not being exposed to oxygen, it is sometimes grayish brown. Only when 'all the meat' in a package is grayish brown do you have to worry that it 'may be beginning to spoil.' "

I catch the attention of the presumed butcher, a young, approachable Indian man with happy eyes, a plump face, and a ponytail hanging to the middle of his back. I ask him about the sign. He smiles, says, "People around here really like their hamburger, but they don't understand why the meat isn't red all the way through. They try to bring it back, or worse, they complain to the tribal council. We only want to educate them."

I can't help but remark, "I don't like it when my hamburger is brown."

"We sell a lot of hamburger here; it is really, really fresh."

"Where do you get your hamburger?"

A little less friendly now, Butcherman moves closer, puts his hands on top of the counter, stares at me. "It comes frozen from the meat-packer in Omaha. We thaw it out."

I can't help but press on. "Why don't you buy it from local ranchers?"

"Too expensive. Where you from, anyway?"

I tell him I once taught school in Kyle, shopped here many times, but I don't remember any problems about the hamburger.

"Well," he adamantly replies, "you should know that this store is important to the people. So what if some of our hamburger isn't as red as the hamburger you can get wherever the hell you live these days."

"OK, sorry to bother you."

"No hard feelings," he calls after me as I walk away.

Butcherman is right, of course. Without the Sioux Nation Shopping Center, people would have to drive a hundred miles to Rapid City or Chadron to get their groceries—other than Big Bat's and the junk food you can buy with your beer in Whiteclay, there aren't many choices on the rez; no corner produce market run by a nice Korean family, no stand-alone butcher shops, no weekend farmers' market; no Safeway or Dean & Deluca. A couple of years back, the tribe tried to shut down the Sioux Nation Shopping Center after it was cited for food safety violations. There was a virtual uprising. People signed petitions, phoned in to complain on KILI Radio, organized a protest horse ride, put on their war paint. They seemed to be saying, "It's not a great shopping center, but this is *our shopping center*—it is here, it is convenient. Many don't have cars and those who do can't afford the gas."

There's just one little problem: it *isn't* their shopping center. While the name "Sioux Nation" might indicate that the tribe owns the place, in actuality, it merely licenses the rights to an outside group, collecting a fee roughly equivalent to rent. When the store opened in 1968, it was inconceivable that someone from the tribe would be competent enough to run a grocery store! To avoid mismanagement, malfeasance, embezzlement, you needed to find an outside professional grocery store management company. But today things are different, and some tribal members have suggested that the tribe should take back the license and open a new grocery store, rename it Oglala Nation Shopping Center. Hopefully, this will happen.

I stash my groceries in *Villa VW*'s trunk, grab my camera, and go for a stroll around the building, not caring if I might be mistaken for a nosy tourist. A large black shipping container sits behind the store on a patch of barren space, a dirt surface. In front of the container is a long table with a standing display rack of rugs and blankets, clearly not

Indian made, cheap, the kind you might buy at the Oakland Coliseum flea market. I see no one nearby; it appears abandoned.

About fifty feet beyond the rug display, a young boy stands next to the open door of an old white Mitsubishi Lancer wearing a Jalen Rose Chicago Bulls shirt. I notice a hand-lettered sign on his dashboard, which reads BURRITOS & POP, $5, and I wonder, is this the Lakota equivalent of a taco truck?

I shout out, "Hi, there. What kind of burritos do you have?"

He looks up at me and says, "We got both kinds. Beans, and beans with buffalo. Two kinds of pop too, orange and grape."

Healthy looking, at that age when baby fat is just beginning to turn into muscle, the kid is urban in his appearance: in addition to the Jalen Rose jersey, he sports jet-black spiked hair, a stud earring, sagging pants, Air Jordans. Recalling my conversation with Butcherman, I ask him, "Where do you get your meat?"

The boy shrugs, turns to ask someone sitting in the car whom I hadn't noticed before. Must be his mom; she's a pretty young woman, no makeup, black hair, not-quite-perfect teeth. Her skeptical dark eyes give me the once-over, lock on mine.

"Why do you want to know?"

"Just curious."

"My *husband*," she continues with decided emphasis, "buys surplus buffalos from Custer State Park. We butcher them ourselves, usually in the winter when the coat is full because my cousin is a buffalo hide painter. We boil the meat for burritos, donate leftovers to the elders or for ceremonies and powwows."

Surprised at the preciseness of her answer, I can only say, "That's amazing."

"Don't you think us Indians can be entrepreneurs?" she asks. "You surprised I know that word?"

"No, I think that's great."

"I went to college," she adds.

I hand the boy five bucks, ask for a burrito with buffalo meat and beans, tell him to keep the orange soda for himself, and wander back to the front of the shopping center thinking, *Here's one boy who doesn't have to live with his grandmother.* Delicious beans obviously made from scratch, juicy meat, salsa with a kick—this burrito rocks.

Damn, who would have thought you could buy something so grubbin' on the rez?

Away from the main drag, Pine Ridge neighbors fill their yards with the flotsam of American advertising—used Pampers, dead cars, punctured tires, and empty beer cans—until buzzards swarm like flies and carry away their unwatched children, young boys riding banana bikes through mud puddles. Bored teenagers hang about—at least they have each other—along with elders holding hands. And then there's a busy Taco John's, a thriving Subway sandwich shop, and churches: lovely white Sacred Heart Catholic, sturdy log-building Lakota Baptist, corrugated-metal Episcopal Mission, modern pointy-roofed Presbyterian. All reservation churches that collect substantial donations from well-meaning people all over the world who have no idea that native people have their own spiritual beliefs, "don't need no white-man Jesus." The priests and pastors live in tidy houses with neatly kept lawns, hedges, and thriving gardens; why should they suffer?

Regardless of who you are, however, the pace in Pine Ridge is infectiously *slooooow*, cars and trucks crawl along, no hurry . . . there is no place to go. But I can't let myself fall into this rhythm; it is already past ten a.m., there are fifty more miles to Kyle, and I simply must stop at Wounded Knee.

ACT TWO

All Indians must dance, everywhere, keep on dancing. Pretty soon in next spring Great Spirit come. He bring back game of every kind. The game be thick everywhere. All dead Indians come back and live again. They all be strong like young men, be young again. Old blind Indians see again and get young and have fine time. When Great Spirit comes this way, then all Indians go to mountains, high up away from whites. Whites can't hurt Indians then. Then while Indians way up high, big flood comes like water and all white people die, get drowned. After that, water go way and then nobody but Indians everywhere and game all kinds thick. Then medicine man tell Indians to send word to all Indians to keep up dancing and the good time will come. Indians who don't dance, who don't believe in this word, will grow little. Just about a foot high, and stay that way. Some of them will be turned into wood and be burned in fire.

—WOVOKA, PAIUTE MESSIAH,
TEACHER OF THE GHOST DANCE

CRAZY HORSE SIGN

NO POETRY FOR TASUNKA WITKO

Once *Villa VW* chugs across the Pine Ridge "city limits," I can drive faster, but not too fast; reservation roads are notoriously treacherous: slick when it rains, icy during winter, clogged with foot traffic, stray dogs and horses, inebriated drivers, blown tires, and potholes to China. In 1973, on my way to Rapid City, I nearly ran over two drunk men who lay passed out on the road near Scenic, South Dakota, then a liquor-soaked border town like Whiteclay.

It was mid-morning; the men lay perpendicular to the road, three-quarters of their bodies on the blacktop. I would have killed both if one hadn't been wearing a bright red shirt, which from a distance I saw as a pool of blood. Fearing they were dead, I screeched to a stop . . . perhaps they had fallen or been thrown out the back of a truck. But the moment I got out of the car, it was apparent they were alive. There was an overwhelming stench of beer, cigarette smoke, urine; and then came the snoring, loud and sustained like the rumblings of a passing Chicago elevated train. Waking them was a lost cause. Neither stirred when I grabbed their ankles, pulled one and then the other off the road. It was nasty work. There was no way I could have gotten them into the back-seat of my car, nor did I want to. This was before cell phones, so I couldn't call the tribal cops, not that they would have given a damn. Shit happens—drunks stumbling down the dark highways, drunks driving blind without headlights, drunks falling asleep at the wheel, whole carloads of the oblivious rolling down embankments. Heads spinning in the starry night.

The land east of Pine Ridge is flat again—once lush buffalo grass as far as the eye can see now plowed under, pulverized, replanted, turned into dull-brown yellow wheat fields, dusty pastures, fallow land, a few farmhouses, fences, barns, domesticated animals, and domesticated people. I am still on the reservation, but most of what I see belongs to white farmers and ranchers, a consequence of the notorious 1887 Dawes Act, which divided tribal lands into individual parcels, 160 acres to each head of a family as long as they were registered members of the tribe, 80 acres to unmarried adults. Well-intentioned, the act's stated goal was to encourage native people to adopt the ways of whites by giving them their very own farms. A transformative experience—Indians would learn the pride of ownership, the value of hard work; they would see the shortcomings of their primitive ways. Soon they would talk like, dress like, and act like proper white people. Indian men with short haircuts, Indians baking cherry pies, and parents happily packing their little ones off to boarding school. Everyone, of course, free to join the Christian church of his or her choice. But the reformers forgot one thing: in America, if you own a little piece of land, you have the right to sell it . . . right? And thus the Dawes Act became a cruel joke. White speculators moved in to buy up the best reservation land. When I taught at Little Wound School, one of my first surprises was how many of my students were the privileged white children of parents who owned sizeable farms and ranches on the reservation.

The intersection to Wounded Knee and ultimately Kyle is straight ahead. As I slow down and turn left, I remember the makeshift memorial sign on this spot that honors the great warrior Crazy Horse. Just words, lots of words on a large metal plate suspended between two metal poles implanted into a cement base. Ah, the poetry on this sign, powerfully stated; the words written and the letters hand painted by Vernell's revered father, Chief Guy White Thunder, now eighty-nine, one of the oldest living Lakota. I am excited to read it again, and to take photos, something I failed to do all the times I've been here before.

What the holy crap!

The sign is no more—I can see only the base, the metal poles pointing skyward like solitary sentinels with blank space between them. There is nothing to hold up or defend, no tribute, no poetry for Tasunka Witko, the Spartacus, Miyamoto Musashi, Hannibal Barca of the Lakota Oglala, great war chief who humiliated, then *defeated*, the U.S. Army. Who took down this sign, and why? Tribal dispute? Rowdy teenage boys just being teenage boys? Seething, I get out of the car to take photos anyway. The concrete base is defaced with graffiti; there are beer cans, bottles, and wrappers strewn about. I stopped here so many times in thc past, never got tired of reading the sign, dedicated in 1964. Across the top in large letters was the heading, which I still remember:

OGLALA SIOUX
1840—WAR CHIEF CRAZY HORSE—1877
TASUNKA WITKO

Underneath was a lyrical summation of Crazy Horse's remarkable life, how his mother delivered him by a stream near the holy mountain Mato Paha (Bear Butte) and wrapped him in a piece of soft deerskin; how he was different, with light skin and sandy-brown curly hair; how they called him Curly. When they were only eleven, Curly and his best friend, Hump, emulated the warriors of the village—went on horse-catching expeditions, snuck away to join war parties and buffalo hunts. Still in his teens, Curly famously took part in a battle with the Arapahos; he bravely charged straight into them, counted coup three times, and came back with a painful but not debilitating shoulder wound. Impressed by his son's brave deed, his father gave him his own name, Tasunka Witko; took up the new name Waglula (Worm); and told his son to go on a vision quest. On this quest, Crazy Horse saw a magnificent war pony floating above the ground, mounted by an unpainted warrior who had a single feather in his long brown hair, a small brown stone tied behind his ear. This unpainted warrior spoke to Crazy Horse, instructed him before battle to streak his pony with dirt thrown up by a burrowing mole, and to touch the dirt to his hair, so that the mole's blindness would make him and his horse harder to see. "Live for the people and never take anything for yourself," the warrior said, "and you will have the power to ride straight through your enemies. You won't be killed or wounded by their lead balls, flying arrows. You can only be hurt by your own people, who will someday betray you."

Crazy Horse lived by these rules. He never bragged about his exploits. He gave his captured ponies to the needy boys of the camp, and he always honored the old ways, refused to live the life of an agency Indian, never touched the pen to a treaty. As foreseen in his vision, his own people spread rumors about him, said he was planning an uprising at Fort Robinson, when he only wanted to live in peace. They conspired with the soldiers to put Crazy Horse in jail, but their plans went horribly wrong. Crazy Horse struggled to get free, but one of his old warrior friends held him tightly. Just as Longinus killed Jesus at Golgotha, a soldier thrust his bayonet into Crazy Horse's backside. Refusing a bed at the agency clinic, Crazy Horse lay bleeding on the floor throughout the night, and as the sun came up, he died. His parents took his body on a travois to be buried in a secret place some twenty miles southeast of here. Crazy Horse was never photographed. No one knows exactly what he looked like.

All these things were beautifully written by Vernell's father, and beautifully inscribed on this remarkable sign. Poetry more powerful than any gigantic mountainside carving.

The Crazy Horse figure carved into Thunder Mountain near Custer Park in the Black Hills, when finished, will be by far the world's largest sculpture, dwarfing the Mount Rushmore presidents. Already visited by millions every year, it makes a statement: *Indians too had great leaders!* (And they merit big monuments.)

Shortly after moving to the rez from Chicago in 1971, I made a trip to the Black Hills, and was fortunate to meet Korczak Ziolkowski, the Polish-American sculptor responsible for this great work. It is impossible for me to forget his carefully cultivated French fork beard and mustache, his battered cowboy hat, his eyes squinting as if he were facing the sun even when he wasn't, and of course the Polish accent. Considering that Ziolkowski had a lot of work to do and I was just an idealistic young teacher from Chicago, he was extraordinarily generous with his time. What a thrill it was when he handed me the letter sent to him on November 9, 1939, by Henry Standing Bear, an Oglala chief, Crazy Horse's maternal cousin. "This letter is what got me started," Ziolkowski said.

The letter must have been written with black ink using a fountain pen as it was smudged in several places, but I could clearly read it, and I was struck by the directness and casualness of Standing Bear's prose—and its correctness. "My fellow chiefs and I," he wrote, "are interested in finding some sculptor who can carve a head of an Indian Chief who was killed many years ago."

Standing Bear was one of the first Indian children educated at the Carlisle Indian Industrial School in Pennsylvania, a notoriously racist boarding school set up to transform Indian children into little white Christians. (The motto of its founder, Captain Richard Henry Pratt, was "kill the child to save the man.") Standing Bear learned to speak and write English at Carlisle and used his skills to advocate for his people . . . his Indian culture apparently intact. He and Ziolkowski became great friends. Together they made the plans for the Crazy Horse Monument, selected the site, and got the project off the ground.

As the former assistant to the sculptor who created Mount Rushmore, Ziolkowski was eminently qualified to handle such a huge task. He obsessively worked on his Crazy Horse stone sculpture for thirty-four years, honoring Standing Bear's request not to accept any government monies, to rely totally on donations. When he died from pancreatitis in 1982 at the age of seventy-four, his wife, children, and grandchildren continued the project.

It has been nearly seventy years since the first of thousands of dynamite blasts made a small dent in the side of the iron-ore-rich mountain. When I visited Ziolkowski, you could see that someone had blown the crap out of some rocks, the beginning of what could conceivably be a face. Today you can clearly see what is supposed to be Crazy Horse's head, even though no one knows what Crazy Horse looked like. Though there is no target date for completion, millions of tourists visit the site every year, which includes a museum with one of the world's largest collections of indigenous artifacts. The tourists buy admission tickets and souvenirs, eat in the cafeteria and help fund the project for the Ziolkowskis, who live on the site. There doesn't seem to be any sense of urgency to finish the carving; blasting is frequently halted to focus on fund-raising.

Is this something Crazy Horse would have wanted? I must ask Vernell what he thinks; but more important, does he know who stole his father's sign?

WOUNDED KNEE

THE BABY WAS STILL ALIVE

I send Vernell a text to let him know I'm traveling his direction: *Headed your way!*

He replies: *I'll put on the beans.*

Only two or three more miles of rolling flatness beyond the virtual Crazy Horse sign, I am again metamorphosed by the rugged beauty of the Pine Ridge I love: the Jurassic formations, waves of evergreen, golden-brown underbrush, chalky cliffs, and, popping up to my right, a village I've never seen before; I have to pull over, investigate, take a few photos. A quiet little cluster of BIA houses nestled at the base of a forbidding pine-coated hill, no road sign to indicate the name of this place, no water tower, no gas stations, post office, or churches. The people living here must have recently moved in from the remote areas where they lived in one-room log houses or battered trailers, kept a horse and a few chickens outside, maybe a garden; it's doubtful they had plumbing or electricity. If my mother were alive, she would say, "How can they live like this?" as if there were a choice. But I see no evidence of life. No kids playing outside, no barking dogs, no horses, no one walking on the roads—yet there are a few cars and pickup trucks parked about . . . and the air is deadly still. Is this village with no name a ghost village, a mirage, a hunting ground for hapless lost souls? It scares me; I drive on.

Around the next curve and up a steep incline, I'm suddenly looking down at Wounded Knee, so barren you could easily miss it; the saddest little hill in America positioned near the middle of an unremarkable valley carved out of the plains by "the creek of a wounded knee" (*chankpe opi wakpala*). You have to squint your eyes from here to see fencing on top of Wounded Knee, the odd-looking portal—two white, maroon-checkered columns made from cinder blocks and bricks, joined together by an iron lattice archway, topped off with a small cross; the entrance to a cemetery. The cemetery where they unceremoniously dumped the grotesquely deformed, frozen corpses of Chief Big Foot and his scraggly band of warriors, old men, women, children, some shredded beyond recognition by .45-70 cartridges from the 9th Calvary's Hotchkiss Gatling guns. Dumped in a long narrow trench on a blustery cold New Year's Day, 1891. According to the army burial-brigade count, there are 146 souls here, yet only forty-three names are chiseled into the obelisk stone marker at the foot of the mass grave. Some say there are many more buried here, up to 300.

As I drive into the valley, I think about the pretty Sacred Heart Catholic church that once stood by the side of this cemetery, the crown of its stately bell-tower steeple pointing high into the prairie sky. Except for the bright red door, the whole church, even the roof, was painted white—such an idyllic sight, you would never know by looking at it that the Catholic missionaries were determined to destroy native culture, that they built a system of oppressive boarding schools on reservations across America where Indian children were denied the right to speak their native tongue, not allowed to go home, often beaten and sexually abused. Looking at it, you would think these missionaries really cared about their native flock, protecting people, providing love and sustenance.

Across the road from the little hill was a trading post that also served as the post office, and a large log building, the Wounded Knee Museum, curated by a gregarious, wheelchair-bound old man, Wilbur Riegert, who could have easily been mistaken for a South Dakota farmer of Belgian origin, though he claimed to be part Chippewa. I liked him very much. Obviously intelligent and dedicated, he had been collecting Lakota artifacts for many years. In addition to the usual quillwork, moccasins, breastplates, flint scrapers—both flint and steel arrowheads—and other relics you might find at the Crazy Horse Memorial Museum or in Rushville's Pfister Hotel, Riegert had a magnificent, priceless painting of the last known keeper of the Sacred Pipe, Martha Bad Warrior, and two rare buffalo hide paintings depicting the Lakota's complete knowledge of the stars. There was also a haunting display of black-and-white photographs taken in the aftermath of the 1890 massacre: Chief Big Foot lying on the frozen ground, his fingers and legs twisted like pretzels; soldiers standing by their horses, smoking and looking around at the charred piles of blankets and buffalo robes; soldiers dutifully piling corpses in a trench; more frozen corpses; the remains of the burned-out wagon that carried Chief Big Foot on his final earthly journey.

Stooped over in his wheelchair, Riegert was clearly in decline, but his neck snapped to attention and he smiled warmly whenever someone came through the museum door. He loved to share his encyclopedic knowledge of Indian culture and history, would talk for hours and hours if you let him, had a story to tell about each object in his collection. Sadly, when radical Indians occupied Wounded Knee in 1973, they couldn't see much value in maintaining Riegert's lifework. Their view was that all these things were stolen property and since there was no way to determine the original owners, it was perfectly OK to repossess them. While being held hostage with his wife and twelve-year-old granddaughter, Riegert watched in silent horror as object after object was removed from the museum until there was nothing left, not even an arrowhead.

The unpaved road up the hill to the graveyard is dry, yet deep tire ruts make the going slow; this is not the type of terrain German engineers had in mind when they decided to manufacture my poor underpowered *Villa VW* in Mexico. As I near the top, I see a few people milling about; Indian schoolchildren with their teacher, a couple of tourists, a boy selling dream catchers. I park in front of the portal; it is only a few steps to the mass grave protected by a short chain-link fence, easy enough to hop over if you wanted to. Outlined by a narrow strip of concrete, the grave is a single trench less than six feet wide and about eight feet long, a rough surface of grass, dirt, and weeds. Someone has disrespectfully tossed a cigarette butt near where I am standing. I find it hard to imagine the mangled bones beneath this surface.

Alongside the middle of the tomb stands an eight-foot-tall obelisk grave marker topped with a four-sided Ming Dynasty roof and temple vase. This strange but appropriately somber granite monument was placed here by relatives of the deceased in 1903. Carved into the side facing the rising sun is an inscription followed by the names of forty-three people known to be buried here. It is barely legible; if someone doesn't restore it, it will soon fade away, perhaps forever:

> *This monument is erected by surviving relatives and other Ogallala and Cheyenne River Sioux Indians in memory of the Chief Big Foot massacre December 29, 1890. Col. Forsyth in command of U.S. troops. Big Foot was a great chief of the Sioux Indians. He often said "I will stand in peace till my last day comes." He did many good and brave deeds for the white man and the red man. Many innocent women and children who knew no wrong died here.*

This is followed by a list of names, of which I can make out a few:

> *Chief Big Foot, Yellow Robe, Long Bull, Wounded Hand, Red Eagle, Pretty Hawk, He Crow, Spotted*

Thunder, Chase In Winter, He Eagle, No Ears, Shoots the Bear, Red Horn, Wolf Skin Necklace, Weasel Bear, Big Skirt, Pass Water In Horn, Kills Seneca, Yellow Bird, Picked Horses, Bird Shakes.

A large blue prayer ribbon is tied around the vase; multitudes of colored ribbons are tied to the fence and nearby tree branches; sage and wilted flowers are scattered about. Just as I turn to walk away, a millennial tourist couple solemnly approaches the monument, squats before it at a respectful distance, takes photos. Lost in thought, they stand, silently peruse the scene. Better dressed than most tourists—he wears khaki pants and a polo shirt buttoned at the top instead of the stereotypical tattered cargo shorts and Duck Dynasty Mount Rushmore T-shirts you see on so many tourists these days, and she has on a fashionable floral-print maxi dress suitable for a summer backyard party in the Hamptons—they could be Ralph Lauren models if they were only a bit thinner. They look stunned . . . it must be incomprehensible to many Anglo-Americans that their government of the people, for the people could commit such an atrocity; U.S. soldiers gunning down women and children on U.S. soil (never mind the My Lai or Al-Ishaqi massacres). It's sad for anyone to see this, but I am happy they are here; everyone should come to Wounded Knee at least once.

The Indian boy selling cheap factory-made dream catchers rudely brings the contemplative couple back to reality. "Hey, where you from?" he asks aggressively.

The woman replies, "From Cincinnati. On our way to the 'Faces.' Heard about this place from my father-in-law. He loves *everything* about the West."

The boy shows them the dream catcher, says he made it himself; many hours of fine craftsmanship. He smiles as they pay him twenty dollars.

Not sure I approve of what he is doing, I avoid eye contact, but this doesn't stop him from approaching me. I give in . . . look up at his glowing, girlish baby face and see he is wearing an old Michael Jordan basketball jersey.

"Hey, where you from?" he asks.

I tell him I once lived near here but now I am from California and no thanks, I don't want to buy a dream catcher; I have more dream catchers than I could ever need.

He laughs, quickly shifts gears as if he realizes that I realize what a fraud his dream catcher scam is, tells me his name (I'll call him George), and asks me if I want to take his picture.

George stands underneath the Wounded Knee portal, raises his fist as a sign, he says, of "Indian pride," gives me a big smile. He's obviously a bright kid; he tells me he goes to the Red Cloud Indian School in Pine Ridge, where his favorite class is computer science . . . *So what*, I now think, *that he makes a few bucks selling dream catchers he buys in Rapid City for a dollar ninety-five?* When he asks me to send him a copy of the photo, I enter his address into my phone, and when he asks for a donation, I give him five dollars.

George wanders off. I survey the rest of the cemetery; there are many other graves here, some sweet little ones just as poignant in their way as the mass grave—mound of dirt, simple wooden cross, name painted or carved into the crossbar: Mike Shot, Marvin M. Two Two, Zandra R. Shot, Ann T. Respects Nothing, and one that conjures up an especially sad story, Zintkala Zi (Yellow Bird).

The marker implies that she was a baby who died in 1976, but actually she was still a six-month-old fetus when a brutish cop, Clifford Valentine, viciously kicked her mom in the stomach outside a bar in Gordon, Nebraska. After being kicked, Jo Ann Yellow Bird fell against a parked car and slid to the ground. She experienced pain in her stomach and lower back, and later testified in a civil lawsuit, "I felt the baby kick once, real hard, and then I never felt it." She begged, "Take me to a hospital," but Valentine handcuffed her, threw her in the back of his squad car, and sped off toward the Sheridan County Jail, some twenty miles to the west.

As she sat thrashing about, kicking the front seat, she continued to scream, "Motherfucker, I need a doctor." Valentine began swerving across the road, turned his head, and yelled; "Shut up, squaw bitch, or I'll push you out of this goddamn car and shoot you."

"Why don't you?"

Valentine laughed. "I don't want to waste any good bullets."

Once in jail, Jo Ann continued her pleas to see a doctor. In her support, other inmates started yelling and banging on the cell bars, but the sheriff's deputies ignored them. Next morning she was driven in handcuffs to Gordon Memorial Hospital, where doctors were unable to detect a fetal heartbeat. They called for an ambulance to the Pine Ridge hospital. It was too late. Jo Ann delivered a stillborn baby.

Zintkala Zi is a direct descendant of the Yellow Bird who is buried in the mass grave, one of the names still visible on the obelisk. Some say it was this Yellow Bird, a fanatical medicine man, who set off the series of missteps that provoked the soldiers to start shooting on the morning of December 29, 1889. When the soldiers went into the camp to search for weapons, Yellow Bird began dancing the Ghost Dance (Wacipi Wanagi), throwing dirt on himself, shouting to the other warriors, "Do not be afraid, because the soldier's bullets cannot hurt you." Most agree that Yellow Bird played a role in the start of the events—it may have been simply a cloud of dust thought to be gunfire; it may have been the firing of a hidden weapon. Regardless, a crack rang out through the camp of soldiers and American Indians. A tragedy ensued that continues to haunt American history.

There are flowers and bows on Zintkala Zi's grave, and on many others, perhaps because it is Good Friday.

Not all of the graves are marked with wooden crosses; a few have modest granite tombstones. One of these is on the grave of Zintkala Zi's father, Bob Yellow Bird. A U.S. Navy Vietnam veteran who lived much of his life in Gordon, he was the leader of the Nebraska American Indian Movement (AIM). In 1996, while drinking in a bar in Martin, South Dakota, a border town near the southeast corner of the rez,

Yellow Bird shot himself in the head while playing Russian roulette with a group of fellow veterans (they must have seen *The Deer Hunter*). Somehow, Bob survived but was paralyzed on his left side. A heavy smoker his entire adult life, he died a year later from lung cancer.

I see the name Phillip J. Black Elk on the next tombstone and remember meeting him during the 1973 Wounded Knee occupation. A nephew of the great Lakota spiritual leader Black Elk (made famous by the book *Black Elk Speaks*), Phillip Black Elk was blown to smithereens a few days after the occupation when he tried to light his propane burner to heat up a cup of coffee. Because he was an AIM supporter, many people believe he was assassinated, but because an FBI investigation revealed there had been an earlier gas leak in his house, the odds are pretty high it was an accident.

There's a gravestone for Vincent Fast Horse, a Lakota Vietnam veteran, who was only twenty-seven when he died in an automobile wreck involving alcohol in 1975.

And then there's Lost Bird.

On a bittersweet slab of reddish-gray granite, the inscription inside a fancy border simply reads: LOST BIRD, BORN MAY—1890, DIED FEB.—1919. Something is terribly melancholic about this tombstone: the name, the simplicity. Lost Bird was only three months old when she was found frostbitten but still alive under her mother's frozen corpse on the site of the Wounded Knee massacre. Carefully bundled in a buffalo blanket, she wore a warm cap decorated with tiny red, white, and blue glass beads. Dehydrated, her breathing labored, Lost Bird somehow managed to cry out just loud enough. The first to hear her was a half-blood Santee Dakota doctor with the white name Charles Eastman. He yelled, "Someone is alive. A baby, a baby is alive!" The same soldiers who had gleefully murdered Lakota women and children only three days earlier began frantically searching for her; it was a miracle that any human could have survived for even a few hours in the subzero weather. Dr. Eastman rushed Lost Bird on horseback to the Pine Ridge Agency, where he revived her and nurtured her back to good health. Indians and whites alike who knew about Lost Bird came forward to adopt her, some out of compassion, others because they thought she would bring them good fortune.

Stolen, retrieved, and stolen again, Lost Bird had four different names before the commander of the Nebraska National Guard, Brigadier General Leonard Colby, disobeying military orders, adopted the small living "curio" of the massacre, and later—after resigning as assistant attorney general of the United States—used her to convince prominent tribes to hire him as their lawyer. As an adolescent, Lost Bird was sexually abused by the general, and her adoptive mother, Clara Colby, divorced him. A suffragist and prominent newspaper columnist, Ms. Colby spoke up against the exploitation of Indian culture and defied her friends Susan B. Anthony and Elizabeth Cady Stanton by raising the girl alone.

Lost Bird was brought up to be independent and strong willed. She lived a charmed life full of special privileges—private schools, music lessons, shopping trips to New York, fashionable clothes—but Lost Bird had trouble resisting the many diseases of the white world; she caught colds easily, had allergies, came down with severe measles and mumps, and suffered her whole life from migraine headaches. As she grew into her teenage years, her exotic good looks, gold-brown skin, and long onyx ponytails attracted unwanted male attention, and jealousy from the white girls. Mean and spiteful, they called her names, sometimes shouting them out, other times whispering in her ear: "Squaw whore," "Pocahontas bitch," "Prairie nigger." Confused about her identity and the animosity it created, she ran away from her boarding school, fled across country seeking other Native Americans, and even spent a few weeks in Pine Ridge, only to be more devastated as these girls too saw her as some sort of freak, a "Lakota white girl" who looked like them but acted white.

Slapped in the face at every turn, Lost Bird sought solace in alcohol and in the men who were always making passes at her—she became the promiscuous Indian princess of their lusty dreams, and when she got pregnant, she turned to her adoptive father for help. No doubt thinking he was doing the right thing, General Colby put her in the Nebraska Industrial Home for unwed mothers in Milford, which was established with good intentions as a rehabilitation home for "penitent girls" who had "no specific disease," where, for a minimum required period of one year, they could bear their babies and "be trained in practical arts, homemaking, health and moral teachings." The children, when born, could be kept by the mother, adopted out, or sent to an orphanage.

Soon after her arrival, Lost Bird gave birth to a stillborn son, and yet she continued to be confined against her will in the home for another year. She eventually returned to live with her mother in Washington, D.C., where one of the several men Lost Bird married gave her syphilis. Dressed as an Indian maiden, she worked in vaudeville and in the early movie business, and for a short time joined Buffalo Bill's Wild West Show. She had two more children: one daughter, who died, and a boy, whom she gave to an Indian woman friend because she was too poor to take care of him.

Living in California, Lost Bird was only twenty-nine when she fell victim to the Spanish flu and was buried in a pauper's grave in the remote town of Hanford. Seventy-one years after Lost Bird's death, on August 8, 1990, Renée Sansom Flood, author of *Lost Bird of Wounded Knee: Spirit of the Lakota*, was invited to Wounded Knee, South Dakota, for a meeting of the Wounded Knee Survivors' Association, a group of Lakota elders who mostly wanted to know where Lost Bird was buried and how to teach others how to deal with "Lost Bird syndrome," moving from one foster home to another. It was at this meeting where someone spontaneously said, "We should bring Lost Bird home, and bury her with her relatives at Wounded Knee."

Marie Not Help Him was put in charge of fund-raising, and thanks to Nelson Rockefeller's daughter, Ann R. Robert, who provided the bulk of the money, a year later, on July 11, 1991, the Pine Ridge Wounded Knee Survivors Association's painstaking efforts to return Lost Bird to her homeland became a sacred reality. This time she was buried as a symbol for all people of the world who have been deprived of their heritage.

Lost Bird lies at Wounded Knee now. And I suppose you might even say she was lucky, as the soldiers deliberately killed many children that day. In testimony to the Commissioner of Indian Affairs in Washington, D.C., on February 11, 1891, Chief American Horse reported, "The women and children . . . were strewn all along the circular village until they were dispatched. Right near the flag of truce a mother was shot down with her infant; the child not knowing that its mother was dead was still nursing. . . . The women as they were fleeing with their babies were killed together, shot right through, and the women who were very heavy with child were also killed. All the Indians fled in . . . three directions, and after most of them had been killed a cry was made that all those who were not killed [or] wounded should come forth and they would be safe. Little boys who were not wounded came out of their places of refuge, and as soon as they came in sight a number of soldiers surrounded them and butchered them there."

The grandest grave marker is just to the right of Lost Bird's grave—a large block of granite resting on a separate, rectangular slab that covers the entire grave. It honors a young Lakota man, Lawrence "Buddy" La Monte, who was shot dead by a federal marshal sniper eleven days before the end of the 1973 takeover. The headstone is simply engraved "SON" above the image of the sacred pipe. There is a longer message on the rectangular slab:

TA CAN NUPE WAKAN
2000 AND 500 CAME TO WOUNDED KNEE 1973
ONE STILL REMAINS
LAWRENCE "BUDDY" LA MONTE

Etched below is a scene of a Lakota village: several tepees at the foot of a hill, a traditionally dressed Indian boy, bow slung on his back. About to jump on his horse, he waves good-bye to an old man wearing a war bonnet. Below this is inscribed in cursive:

Although he went away traveling alone,
we'll meet one day at our final home.

The American Indian Movement was founded in 1968 by Native American leaders as a militant political and civil rights organization. Shortly before dawn on November 20, 1969, eighty-nine radical American Indians led by Russell Means and Dennis Banks boarded boats in Sausalito, California, and made the five-mile trip across foggy San Francisco Bay to Alcatraz Island. Upon landing, they declared the former prison Indian land "by right of discovery" and demanded the U.S. government provide funding to turn it into a Native American cultural center and university. No surprise, their terms were ignored, and in defiance of the authorities, the island was occupied for nineteen months, until June 1971. In November 1972, AIM members briefly occupied the Bureau of Indian Affairs headquarters in Washington, D.C., to protest programs controlling reservation development. This represented the culmination of a cross-country journey called the Trail of Broken Treaties, intended to bring attention to American Indian living standards and treaty rights issues. Protesters vandalized the building, overturned tables and desks against the windows, and set fire to the interior offices and the marble lobbies, destroying many historical documents.

The man who caused the American Indian Movement to gain worldwide attention was an Indian cowboy from Kyle, older than but related to Vernell White Thunder, who, like Vernell, lived his early days in a one-room log house, and who had a reputation for being friendly and always dependable. His name was Raymond Yellow Thunder, and on February 13, 1972, he was brutally killed by two racist thugs, brothers Melvin and Leslie Hare. After savagely beating him, they stripped Yellow Thunder of his pants, underwear, and shoes; put him in the trunk of their car; and drove around the racist border town of Gordon, Nebraska. They pushed him into the American Legion Hall to be ridiculed by those attending a dance before finally dumping him back where they'd found him. He later died of his injuries. The actual memories of the Wounded Knee occupation flood my mind. How it began on a perfectly still, cold winter night, February 27, 1973; snow was on the ground, the roads were icy, and it felt like a blizzard was on the way. Vernell and I both were living in the northeastern corner of the reservation, in the little village of Wanblee, about seventy miles from Wounded Knee. Melvin White Bull, one of the students I knew from Wanblee Crazy Horse High School, ran up to me as I was out walking with my dog, alternately smoking marijuana and tobacco in my pipe. He was so out of breath, I had a hard time understanding him. "Mr. Bunnell, have you heard? AIM took over Wounded Knee!" His mom had received a call from one of her cousins . . . a call from Wounded Knee, not from the pay phone outside the post office, but from the phone inside the museum. "AIM shot out the streetlights, set up roadblocks. The GOONs are coming," Melvin said, referring to newly elected tribal president Dick Wilson's vigilante group, Guardians of the Oglala Nation.

The night the occupation took place, a meeting with traditional Oglala elders took place in Calico, a tiny hamlet north of Pine Ridge. Speaking in Lakota (he never spoke English), Frank Fools Crow, the head medicine man, said to his followers, "Go ahead and do it. Go to Wounded Knee. You can't get into the BIA office and the tribal office, so take your brothers from the American Indian Movement and go to Wounded Knee and make your stand there." Fools Crow rode in the lead car along with AIM leaders Dennis Banks and Russell Means, and along the way he reminded them that Dick Wilson was "a heavy-drinking bootlegger known for corruption, who favor[ed] giving up more Lakota land, even the sacred Pahá Sapá itself."

The takeover was hardly well thought out. People just jumped into their cars; drove through Pine Ridge yelling, honking their horns, and giving the finger to the Feds; and raced on to Wounded Knee. I feared for them. Hatred on the reservation was so thick, it made breathing difficult—another massacre, bloodier than the 1890 original, was not out of the question. I had to do something, so I rushed back to the trailer house where I then lived and called my dad, who was working late that night at the newspaper office. After telling him what I knew, I pleaded with him, "Dad, you need to post a bulletin on the Associated Press wire and do it now . . . or there will be bloodshed. The government will sit back and let Wilson's armed thugs kill everyone."

Killing a bunch of radical Indians was no problem, I figured, but it would be politically embarrassing to shoot reporters and TV anchormen. I don't know if Dad believed it was really that serious, but he put a report out on the wire, which was instantly transmitted to TV, radio, and newspaper offices around the world. I will never know for sure what impact this had, but AIM leader Russell Means had similar ideas. When he showed up in Wounded Knee about an hour after the initial arrivals, having failed to stop people from looting the trading post, he got on the museum phone to call the media. By sunrise (6:31 a.m.), a CBS news truck from Denver was broadcasting from Wounded Knee, sending out reports and special bulletins. For the time being, the Wounded Knee occupiers were safe; no one was going to launch an attack while the whole world was watching.

I admit it was pretty exciting to go from living in the middle of nowhere to living in the middle of a media firestorm. Friends and family called to see if my family was safe, to learn what was happening. Nightly newscasts from Wounded Knee reported on the latest developments, stalled negotiations, new demands, the occasional glimmers of hope, disappointments. They interviewed the parade of celebrities, politicians, and self-proclaimed revolutionaries who came to Wounded Knee to show their support and get some free worldwide exposure. Among them were Marlon Brando, Jane Fonda, Johnny Cash, Abbie

Hoffman, William Kunstler, Ralph Abernathy, Angela Davis, and South Dakota senators George McGovern and James Abourezk.

FBI operatives and federal marshals armed with M-16 rifles, grenade launchers, C-S gas, M-40 explosives, helicopters, and at least seventeen armored personnel carriers surrounded Wounded Knee, set up roadblocks, bunkers, sandbagged trenches, and communication outposts. They said their mission was peaceful—to keep people, guns, and ammunition from getting in, and keep the GOONs from trying to storm the place. They were successful with the latter but not so much with the former. There are too many gullies and trails going into Wounded Knee; within days, the population had more than doubled, as had the quantity and quality of the weapons. At five o'clock one morning, three single-engine planes swooped down on Wounded Knee and dropped ten giant, colorful parachutes, each balancing hundreds of pounds of food and supplies. Ironically, Vista workers, employed by the government to repair schools and provide services to Pine Ridge residents and students, were among the most active smugglers, sneaking ammunition and high-powered rifles into the village at night. Vista workers were young idealists; they saw themselves as Contras during the day, Sandinistas at night.

Hunkered down in my trailer house trying to stay warm, I felt goose bumps when I saw Russell Means on *CBS Evening News* with his long braids and ferocious eyes, wagging his finger, saying some of the most outrageous things ever broadcast: "We declare Wounded Knee an independent country!" "We demand the immediate return of the Black Hills!" "We insist Secretary of State Henry Kissinger come to Wounded Knee to negotiate an end to these hostilities!"

So utterly defiant, proud, unafraid; in my mind, Russell Means was the Lakota equivalent of Malcolm X, Eldridge Cleaver, and H. Rap Brown; he was the American Indian Movement's most important leader because he had by far the most charisma. It never mattered to me that AIM made a habit of occupying and trashing government buildings and burning down courthouses; nor that like the Black Panthers, they marched around with guns. Watching Russell Means on TV, I knew that no matter how things turned out, despite all the theatrical pretentiousness, there was a watershed of change going on, a watershed of historic proportions. Whatever happened from here on out, pride had been restored to the American Indians, pride that would never again under any circumstances be taken from them.

I was, of course, anxious to do more, but it was complicated. Fired from my first teaching job in Kyle, I had moved with Linda to a nearby village, Wanblee (meaning "Eagle"), where she'd landed a position at Crazy Horse High School. I took care of our toddler daughter, Mara, during the day while Linda was working, as there were no day-care centers, nor babysitters. I couldn't drop everything, head over to Wounded Knee with a tent and my sleeping bag, stay for the duration, write down my observations in a notebook, take photos. But I couldn't stay away either.

Before sunup one morning about two weeks into the occupation, I bundled Mara into our blue 1970 Pontiac station wagon and took the 150-mile back route through Martin, South Dakota, and Gordon, Nebraska—which bypasses Wounded Knee—to Alliance. I left Mara with her more-than-happy-to-oblige grandmother and headed downtown to my father-in-law John Essay's grocery store. He wondered why I needed a whole shopping cart filled with chicken and hamburger, another of canned food and produce, another of cereal, bread, rolls, and chips—and yet another of milk and soft drinks. I wasn't sure what his reaction would be, so I opted for the truth. I was taking this food up to the Indians at Wounded Knee. He only laughed; he knew me well and wasn't a bit surprised. John had inherited the store from his father, who immigrated to Alliance from Lebanon. Having faced discrimination all his life from some of the locals who distrusted "Arabs," John was sympathetic to Indians, many of whom shopped in his store; he even spoke a few words of Lakota, and he was the only merchant in Alliance who gave them credit. I loaded up as quickly as I could to get back on the road, and by noon that day I found myself pulling up to a federal roadblock two miles south of Wounded Knee.

A personnel carrier blocked the road. Four or five federal marshals stood beside it with assault rifles, ammunition belts, high-powered binoculars, bulletproof vests—but they looked relaxed; one was eating sunflower seeds, another smoking a cigarette. Driving up to them, I worried I was doing something really stupid, but it was too late to turn back. Both sides had agreed to the first cease-fire, but shooting was still frequent. A U.S. marshal had been shot and paralyzed in March, and a Cherokee and an Oglala Lakota were killed in April 1973—plus Ray Robinson, a civil rights activist who joined the protesters, disappeared during the events and is believed to have been murdered.

After checking cars for weapons and taking down names, the marshals were letting people in, but not without comment. While one rummaged through my groceries and another looked underneath the car, a third sneered at me and sarcastically said, "You taking food to the Indians so they can keep shooting at us?"

"No, sir," I replied. "Not in favor of shooting anybody."

"You tell them that, OK?"

"Yes, sir. I'll tell them that," I lied.

One of the marshals got into the personnel carrier and drove it off the road just enough so I could get by. I was elated; this had been much easier than I had hoped.

The silly grin on my face quickly disappeared, however, when I came upon the next roadblock—two junked-out pickup trucks, their tires flattened, loaded up with sandbags, scrap metal, and cinder blocks so they would be too heavy to easily move aside. The words AIM CONTROL were spray-painted on their doors, and they were positioned so you could get past them only if you zigzagged around the first and then zigzagged the opposite way around the second. Two Indian men—boys, really—their scrawny arms hanging out of loose-fitting T-shirts like sticks of dried spaghetti, sat back-to-back on the road in front of the trucks, one holding a 12-gauge shotgun, the other a .22. A third Indian, who stood on the front truck bed, had a tired look on his face, and for some reason I tagged him as a Vietnam vet. He held up a hand and spread his fingers as a signal for me to stop.

"Where the fuck do you think you're going?"

"Brought food; I'm delivering it to the people."

The boys stood up and moved to each side of my station wagon. I noticed two things about them: each had droopy long hair much in need of a shampoo, and each had a finger on the trigger of his weapon. The older man hopped down from the pickup bed and approached my car with purposeful, authoritative steps. "We'll see about that," he said as he waved the boy on the passenger side away from the door, which he opened; he slid in and sat next to me. Signaling again with his hands, he motioned for me to drive around the barricades. I took it as a hopeful sign that he was unarmed.

"Good you brought food, but you need to get clearance from security. We need to make sure you aren't trying to poison us. You aren't trying to poison us, are you?"

"I got all this food from my father-in-law's grocery store. I'm on your side."

Too nervous to get a good look at him, I kept my eyes straight ahead as he directed me off the main road and down the deeply rutted dirt turnoff that leads to the museum, a road I was familiar with. The front of the old log structure looked much the same as it had the last time I'd been there, except the sign above the entrance had been changed. Instead of WOUNDED KNEE MUSEUM, it read INDEPENDENT OGLALA NATION WOUNDED KNEE.

Inside was a shock. It was as if the entire museum had moved to a new location and the new tenants were now camping out until they figured out how to redecorate the place. Everything was gone: all of the display cases, picture frames, cabinets, and presumably their contents . . . gone, hidden away, or stolen. No quillwork, arrowheads, scrapers, war shirts, no painting of Martha Bad Warrior, no big mounted moose head, and no historic photographs of Big Foot's frozen body. Same unpolished wooden floors, exposed log walls, and open ceiling. Chairs scattered all around, a long table or two, a few smaller tables, rolled-up sleeping bags and duffel bags pushed against the walls, kerosene lamps, typewriters, and a mimeograph machine. A noisy generator out back powered a coffeepot and a CB radio. I saw few Indians but a surprising number of white people, obvious radicals, typing and collating documents, looking at maps, chatting on the radio, discussing tactics—this was clearly the operational heart of the movement, and I wondered who was really in charge here. I was twenty-eight at the time; everyone else, it seemed, was *really* young, under twenty-five, men and women dressed in blue jeans, boots, cowboy shirts, and regardless of ethnicity wearing some sign of Indian identity—feather in the hair, choker, headband, bracelet. My "tour guide," who had refused to give me his name on our trip over, escorted me to a table with a sign on it reading AIM SECURITY. He mumbled something to the huge man sitting there, part native; his long hair dishwater blond, he was wearing a red-checkered handkerchief headband, had bloodshot but otherwise brown, piercing eyes, and looked to me to be an extremely serious person. When the huge man stood up, I cringed; he was at least six foot five and had a powerful frame, more like that of a champion woodchopper than a weight lifter. He hovered over me, glaring down, and then turned to pick up the rifle (as if he needed it!) that was leaning against the back wall, pointed the barrel to within a few inches of my nose, and said, "Couple spies came in here yesterday pretending to be telephone repairmen. How do we know you ain't another goddamn spy?"

I was too scared to answer.

He shoved the table aside, yelled at me to turn around. Handcuffed, I was pushed to the floor, the rifle barrel still inches from my nose. "Maybe we should take you outside and shoot you right now."

Someone from the far side of the museum shouted, "Yeah, let's shoot the motherfucker!"

Others joined in: "Shoot him! Shoot him!"

Things were not looking good . . . could this be real? Would they really put me up against a post, offer me a blindfold and a cigarette, ask me if I had any final words? Would they shoot me or fire a blank, laugh their asses off, and point at the big wet spot on my trousers? Just then came divine intervention from Wakan Tanka, Tunkashila (Grandfather), the Strong One Above. Russell Means walked into the room and my voice returned; I shouted, "Russell Means! Save me. I brought you food—what the fuck?"

And now you are going to know why I will always hold Russell Means in reverence. His entire face turned red as he stared down the scary man with the rifle and growled, "This dude brought food, and you are going to shoot him?" Means ordered the security man to take off my handcuffs, and then impulsively grabbed a notepad and wrote me a note, a security pass signed by Russell Means giving me permission to go anywhere I wanted to go in Wounded Knee as long as I left by sunset. Two years later, when AIM leaders were put on trial in St. Paul, Minnesota, I learned the identity of the huge man who pushed me to the floor and stuck the rifle in my face. He was an FBI informant named Douglass Durham, the *real* spy, an agent provocateur. Durham would not have shot me himself, but to discredit AIM he might have encouraged someone else to do it, and on that day in that place, there were plenty of trigger-happy fools hanging about.

From the moment of my release, I had a goddamn marvelous day. It was cold, clear, and sunny. Perhaps due to the cease-fire, people were relaxed, smiling, the energy upbeat. I walked up the hill from the museum, crossed the road, and wandered toward the white church. A simple hole dug in the ground in front of the church served as a bunker; there was a wall of cement blocks in front, pillowcases filled with dirt; two large wood posts provided overhead protection. A beautiful round deerskin shield was propped up against the outside of the wall, an eagle painted on its surface. Perhaps it came from the museum. An upside-down American flag was attached to a steel fence post—this was the steel fence post that marked the spot where the 7th Cavalry positioned its Hotchkiss guns that terrible day in 1890. A small metal sign on the post read:

BATTERY
HOTCHKISS GUNS
1st Field Artillery
Capt. Allyn Capron

Captain war criminal Capron! After his death in 1898, he was posthumously awarded a Silver Star for gallantry for his role in the Sioux Campaign at Wounded Knee. They sent the citation to his widow in Washington, D.C. Widows of the twenty soldiers who actually died in the "battle" (no doubt from the army's own crossfire) fared better—their husbands received the Congressional Medal of Honor.

I wondered if the robust Indian man with a double-barreled shotgun standing guard behind the cement blocks knew the significance of this sign. Did he realize that his modern-day weapon would not stand a chance against the Hotchkiss? Much too fat for such a young man, with long hair and loose-fitting clothes, he paid no attention to me. Walking around to the other side of the bunker, I saw two men sitting inside on dusty old upholstered chairs, one with his feet resting on a tattered ottoman, smoking a cigarette, reading a comic book. Both men had rifles, one with a clip, the other a single-shot bolt-action gun probably more useful for hunting rabbits than shooting at the machine-gun-toting federal marshals positioned behind personnel carriers. The man not reading had short hair and restless eyes that darted about; he wore a fancy embroidered vest over his *I am popular in South Daḳota* T-shirt.

"Hi, honky. How's your day?" he said with a laugh.

They were both young, talkative. I pulled the notebook and pen from my shirt pocket, told them I was a writer working on a story for the *Chicago Tribune*. The man reading the comic book claimed to be a Vietnam veteran, said he lived on the reservation. The other was from Minneapolis, where AIM started, had been with AIM since the very beginning. They were there to support the cause, for sure, but I had the sense there wasn't much else going on in their lives.

Just beyond the bunker, a group of older men—who from this distance looked more like cowboys than Indians with their crew cuts, cowboy hats, and cowboy boots—stood on the front steps of the church. All of them were looking eastward across the valley where Big Foot had camped, the site of the massacre, to the ridge beyond. One had binoculars; another was peering through a surveyor's leveling instrument. I realized they were watching the movement of the personnel carriers, perhaps being positioned for when the cease-fire inevitably came to an end.

Draped on the belfry was a large, flurrying banner—red, yellow, black, and white, the symbolic colors of the Lakota people, representing the four directions. To the left of the steps was a traditional sweat lodge, a dome-shaped structure covered with tarps and blankets. The entrance was just big enough for one person at a time to stoop down and squeeze through it; behind the sweat lodge was a traditional but unadorned tepee. The tepee was for negotiations between AIM leaders and government officials. As someone who had experienced the sweat lodge, I found it extremely funny that AIM insisted that before anyone entered the tepee to negotiate, they first had to be purified in the sweat lodge. *If Henry Kissinger shows up*, I thought, *they will have had a hell of a time squeezing him into this sweat lodge, getting him to say* mitakuye oyasin *[all my relations] at the end of each of their chants.*

There were mud-splattered cars and trucks haphazardly parked here and there, including a U-Haul van riddled with bullet holes, its back window apparently shot out; patches of snow; a half-melted snowman holding a BLACK HILLS NOT FOR SALE sign. People sat in small groups or strolled about, mostly young men but women and elders too, along with children playing, dogs yapping, horses grazing. Four men sat in a circle beating a large drum that lay flat between them, singing the hauntingly beautiful AIM song that some Cheyenne singers gave to the movement. The atmosphere was serene, like the Lakota version of Sunday in Central Park.

The more I walked about, the more relaxed I felt, and the easier it was to talk to people. I met an elderly couple who lived outside Kyle near the camp of Frank Fools Crow, the great spiritual leader, nephew of Black Elk, who, they say, was guiding AIM on strategy and tactics. I asked them if they felt safe here. They answered that as long as people followed the right path as prescribed by Fools Crow, no one would be hurt. "Eventually, the *wasicu* [white people] will get tired and go away. We will declare victory, and everyone will go home." Contrary to the impression that the occupiers of Wounded Knee, like the ones inside the museum, were largely outsiders, radicals from Oakland and Minneapolis, nearly everyone I talked to the rest of that day was from one of the nearby villages: Porcupine, Kyle, Potato Creek, Oglala, Loneman, Manderson, Wanblee, Medicine Root, and Pine Ridge.

I asked one boy if he was missing school. He laughed. "This *is* my school."

Inside the Sacred Heart Church, another surprise: everything looked normal, neat and tidy, from the baptismal water bowl to the flowers on the altar, the statues of Jesus and Mother Mary, even the candles. The hymnals were tucked into the racks behind the pews, the kneeling benches were in place; there were a few muddy footprints, but that would have been almost impossible to prevent. The militants clearly didn't respect the museum or the trading post—they had trashed both thoroughly—but apparently they respected the church, a holy place if not their holy place. Except for bullet holes, the Sacred Heart church remained unscathed for the entirety of the seventy-one-day occupation, only to be mysteriously torched a few days later, no one knows by whom or why.

As the sun sank behind the pine-covered hills on the western side of Sacred Heart, the temperature dropped and people moved toward the church, the bunkers, the trading post and museum. There was a ceasefire that day, but most of the gun battles happened at night; it could start up again any moment. I hated to leave, and reluctantly I made my way back to my blue Pontiac wagon, still parked in front of the museum. Russell Means thanked me again for the groceries and waved good-bye as I pulled out onto the road and headed back to Alliance, reflecting on a trying but adventuresome day. The same Indian boys guarding the AIM checkpoint waved me through, as did the federal marshals at the government checkpoint.

I waved back at the Indians, ignored the marshals.

Of the 130,000 total bullets fired during the Wounded Knee Takeover, 129,995 missed their intended targets. One severed the pulmonary artery near Buddy La Monte's heart. Visitors to the cemetery who see his tombstone and don't know the history might get the impression that La Monte was the only Wounded Knee shooting victim, but he wasn't. Another bullet went through the wrist of FBI agent Curtis Fitzgerald while he was sitting in his car at one of the checkpoints. A third shattered federal marshal Lloyd Grimm's spine, paralyzing him for life. Rocky Madrid, a medic working for the Feds, was shot in the stomach but survived. And a fifth bullet blew off the top of Frank Clearwater's head in much the same fashion the bullet from Lee Harvey Oswald's Carcano rifle blew off the top of John Kennedy's.

I know about Frank Clearwater because I was at his funeral, peered into the open casket, saw the ugly wound—he was shot while sleeping on a pew in the church, just two days after he smuggled himself into Wounded Knee in late April. One of his Indian comrades who carried him out of the church on a stretcher held the top of his skull so it wouldn't fall to the ground. Under a white flag, they put Clearwater in back of the U-Haul van and drove him ninety miles to a hospital in Rapid City. He was dead by the time they pulled up to the emergency door. Called into emergency session, Dick Wilson's tribal council passed a resolution barring Clearwater's burial on the Pine Ridge reservation. Clearwater was obviously not full-blood, nor was he a member of the

Oglala or Brulé tribes, so it was decided to bury him on the adjacent Rosebud reservation, as long as the burial took place on private not public land. From this point on, only full-blooded Oglala could be buried on the Pine Ridge reservation, and permission from elders would be needed to be buried at Wounded Knee itself.

I joined the procession of vehicles escorting Clearwater's body to Leonard Crow Dog's camp, sometimes referred to as Crow Dog's Paradise, on the Rosebud reservation. Leonard Crow Dog, like Frank Fools Crow, was a spiritual leader; his grandfather was *the* Crow Dog, who in a fit of jealousy murdered Chief Spotted Tail in 1881. A long-haired journalist from Denmark named Jacob Holdt hitched a ride with me. Clearwater's body was in a plain plywood casket hanging out the back of a pickup truck, second in line behind a tribal police car with lights flashing. There were a dozen or more vehicles. My car was last.

Finding Holdt infectiously friendly, I merrily chatted away with him as if we were on our way to an after-work cocktail party. In the United States since the previous August, he said he had originally come to cover the 1972 Republican Convention in Miami. The Secret Service had given him security clearance that allowed him access to the main convention hotel, the Fontainebleau Miami Beach, where he interviewed Julie Eisenhower, John Wayne, Ronald Reagan, and others. He spun a good tale; ironically, on this particular day, it turned out his Secret Service security clearance did him a fat lot of good.

Up ahead, just before the Pine Ridge/Rosebud border, was a roadblock manned by tribal police and some not-very-nice-looking Indian men with crew cuts and double-barreled shotguns. Along with the others, we stopped. The police were going car to car checking IDs. When Holdt showed them his Secret Service security clearance and his Danish passport, one of the officers told him to get out. He was handcuffed and slammed against the hood of my car.

"Didn't anyone tell you we banned foreigners from the reservation?"

And it was oddly true. In a brazen act of tribal sovereignty, the Pine Ridge Tribal Council had banned whole groups of people—movie stars, network TV commentators, reporters from *The New York Times*, members of AIM, and *all* foreigners—from treading on tribal land *forever*; doing so was punishable by a thousand-dollar fine or six weeks in the tribal jail. I wasn't sure if I should go on ahead with the funeral procession or if I should go to Pine Ridge to see if I could bail Holdt out; but then they released him, saying that since the ban had gone into effect after he arrived in Pine Ridge, he could go, but only after he promised never to come back. Once our caravan crossed into the Rosebud reservation, the Pine Ridge tribal police and the FBI quit following us and we seemed to be home free, but there was another roadblock, this one manned by Rosebud tribal police. Unlike their Pine Ridge counterparts, they were relaxed, not interested in checking IDs; they just wanted to hold us up so their tribal council, convening nearby, could decide if Clearwater could be buried on their reservation. We waited for a long time. People got bored, someone honked a horn, and suddenly tires screeched and the pickup truck took off; somehow the casket did not slide off the back. The next car in line followed, and soon everyone was barreling past the Rosebud police, who hollered at us but didn't bother giving chase. Apparently, they really didn't give a damn.

The Rosebud reservation is beautiful, similar to Pine Ridge, but somehow its features are less pronounced; same buffalo grass, Ponderosa pines, but fewer ridges, more rolling hills. The roads are equally bad, potholes in potholes, puddles of mud and water. We pulled off the main road onto an even more wretched road, plunged across a small creek onto a flat patch of lush meadow bordered by evergreen shrubs. In this meadow was a traditional Sun Dance ground, a painted pole made from the trunk of a forked cottonwood, draped with dozens of colorful cloth fragments, sacred colors. Called the Tree of Life, this pole was surrounded by an arbor; twenty-eight smaller tree poles were aligned with the rising sun.

Nearby was a sweat lodge where the dancers purified themselves, bigger than the one I'd seen at Wounded Knee, with a buffalo skull in front of the opening. Crow Dog's simple log house was on the far side of this meadow. The pickup truck was already parked; I could see men carrying the casket inside.

Along with the others, I parked my car and went inside with Jacob Holdt to pay my respects. Clearwater was resting peacefully in the now open casket placed in front of a beautiful yellow morning star quilt, the link between living and dead, a quilt that would be buried with him. I was surprised to see he was much older than I had expected; bare-chested, eyes closed, he had long straight hair, wore a Lakota bone choker. There had been no attempt to hide his massive head wound. An elder was sitting in the corner, playing the funeral drum and singing while Crow Dog passed a smoldering sage smudge stick over Clearwater's body, around the casket, and throughout the room.

In the kitchen, the women were cooking *wohampi,* a traditional stew made with buffalo meat, prairie turnips, wild potatoes, and wild onions. There were about a dozen mourners, all ages, with more coming. No one really knew Frank Clearwater; the woman who arrived with him at Wounded Knee was just a hitchhiking companion and he had no known relatives. But now he was a martyr and a brother. Regardless of his true origin or how much Indian blood flowed through his veins, we were here to pray for his safe journey to the Happy Hunting Grounds. Jacob Holdt was determined to stay for the whole affair (probably not anxious to get back to Pine Ridge), but I needed to get back to Wanblee, resume my stay-at-home dad routine. And, to be honest, I was a bit uncertain about spending the night at Crow Dog's Paradise.

It was late afternoon, a warm day, the air conditioner on full blast, the radio tuned to the nearest country station (KILI didn't yet exist). I was feeling pretty good about myself. An article I'd written about life in Wanblee had been accepted for publication in the Sunday magazine of the *Chicago Tribune,* my little girl was beginning to walk, my wife had a good teaching job even if I didn't. While life on the rez was hard, we had many friends—Indian and white. Once I was off the Rosebud, I turned up Highway 73 and drove on the dirt road through Allen, South Dakota; there was no traffic, and I must have been going ninety.

I didn't think much of the car approaching me. Tilted to one side, it looked like a typical misaligned rez car, trailing dust and black exhaust, except it was moving really fast, and Indians mostly drive agonizingly slow. As it got near, I could make out the forms of three men in the car, six eyes intently fixed on me, and a rifle. The man in the backseat stuck his head and then his torso out of the window. He was the one with the rifle.

Hanging on tightly to the steering wheel, I hit my brakes, swerved, skidded, and slid down the gravel embankment. I never heard the shot but could feel the force of a shattered window. Luckily, it was the passenger window behind me. Somehow I managed to come to a stop. My hands shaking, heart racing, I struggled to breathe, scared shitless. I needed to regain some composure so I could get out of this ditch, get the hell out of there before they turned around and came back to finish the job.

Except for a tiny sliver of glass embedded in my neck, I was unscathed. Somehow I recovered, got back on the road, and revved it up again to ninety. I made it all the way back to our little trailer house without seeing another car. I told Linda and anyone curious that the window had been broken when a piece of gravel flew up from a passing vehicle.

No big thing.

BIG FOOT TRAIL

CHIEF BIG FOOT SURRENDERS

The next segment of my journey follows the last leg of the Big Foot Trail, the route Chief Big Foot followed with his starving band of Minneconjou and Hunkpapa Lakota in late December 1890. It was a deadly winter, with temperatures below zero and an unforgiving wind; snowflakes turned into ice bullets that bruised the face, blinded some of the horses. Not a good time for such a trip, but people were afraid not to go. At sunrise on the morning of December 15, Big Foot's half brother, the great Tatanka Iyotake (Sitting Bull) had been gunned down outside his lodge, murdered by one of the forty Indian police who had come to arrest him. It was not safe to be near Sitting Bull's Standing Rock reservation, and Chief Red Cloud had offered Big Foot refuge on the Pine Ridge reservation; he decided to accept. There was no time to waste.

Tensions in the Dakotas were higher than they had been since the Battle of the Greasy Grass. Thousands of Lakota had abandoned the agencies to take part in a huge nonstop ghost dance at the Stronghold, a natural fortress in the Badlands on a high plateau between the Cheyenne and White Rivers. These Indians believed that ghost dancing would bring back their dead relatives and the buffalo—Mother Earth would return as she was before, the white people would disappear. Whites living near the reservations were terrified. Their paranoia intensified by false newspaper stories, they lobbied the federal government to protect them. "Lock the savages up in stockades before they go on a bloodthirsty rampage," they demanded. "Exterminate them if necessary."

Agency officials knew the dancing was harmless but outlawed it anyway and asked the 7th Cavalry to enforce the ban. Big Foot could have chosen to take his people to the Stronghold; his fellow chief Kicking Bear would have welcomed them, and nothing bad had so far happened to the ghost dancers. But Big Foot saw that Kicking Bear's people had been dancing a long time, and nothing had changed. He also feared that the soldiers would attack the Stronghold. And if he stayed put, some would leave anyway, splitting his dwindling followers into two camps.

Of the 350 people with Big Foot, only 40 were warriors, the rest women, children, and old men. Many were sick. Big Foot himself had pneumonia, was hemorrhaging blood in a handkerchief. This 190-mile journey seemed impossible, suicidal; still, the collective will of the Lakota could never be discounted. With only a few horses and one wagon for their chief, the people fought their way through the never-ending blizzard, and on the seventh day they were within thirty miles of Pine Ridge. Big Foot's warrior scouts spotted the first horse soldiers. To show peaceful intentions, one of the warriors hoisted a white flag over Big Foot's wagon while another galloped off to greet the soldiers and ask them for a parley. Major Samuel Whitside, who was leading the 7th Cavalry Regiment, wanted to take the Indians in peacefully and was happy to oblige.

Whitside and his interpreter met with Big Foot in his wagon with his sixteen-year-old nephew Joseph Horn Cloud, who in 1906 was interviewed about this encounter by Eli Ricker, the Nebraska rancher and reporter who recorded dozens of eyewitness accounts of historical "Indian War" battles, some fifteen hundred pages on ruled tablets that have become invaluable for documenting the history of the American West. According to Ricker's notes, Horn Cloud said the conversation went as follows:

"What is your name?" Major Whitside asked.

"My name is Big Foot."

"Where you going?"

"Going to Pine Ridge to see the people because they sent for me."

"Do you want peace or a fight?"

"My great fathers were friendly to the whites and died in peace. I want to die the same."

"If you are telling me the truth, I want you to give me twenty-five guns."

"I am willing, but if I do, your soldiers will do some harm to my people. Wait until we get to the agency. I will give you all you ask and return to my home."

Horn Cloud commented on Big Foot's condition. "He was talking in a hoarse whisper; blood drops fell from his nose, froze on the icy bottom of his wagon."

He continued: "Whitside agreed. He extended his arm and they shook hands."

Whitside moved Big Foot to the army ambulance, where he would be more comfortable, and had his soldiers escort the band to the Wounded Knee valley, about five miles away. Horn Cloud and other survivors said Whitside had a big heart. Once they were at Wounded Knee, he put Big Foot in a Sibley tent with a warm stove and instructed the army physician to do everything he could for the suffering chief. Had Major Whitside stayed in command, Big Foot's band surely would have made it safely to Pine Ridge, but a few hours after they'd settled down, Whiteside's commanding officer, Colonel James Forsyth, arrived from Pine Ridge. The kindness evaporated. Forsyth told Whitside he had orders to escort Big Foot's entire band to the railway station in Rushville, where they would be transported in boxcars to a military prison in Omaha. He had his soldiers surround the camp and placed four Hotchkiss guns on an overlooking hill, the very same hill where the mass grave is today.

James Asay, who owned a trading post in Pine Ridge and was a prototype of today's Whiteclay liquor dealers, tagged along with Forsyth. He brought a ten-gallon keg of 120-proof Tennessee sour mash, which he generously shared with soldiers who were not on guard duty. These 7th Cavalry troopers had made a long trek, over five hundred miles from Fort Riley, Kansas. Tired, some were pissed; it had been less than fourteen years since Crazy Horse and his gang of scalp takers had wiped out Custer and his men. They itched for revenge. Liquored up, a few rowdy soldiers even hassled the captives at gunpoint. The whiskey-soaked soldiers demanded to know: "Were you at Little Bighorn? Which one of you savages killed Custer?"

By morning, the stage was set for the tragicomedy that followed. Colonel Forsyth ordered his troopers to search Big Foot's camp and confiscate anything that could conceivably be a weapon, not just guns but cooking knives, scrapers, riding crops, even tent stakes. Yellow Bird did his dance, shots were fired, and once the madness got rolling, the only thing that could stop it was exhaustion. Some of Big Foot's people were found up to ten miles away, lying bloodied and dead in the snow.

One survivor treated by Dr. Eastman at the makeshift hospital he set up in Pine Ridge told him she was hiding in a clump of bushes when two terrified little girls ran toward her. She grabbed them, put her hands over their mouths to keep them quiet, and tried to hide them with her in the bushes, but a mounted soldier spotted them. The soldier rode over, fired a bullet into the head of one girl, calmly reloaded his rifle and fired a second bullet into the head of the other girl. Then he shot the woman, who feigned death, living long enough tell her story to Dr. Eastman. Sadly, a few hours later she too died.

It is said that the sacred hoop of the Lakota was broken that day, that it would remain broken for seven generations before the Lakota nation could heal. And it has been a long hard wait, but now the seventh generation is here. Today's teenagers and young adults are seven generations removed from those who died at Wounded Knee. As prophesied by the holy man Black Elk, they are mending the sacred hoop; the rebirth of Lakota culture and spirituality is upon us. Where once there were only two or three Sun Dances on the Pine Ridge reservation during the summer months, now there are fifty or sixty. Sweat lodges are everywhere; powwows are huge and frequent. Hostility between full-bloods and half-bloods is fading away. There is a Lakota language teacher in every reservation school. The tribe is asserting its sovereignty.

Nothing symbolizes the rebirth of Indian pride more than the annual Chief Big Foot Memorial Ride, seven grueling days on horseback tracing Big Foot's torturous 190-mile ride in the dead of Dakota winter, starting at the place in Sitting Bull's camp on the Standing Rock reservation in northeastern South Dakota where Sitting Bull was killed. Here up to five hundred riders assemble for an opening ceremony of prayers and remembrances before riding on to Big Foot's camp on the Cheyenne River Indian Reservation, and then turning west to Wounded Knee and ending in Pine Ridge, much of the route through the Badlands. There were seventeen riders on the first of these Big Foot Rides in 1986; in more recent years there have been as many as five hundred.

There have been many harrowing adventures during these rides. On the third ride, in 1990, temperatures dropped to 30 degrees below zero with a windchill factor of minus 140; the riders were slammed by a whiteout blizzard, and drifts got so high that the tallest horses had to punch through the snow for the others. On another ride, Charlie New Holy's horse, Nutcracker, plunged into a snow-covered pocket and fell on Charlie's left leg, severely tearing the ligaments in his knee. An ambulance took Charlie to the emergency room at the Pine Ridge hospital, where doctors bound his leg and gave him a brace and crutches to use for walking. People cheered when he unexpectedly rejoined the riders. Charlie couldn't get on and off his horse without assistance, but he finished the ride.

On Christmas Day during another severe blizzard, the Big Foot main support group had to abandon three of their vehicles—a car and two pickups—along the highway in the Badlands. When they went to retrieve them the next day, they discovered that Absolute Towing, acting on a request from the South Dakota Highway Patrol, had towed them to Rapid City during the night. The car and trucks were crammed with much-needed supplies, including a few replacement saddles and bridles, bottled water, and hay for the horses. Informed in advance about the upcoming Big Foot Ride, the highway patrol must have realized that these abandoned vehicles belonged to the riders, that they would return for them as soon as weather permitted. The people at Absolute Towing were sympathetic, but they too were put out; the roads were dangerous that night, and it took hours to finish the job.

"Sorry for the inconvenience, folks, but we refuse to release these vehicles or the stuff in them until you pay the eleven-hundred-dollar towing fee!"

Not all the memorable anecdotes are related to weather. A little black stray dog showed up on the first day of another ride. Every day for the entire distance, it ran out in front of the riders, looking back frequently as if it wanted to make sure the procession proceeded according to plan. There was something holy about this dog; the riders gave him the name Shadow, always made sure he was fed. Their intention was to have someone adopt Shadow, but after the Wiping of the Tears ceremony, which is held in Pine Ridge at the ride's conclusion, Shadow trotted off, never to be seen again.

At the end of each day of a Big Foot Ride (except the last), riders circle their horses to pray and sing the "Warrior Society Song." They take care of their horses, remove the saddles and bridles, feed them hay, and make sure they have plenty of water. Exhausted but hungry, the riders eat dinner, mostly soup or stew and some bread, provided by a local support group that has come out to greet them. After dinner and coffee, they go to bed, sometimes sleeping on the ground in sleeping bags, sometimes in tents.

If you ask anyone who's been on one of these rides what the biggest challenge is, they will invariably say, "Keeping warm." Vernell has ridden in every Big Foot Ride. His father went on the first ride in a horse and wagon (as did Chief Big Foot).

Up ahead I see another familiar road sign I have stopped at many times. It commemorates the spot where Big Foot surrendered, a beautiful piece of land—rolling hills, small patches of snow, gigantic blue sky, high whispery cirrus clouds. The sign is graffiti scarred but still here; it hasn't yet been stolen. I can make out the words, and just in case it is not here the next time I come by, I write them down:

> *CHIEF BIG FOOT SURRENDERS*
> *East 1/2 mile from this point, on the old Cherry Creek–Pine Ridge Trail, Chief Big Foot (Spotted Elk) and his Minneconjou, wagon horse band, with some forty braves of Sitting Bull's Hunkpapa band was intercepted and surrendered on December 28, 1890 to Major Samuel M. Whiteside, 7th U.S. Cavalry. The Band was escorted to Wounded Knee, where they camped for the night under guard. Big Foot who was ill was attended by the army physician that night.*

Just around a bend from the Big Foot sign is the village of Porcupine. The BIA houses here look older, more weather-beaten than the ones in Pine Ridge, with more boarded-up windows. One house has no door, only a tattered blanket covering the front entrance. Dirt roads and dead grass, weeds, garbage, straggly dogs, and a cluster of junked cars and trucks surround the houses; nearby are the Porcupine Trading Post, a simple white building with one gas pump in front; the Porcupine Day School; teacher housing; and a couple of school buses.

Driving on the reservation, one seldom slows down to pass through a village, but I downshift, drive slow, feeling a need to show respect. An

Indian boy on a bicycle acknowledges me with a wave. Russell Means was born in Porcupine, recently died in Porcupine. For the first time today I feel like crying; it's strange, but he did save my life, and while he may have sometimes been more interested in self-promotion than in Indian liberation, Means made a never-to-be-forgotten impression. Some say he will be remembered along with Red Cloud, Crazy Horse, and Sitting Bull, but what makes me particularly sad is the memory of him as an old man, ravaged by throat cancer. Looking haggard, skeletal but still brilliant, champion of Indian liberation, Hollywood celebrity now destitute, respected by some, vilified by others, estranged from Dennis Banks, no longer welcome in AIM, powerless to do much about it.

In his final interview, filmed a few weeks before his death in October 2012, Means said, "Men go from diaper to diaper. You need a woman at the beginning of life to take care of you, and at the end of your life. If you are foolish enough not to recognize that throughout your life, you'll never know love."

It's good to know that Russell Means knew love; his fifth marriage, to Pearl Means, lasted twelve years, and she was there at the end. He had seven children, three of them adopted. Crow Dog, the spiritual leader who passed the burning sage around Frank Clearwater's body, presided at Means's twelve-hour memorial service at the Little Wound School auditorium in Kyle.

"In four days," Crow Dog said, "Russell's soul will enter the Happy Hunting Grounds. He will see all the chiefs in his band, all the families, all the relations, all the stillborn that went to the Happy Hunting Grounds."

Means's family spread his ashes in the Black Hills, and as with only Crazy Horse's relatives' knowing where he is buried, only they know where.

I once visited the Porcupine Day School, a K-8 school. It was Columbus Day 1972, six weeks into my first and last year working as a BIA schoolteacher in Kyle at the newly opened Little Wound School. I was there for a district-wide teacher and administrator meeting in the school gym; nothing too remarkable—there was always a meeting of one kind or another. Naive and idealistic, I had quit my job teaching at an inner-city school in Chicago to teach Indian kids, perhaps thinking I could make a difference. Growing up in Alliance, I knew, of course, how impoverished Indians were, the discrimination they faced. More recently I had read Dee Brown's *Bury My Heart at Wounded Knee*, which had a great impact on me.

I was in a sour mood that day when Marvin Waldner, the principal at Little Wound School whose smile was not much more than a snarl, herded us out to the school bus. Feeling an urge to complain, I sat next to my two best teacher friends, Leonard Running and Lawden Heller. Fresh out of teacher's college, Leonard was a long-haired music teacher who had lost three fingers on his left hand in a childhood accident yet was a wicked guitar player. Lawden was my father's age, a history teacher who grew up in South Dakota; he had been a World War II pilot in the same squadron as Senator George McGovern. Still McGovern's friend, he worked tirelessly on all his campaigns. Leonard and Lawden were excellent teachers, the two best I met during my years teaching, including in Chicago. Sincerely interested in and supportive of Lakota culture, they loved the kids, were the type of teachers I expected to find when I applied for a job on the Pine Ridge reservation. But some of the other teachers were decidedly not. A few were incompetent, too lamebrained to get more secure positions teaching in nearby white schools. Indifferent, blind, uncaring, hateful, these so-called teachers were going through the motions, doing their jobs, plodding along, hoping to land something better next year.

All three of us despised Waldner. For comic relief, we compared him to Colonel Wilhelm Klink, the buffoon commandant of the German POW camp on the then popular TV series *Hogan's Heroes*. Like Colonel Klink, Waldner saw himself as being in absolute command, but the reality was quite the opposite. Little Wound School was chaotic, undisciplined, rudderless, poorly managed—you might say the inmates were in charge of the asylum. Earlier that day, Waldner had unexpectedly appeared in my classroom to berate William Bull Bear, a freshman, because he had long hair.

"This boy thinks he's a girl," Waldner said loud enough for the whole class to hear. "If he wants to play football, he needs to get a haircut."

I was furious. Bull Bear kept his head down, said nothing. Waldner should have known or, if he did know, cared that cutting an Indian boy's hair was an act of cultural transgression. Outraged but new at my job, I kept my anger below the surface.

When I told Lawden and Leonard this story, Lawden laughed. "Waldner is not going to kick Bull Bear off the goddamn football team; he is not going to make him get a haircut either. If he kicks Bull Bear off the team, there won't be enough players to have a full roster, and if he cuts his hair, Bull Bear's grandmother will pull her grandson out of school."

Leonard added, "David, haven't you figured out that football is by far the most important thing about this school?"

I must admit, it was painfully obvious. The boys on the football team got out of class at ten a.m. for early practice, returned in time for lunch, and then had a second practice after school. If one of the boys on the team didn't show up in the morning, Waldner sent the bus drivers out to round him up. No one cared what kind of grades these boys got; just being on the team qualified them for advancement to the next grade and eventual graduation . . . not unlike too many other schools across our land.

Parked at Porcupine Day School, we filed off the bus and into the gym. Along the way, I noticed that the hallway walls were decorated with children's Columbus Day drawings and poems. Several depicted the *Pinta*, *Nina*, and *Santa Maria*; others, Columbus meeting the natives, the natives feasting him, waving good-bye when he sailed back to Spain. Was I in some twilight zone? And it only got worse; once we sat down in the gym, a group of cute third and fourth graders marched onto the stage. Their teacher at the piano, they began to sing:

In fourteen ninety-two, Columbus sailed the ocean blue
He discovered a new land for me and you . . .

"What the hell," I said at the meeting that followed. "Columbus didn't discover land for these kids—their ancestors were already here!"

A murmur ran through the room, a few people nodded, a few of my fellow teachers looked surprised that I would bring up such an unpleasant subject.

"What are we doing to celebrate Lakota culture?" I asked.

District Superintendent Joe Mooney, a gangly, prematurely bald man who favored starched shirts with turquoise buttons and bolo ties, was in charge of the meeting. "Calm down, everyone," he said. "Of course we want our children to be proud of being Lakota, but not all the children who attend our schools are Native American. Some are white; their parents are ranchers, storekeepers. We want all the children to experience everything other American children experience; we don't want them to feel left out. They need to identify with being American, not just Indian."

Exasperated, I looked around to see all but one or two of the teachers nodding; they knew next to nothing about the true history of Native Americans.

"Thank you, Mr. Mooney," I said, as there wasn't much to be gained by continuing my protest. Little did I know then what a useful catalyst Mooney would be in the coming Kyle community struggle to rid itself of Marvin Waldner.

KYLE

GARDEN LEFT UNATTENDED

There are no other vehicles on the road. A few miles past Porcupine, a magnificent ridge, a massive column of steel-gray granite, rises high into the sky; a smaller butte in front oddly reminds me of a London Beefeater guardhouse. Magnificent! *The productive but unappealing flatland might be in the hands of white ranchers*, I think, *but the Lakota still own the most beautiful parts.*

Sharp's Corner is ahead. From the road, all you can see is a prefab aluminum building, a gas pump, a few pickups. The Common Cents Food Store is where I used to stop for a soda on sweltering summer days. The village itself lies down a hill behind the store; I would guess fifty people live here. Across the road from a dramatic cottonwood tree is a Baptist missionary church, a log structure resting on a foundation of cement blocks, with double white doors, no windows, a simple wooden cross, and a school bus parked in the back. I once met the preacher at a community powwow in Kyle, a hardwired white man with a comb-over, sharp features, a food-stained dress shirt, and an out-of-style necktie he must have gotten at the Goodwill. He had desperate, hollow eyes.

I said to him, "Reverend, what do you hope to accomplish on the reservation?"

Refreshingly honest, I guess, he replied, "I am only here to spread the word."

"But don't people here have their own beliefs? Wakan Tanka, vision quests, the sweat lodge, the Sun Dance?"

"Regardless, they still need Jesus. Once they have Jesus, they can solve all their other problems. Jesus is the answer."

"That's it?"

"That's it."

I don't think Reverend Harold liked me much; strangely enough, he avoided me after this.

Turning right at Sharp's Corner onto BIA Highway 2, I am still on the Big Foot Trail; only nine more miles to Kyle. An arthritic old man mindlessly crosses the paved road in front of me; a snarly dog follows him. I brake for him, remember how one night another old man materialized in front of me on this very road. The sky was cloudy—it was so dark it was like driving into a black hole. I heard or imagined I heard a thud, was sure I had smashed head-on into him. I stopped, searched the area with a flashlight, the front of my car . . . there was no body, no blood, no dents. Could he have been a spirit, an old ghost dancer who stayed behind when Chief Big Foot headed off for Pine Ridge?

Was he this very same old man in front of me now?

And I remember the stolen calves. People used to steal calves from the Thompson pasture that runs along the side of this road. Deplorable but funny—a hungry person stops his car on a moonless night, sneaks through the barbed wire to snatch a calf, ties its feet together and clamps a hand over its mouth so it can't bawl too loudly, somehow hauls the piteous creature over the fence, forces it into the backseat, and speeds off to some prearranged spot where it will be butchered. It happened so frequently, I sometimes spotted old man Thompson driving through the fields at night on his tractor, cigarette in his mouth glowing, moving an eerie spotlight back and forth, no doubt with a shotgun on his lap.

Whoa! Sign of serious progress or just another mirage? On my right is the Lakota Prairie Ranch Resort Motel & Restaurant, a tidy collection of small red log cabins and one larger log central office with a blinking VACANCY sign, a for-real tourist spot I haven't seen before. I wonder what it would be like to stay here. Café, yes! Swimming pool, no! Air-conditioning, maybe! Room service, no way! Lobby with roaring fireplace, dream on! No bar; that would be illegal. No matter; I am determined to book a room here one day. When I lived in Kyle, there were no motels or hotels, no B and Bs, no Airbnbs—it was unimaginable that there ever would be. Kyle is the most remote village or town in America, so remote that it is less than ten miles from the exact point of the North American pole of inaccessibility—the single most distant spot on the whole continent: 43.36°N 101.97°W, 1,650 kilometers to reach from both coastlines. Geographically speaking, Kyle is in the middle of nowhere.

At the time, there was a post office and three commercial establishments, Lawrence and Martha Whiting's Trading Post, Richard Keiffe's General Store, and Sally's Homestyle Cafe. Sally's was the only place to eat if you wanted to "eat out"—but calling it a "café" was a stretch. Sally ran it out of the front room of her trailer home, where she set up a couple of card tables and folding chairs. She specialized in *taniga* (tripe) soup, "indigenous tacos" (fry bread smothered in beans and salsa), and well-done double burgers between slices of white Rainbo bread, plus cowboy coffee she made by throwing coffee grounds into a pan of boiling water. And the funny thing was, I did eat there regularly; it had a warm conviviality you won't find at the French Laundry, and I loved it.

I make a sharp left turn and gun *Villa VW* over a long hill; Kyle looms ahead. The usual BIA houses, government buildings, and churches reach out in a jagged pattern to the far horizon from both sides of the highway, making Kyle look much bigger than it really is. You might guess at a population of two or three thousand, but it is closer to five hundred. Like Pine Ridge, Kyle has a brand-new water tower, easily its tallest structure, shaped like a giant poppy pod with its large globe atop a stately column. Painted white, it is unadorned and unlabeled. If you were flying over Kyle in a small plane and looked down, you would see this water tower, but there is no way to identify it. No large KYLE painted around the top.

I wonder, does every town on the rez have a new water tower? Perhaps this is a line item in the recent Department of the Interior budget: *Water towers for Indians.*

As I get closer to the outskirts of Kyle, the traffic picks up; an assortment of the usual rez cars, UPS delivery van, muddy pickup pulling a horse trailer, at least three generations packed into a battered Dodge Caravan, the faces of small children pressed against the back window. They wave to me just as two boys dangerously zip across the intersection between us on a mini-motorcycle sans helmets, spewing a black cloud of toxic gas, their long hair flying behind them. Off to my right is the Kyle Health Center, a sprawling stone building, a huge step forward from the little one-room hovel that once gallantly tried to serve the same purpose with its staff of one medic and a part-time nurse. Nearly big enough to be a hospital, this new health center features an entrance framed by large wooden beams fashioned into the shape of four triangles—the Lakota symbol for the Sun-Earth connection. A strip of beautifully patterned mosaic tiles runs across the top of the entire building. It makes a statement: Lakota culture, once suppressed, is now celebrated; what was once a matter of shame is now a matter of pride. There are more new structures, large and small. One is the Kyle post office, another Oglala Lakota College, a small but serious campus of dorms and classrooms; there are also a modern convenience store and two gas stations. Past the new Kyle is a slice of the old Kyle I remember: a cluster of crumbling government housing; discarded trailer homes; old people and children walking about; an unoccupied car left running, the driver's door open as someone goes inside the post office, a scene you would never see in San Francisco or Oakland. Vehicles coming and going here and there. Kyle is a busy place, but where are the horses?

I'm startled that I see no horses, no young boys streaking across the plains bareback on beautifully speckled Indian ponies. When I lived here, you could not look in any direction without seeing carefree horses grazing or clomping about—horses who some early mornings woke me up as they rummaged through the garbage cans behind my house. These were not wild horses. In Kyle, people let their ponies run about like cows in Calcutta, and like Hindu cows, these horses were sacred; no worry about their being stolen. But all's not lost: as I approach the Allen turnoff, which will take me south to Vernell's ranch, I see a young Indian boy riding in the drainage ditch on a magnificent brown overo American Paint, but he is using a saddle and bridle. I pull up next to him and stop, wave to him.

"Is that your horse?"

"Yes. His name is Cherry Bomb."

"Why Cherry Bomb?"

"When he takes off, he explodes like a racehorse out of the starting gate. Are you a tourist?"

"Long time ago I taught school at Little Wound. Here to visit my friend, Vernell White Thunder. Do you know him?"

The boy smiles. "I go to Little Wound; Vernell is my uncle."

He agrees to let me take his picture with my iPhone, but before I can ask him his name, he says, "See you later," spurs Cherry Bomb up the far side of the ditch, and trots off away from the road. I make a mental note to show this photo to Vernell.

I'm so enthralled with this boy on horseback that I nearly pass right by Little Wound School, perhaps because like the rest of Kyle, it too has changed—once just a boring brick building, it has had a dramatic face-lift. There is a massive brick avant-garde entrance, which I guess suggests a buffalo, with red inward-curving walls and portholes about two feet in diameter positioned to represent nostrils and eyes; the dramatic curvature of its back seems to hold up the sky. Four tall cylindrical sculptures, at least forty feet high, define the front courtyard—I wonder if they are meant to suggest the Tree of Life in the center of a Sun Dance circle.

When they opened this school forty-three years ago, I was the first high school science teacher. I had no experience teaching science, had not majored or minored in science, chemistry, or physics—I had a minor in social science, which I guess is how they qualified me. It didn't matter much, since most of the kids couldn't read the textbooks. There was no chance they could have understood or cared that the number of electrons in the last energy level of an atom is its valence number. So I stashed the syllabus and the science books in a cupboard and tried the best I could for a white dude to teach them something about their history and culture.

I bought all the books I could find on Lakota and American Indian history at the Native American–owned Black Hills State University bookstore in Rapid City and filled the walls of my classroom with posters of great Indian chiefs and bumper stickers such as *This is Indian country*. I even teamed up with one of the few native employees, Leroy Big Boy, who was the career counselor, to teach Lakota language, which too few of them spoke. Principal Waldner didn't care. He was interested only in the sports teams; in his eyes, my main responsibility was to make sure the boys made it to football practice and, when basketball season came, basketball practice. His road to BIA recognition was a South Dakota football championship. When I asked around about the name Little Wound, no one seemed to know who Little Wound was or why the school was named after him. With Big Boy's help, the story of Little Wound became my first lesson.

I taught my students that Little Wound School was named for George Little Wound, son of Chief Little Wound, leader of a Lakota clan known as the Bear People (Kiyuksa). As a young warrior, Chief Little Wound counted coup in the last major inter-tribal battle with the

Pawnee, the so-called Massacre Canyon Battle of 1873. The great Pawnee chief Sky and his party of three hundred warriors were happily dressing buffalo near the bank of the Missouri after an unusually successful hunt when a thousand Lakota warriors unexpectedly attacked them. On a dead gallop, Little Wound charged right up to Sky, touched him with his coup stick, and then retreated. Two Strike followed Little Wound, except he killed Sky with his war club. The Lakota killed sixty-nine Pawnee that day while suffering no casualties. Because counting coup was considered a more courageous act than simply killing someone, Little Wound emerged as the hero of this battle, while Two Strike's exploit was largely forgotten. As one of the main Oglala chiefs, Little Wound rode with Crazy Horse in the Battle of the Greasy Grass and fled to Canada with Chief Sitting Bull. When Sitting Bull returned to the Standing Rock Agency, Chief Little Wound moved to Pine Ridge, eventually settling in Potato Creek, only fifteen miles west of Kyle. He was a ghost dancer, but after the Wounded Knee massacre, he came to the realization that war against the whites was futile.

Chief Little Wound became a peacemaker, devoting the rest of his life to helping his people deal with the many complications of living on a reservation. After he died in 1901, his son George became a prominent leader in the Medicine Root District, which includes Kyle. George Little Wound traveled to Washington, D.C., where he lobbied for the right of his people to have their own day schools to replace the boarding schools where Indian children were forbidden to speak Lakota. He believed in education for Lakota children, except that they should learn about *their* culture, not just European culture.

Unlike the wildly expressive African-American students I taught in Chicago, my Indian students were exceedingly shy; heads down, totally obedient. I found it hard to get them to talk, but I worked hard to pull words out of them. When they mumbled, I asked them to speak up, and kept asking them until they spoke loud enough for all to hear. It took patience and a lot of love, but after a few weeks I had the liveliest class at Little Wound. Once he came out of his shell, Norman Underbaggage was one of my more engaging students. Built like a bear with black ink hair, light chocolate skin, and, most unusual, near-perfect marshmallow teeth, he could be hysterically witty. One day Norman told me his family went to Rapid City for tacos, which he pronounced tay-cos.

"Did you know, Mr. Bunnell, that Rapid City is bigger than Denver?"

"No, I did not know that," I answered, thinking that this poor boy had never been to a bigger place than Rapid City.

"Rapid City is nine letters, Denver only six."

And then he laughed and laughed, and told me the joke a second time.

Tammy May, a classic redhead with freckles, was one of my few studious students; she sat in the back of the class endlessly reading. I had a hard time keeping up with her, which was scary because she *did* understand valence numbers. Tammy's grandpa had bought up land piecemeal over many years, and the Mays lived in a modern two-story ranch house near Allen. They had several hundred head of Black Angus, a new pickup truck every fall, holiday trips to California. Tammy wore expensive Western-style clothes, got along with the other kids, and flirted with Calvin Fire Thunder and Cicero Two Crow. I wonder if Tammy still lives on the reservation; she seemed destined for greater things, a career as a doctor or lawyer, perhaps. I picture her sitting near a swimming pool in Beverly Hills reminiscing to friends about her days on the rez.

Ten percent of the students at Little Wound were white kids. I had a couple of white rancher kids in my class; they were not good students, but they were privileged, had futures to look forward to. I remember many of my Lakota students in part because they had intriguing names: David Black Bear, Charlotte Kills Straight, Theresa Old Horse, Earl Thunder Bull, William Bull Bear, Helen Red Owl, Amos One Feather, Joan Thunder Hawk, Bernadine Iron Cloud, Nancy Broken Rope. And of course Vernell White Thunder, his brother Anthony White

Thunder, and his sister Patricia White Thunder. Suzy Justice, whose mother was a Kyle teacher, was another one of the white kids, a blond girl with intelligent eyes and a permanent smile—she married Vernell, and still lives with him.

During any school day, the population of Little Wound Day School is bigger than the population of Kyle itself, as students are bused in from as far as fifty miles away. The three bus drivers we had at Little Wound during my teaching days, Harvey Zephier, Rubin Clifford, and Art Lafferty, were sweet men who would do anything to help out the students. Walk right into their houses if they were not waiting outside in the morning, get them out of bed and dressed, knowing full well they would go hungry if they stayed home—no food in the house, their hungover parents sleeping—whereas at school they would get at least one meal. When they weren't driving the buses, at the direction of Marvin Waldner they spent much of their time tending to the football field. They watered and carefully manicured the grass, freshly chalked the yard markers, welded new metal goal posts to replace the original flimsy wooden ones, built a new snack shack. And if this wasn't enough, during downtime they went out into the community to knock on doors and remind people to attend the next home game.

Many of the kids came to school too hungry to concentrate, to even stay awake, and in those days, unlike now, Little Wound did not have a breakfast program. The cafeteria wasn't big enough for all the students to eat in at the same time; lunch for grades seven to nine was at noon, but the tenth to twelfth graders had to wait another hour. As a newbie teacher, I was assigned to watch over the upper-grade kids in a mass study hall from noon to one p.m. Unless you have experienced this, you can't possibly imagine what it is like trying to maintain reasonable order over a classroom packed with hungry, hormonally driven teenagers. You might think they would be tired, have their heads on the desktops—but you would be wrong. One student, Randy, usually polite and respectful, could not sit down; his chemistry compelled him to walk around and around the classroom picking up objects, pencils, notebooks, and hurl them at the other students. Nothing I could say or do—requests, threats, and bribes—modified this behavior. I quickly exhausted all the tricks I had learned teaching unruly students in inner-city Chicago and had to accept Randy's bad behavior and that of several other students. They were starving! Lunch at school was their only meal. For all I knew, they had nothing to eat on weekends. When I brought up this matter with Waldner, he shrugged and bragged to me that he included prime T-bone steaks on the list of the food items he ordered for the school cafeteria. "I keep those fat boys in my freezer," he said with a wink. "I'll invite you all over for dinner and grill some up one of these days."

True to his word, Waldner invited me and my wife, Linda, to dinner with several other teachers. His was the slightly larger house on the end of teacher row; it had a double garage that he'd converted into a carpentry shop stocked with screwdrivers, mallets, hammers, a hand drill, various power tools, a sawhorse, and stacks of lumber. There was also a stack of cowhides, which he used to make the miniature teepees he sold through a Rapid City tourist shop under the name Marvin Plenty Horses.

I suppose Waldner wasn't all bad; he established a Kyle Boy Scout group, and he liked to take his son and some of the other boys fishing and hunting. (Vernell earned an Eagle Scout badge.) Until his life in Kyle unraveled, he looked the other way when I completely ignored the curriculum I was supposed to teach. Dinner could have been a dull affair, but perhaps sensing that Linda and I were part of some anti-American subculture, he invited the other rebel teachers: Lawden Heller, Leonard Running, and Mrs. Justice.

I did not expect to see any books in Waldner's house, so it was no shock that there weren't any. It was surprising, however, to find that he was an ardent collector of rocks, beautifully polished agate that he said he found in Buffalo Gap and Railroad Buttes—translucent purple pegmatites, black and pearly white mica, cobblestone, flint, and rose quartz. He was proud of and very knowledgeable about his collection.

A funny realization I had about Waldner that night was that if he weren't the racist principal of Little Wound School, where I happened to be a first-year teacher, I might have liked him. I knew plenty of racists growing up in Alliance, and as long you steered clear of topics such as black people, Mexicans, Indians, or homosexuals, they were jolly good folk. They would help you if you had a flat tire, bring soup to your grandma if she was sick.

I don't remember much of the conversation that evening except for Linda's attempt to get the rest of us to gang up on Waldner, which seemed inappropriate as it was his house. Linda is the only one I know who called him Marvin; even his wife referred to him as Mr. Waldner.

"Marvin," Linda said, "don't you think it's about time you let people have powwows in the school auditorium?"

"No, I don't think so. Ninety percent of the men and half the women will show up drunk. They'll sneak in moonshine, let the kids drink it too."

Lawden weighed in. "You're out of line, Waldner. People are respectful at powwows."

"Are they now? I wouldn't know. I never go to them."

"Doesn't matter," I said, trying to diffuse this conversation. "They have their Lakota community center for powwows."

"That's right," Leonard added. "Let's forget the parents and focus on the kids; we can't do much to help the parents."

We thankfully went on to safer topics, such as whether Rapid City or Chadron was the better place to buy groceries, how bad it had been the previous winter when people were snowed in for several days, and when any of us had last been to a movie. And, of course, we all remarked on how delicious the steaks were.

The outdoor basketball courts and the football field at Little Wound look much the same as they did when I was teaching there, except the football field now has a grandstand. Forty-three years ago, it was just a field. Spectators—teachers, parents, and family—stood on the sidelines. We cheered on the Kyle Mustangs in their pursuit of Waldner's state championship dreams, only they did not win a single game that first year, and the scores were lopsided: 68–13, 56–0, and so forth. Waldner's son, Jerry, was the quarterback, and while he was a gifted athlete, other than Norman Underbaggage, who was a bear of a lineman on both defense and offense, the other boys simply didn't know the rules of the game. They frequently lined up offside and didn't know which way to run if they recovered a fumble. I especially felt sorry for Jerry Waldner, and tried not to imagine the conversations he must have had with his dad when they got home after the games.

Before traveling on to Vernell's White Thunder Ranch, I make a quick pass behind the Little Wound football field through the teacher housing section: at two blocks long, a tiny slice of suburbia plopped down in the middle of the deprivation. This conjures up more memories. Indian students were discouraged from walking through this neighborhood. Some of the teachers didn't feel safe having them around, but that's all changed now as nearly half the teachers at Little Wound *are* Native American. They even teach Lakota language and culture, first grade through high school. I would not be so out of place teaching here now—or would I?

Slowing to a crawl, I pass Waldner's old house, remember that Mr. Dyer, the math teacher, lived next door. The kids called him "Mr. Stinky Breath." He was constantly ducking into the teacher's lounge for a cup of coffee and a cigarette. Two doors down from Stinky Breath's is the house I lived in forty-three years ago with Linda and our infant daughter. Linda and I grew up in Alliance, went to Cornhusker U (University of Nebraska), got married, and were teaching in Chicago public schools when we were both offered jobs in Kyle; but after moving here, we learned that there was actually only one open position. This turned out to be a good thing for us because Linda could stay home with our baby girl, Mara. The rent for our government-subsidized house was cheap, and I could walk to work. On weekends, we drove to Alliance, mostly staying with Linda's parents so I could eat copious amounts of her mom's homemade Lebanese food: baba ghanouj from char-grilled eggplant; kibbeh lovingly hand molded, baked or raw; the world's best tabbouleh and hummus; flat sheets of unleavened bread; homemade goat's-milk yogurt with fresh mint. When we didn't have Lebanese food, Linda's dad, John, brought home prime New York steaks that he grilled in the backyard even if it was minus twenty and snowing. I loved hanging out at their house, watching Nebraska football games and drinking shots of Old Crow with John, flirting with Linda's three younger sisters. I visited my dad too, mostly at the newspaper office, where starting at age twelve I learned everything I know about journalism. Sometimes I hung out with my brother in his massive garage, marveling at his talent for building hot rods and dragsters, his scary collection of assault weapons.

When we didn't go to Alliance for the weekend, like most of the other teachers we went to Rapid City, where we could see a movie, spend the night in a motel, and buy groceries the following morning. I loved teaching at Little Wound School, in spite of Marvin Waldner's clumsiness, the racist teachers, the stupidity of the BIA—which everyone said stood for "Boss Indians Around"—the poverty and sadness, the blowing snow and icy roads. My Lakota students had a certain carefree resilience, a love of life; they lacked the meanness I had seen too much of in the Chicago schools. There were no fistfights, knives, or guns. Some of the students were depressed, but luckily, I never experienced any of the teenage suicides that happen all too frequently on the Pine Ridge reservation.

One morning just after the first holiday season, I woke up feeling horrible. We bundled Mara into the car seat and Linda drove me to Rapid City Regional Hospital, where we checked into the emergency room. The doctor took one look at me and said, "You have hepatitis A." I'd probably been infected by contaminated food in the school cafeteria.

I spent two weeks in the hospital, so tired it was hard for me to get out of bed. Linda took our daughter to Alliance to stay with her grandmother, and then returned to Kyle as the substitute teacher for my classes.

Linda was a much better teacher than I could ever be. Just as compassionate about Indian students and curious about Lakota culture as I was, she kept my students on track with their Lakota language, plus she made an effort to add in a little science. She was friendly and more open than I could ever be, and the other teachers—and even Waldner—really liked her. If I'd had any sense, I would have stayed home the rest of that semester, let Linda do the teaching, and worked on that great American novel I'd always wanted to write. But foolish me, I went back to Little Wound just in time for Waldner's downfall and the cascading events that followed.

About this time, 1973, the BIA stumbled into a new Indian policy that they called "self-determination." After years of learned dependency, their native clients, it was assumed, were now ready to manage their own affairs. In Kyle, this policy manifested itself in the election of the first local school board: four natives and one white rancher. One of the Lakota was a full-blood named Cecelia Bull Bear. She was the grandmother of William Bull Bear—the boy in my classroom whom Waldner harassed about his long hair. Cecelia had outlived her husband by many years and was looked up to as one of Kyle's most respected elders.

Linda and I were at the historic first meeting of the Kyle school board, along with Principal Waldner, most of the teachers, other administrators, several parents, and a couple of BIA bigwig observers from Pine Ridge. No one expected what was to follow. As soon as the meeting was called to order, Mrs. Bull Bear raised her hand. "I have a motion to put forward," she said. "I move that we terminate Marvin Waldner as the principal of Little Wound School. He has no respect for Lakota culture, steals food from our cafeteria, and is abusive to our students." Of course, all hell broke loose. Some of the older teachers, led by foul-breathed Dwyer and the mixed-blood football coach who seemed to loathe his Lakota half, threatened to resign.

"If Waldner goes, we go," they said.

On impulse, I jumped up. "I'm staying. I'll teach for free if I have to. We know some great teachers in Chicago who would love to come out here to teach."

Linda raised her hand to gesture "Me too," and looked at Waldner. "Marvin, you got Little Wound started, so why don't you just butt out peacefully?"

At first, Waldner was too shocked to answer. His eyes switched back and forth from pleading to threatening as he looked about the room, for the first time realizing he had created more enemies than friends. After a few moments of silence, he said, "All these things are mostly lies. I would never steal anything, and Mrs. Bull Bear is getting back at me for disciplining her grandson."

"Waldner, you have no respect!" shouted Lawden Heller. "You humiliated William Bull Bear by trying to force him to get a haircut. These kids deserve better." And then he added: "If you leave, I'm staying. If you stay, I'm going."

Leonard Running chimed in "Me too!"

The fifth-grade teacher for over twenty years, Harvey Weiland, who worked part-time as Waldner's assistant principal and who avoided controversy, found a way to say no to Waldner without joining in the rebellion. He simply said, "I'll be here with my students no matter what." Marvin Orr, the gregarious shop teacher who also loved his students, added, "I'm not going anywhere soon." There was some additional back-and-forth, shouts, threats, a few tears, but Mrs. Bull Bear was determined to have her way, and in the end, though Waldner adamantly defended himself, the board voted four to one to fire him.

Waldner appealed to his BIA bosses in Pine Ridge, and fearing their paternalistic instincts, I figured Waldner would soon be back wandering our halls, waiting for football practice to begin. *Letting the school board fire people*, I imagined the bureaucrats thinking, *will create all sorts of civil service entanglements and lawsuits.*

Waldner likely would have been successful if it weren't for Joe

Mooney, the deputy superintendent I had met on Columbus Day at the Porcupine Day School. He spent a lot of time at Little Wound School, but his role was never clear to any of us teachers. Mooney watched Waldner very closely, wrote dozens if not hundreds of memos to Waldner about his shortcomings and the steps he should take to correct them. After Mooney presented his memos to the appeal board, they voted to uphold the Kyle school board's decision. Not actually fired for real, Waldner, like a deviant priest, was transferred to North Dakota to head another BIA school. Linda and I stood in our yard when the Waldner family left Kyle in their packed-up Jeep Cherokee with the cat they called Custer, who would be missed, as he was very diligent about controlling the neighborhood mouse population.

I felt vindicated, but this was short-lived. I had failed to appreciate fully how Waldner's loosey-goosey management style fit in perfectly with my irresponsible approach to teaching. Waldner's replacement was a tall, stern former marine with a crew cut named Phillip MacGyver, who did not like to be called Phil. During his first week at Little Wound, he stood at the front door in the mornings with a clipboard and a pocket watch, noting the exact time of arrival for each teacher. The Waldner party was definitely over. Looking back, it's no surprise that MacGyver called me into his office on the last day of school to tell me my contract would not be renewed for the following year, that I was being fired for not following the curriculum. I halfheartedly fought back, wrote a letter to the school board, kicked up some dust, but knowing there really wasn't much I could do to bring positive change to Little Wound School, I let it go.

I feel painfully sad parked here in front of my old house. Not for getting fired—getting fired by the BIA is for me a matter of civic pride, something I brag about to my grandkids; it's the garden I feel sad about. During the long recovery time following hepatitis, my doctor said I could return to teaching but I needed to get plenty of moderate exercise, preferably outdoors, and gardening was ideal. There was a splendid spot for a large garden behind our house—plenty of sun, access to water, and if it was properly fenced in, the rabbits, gophers, coyotes, deer, horses, and many other varmints that ran free in Kyle wouldn't be able to help themselves to my lettuce. So I hired Vernell and a couple of his friends to build the fence and drove to Rapid City to buy basic gardening tools. I started hoeing the ground in early May, worked in readily available horse manure, and started planting with cool-season crops: spinach, peas, lettuce, and radishes. Soon I was on to cabbage, broccoli, carrots, onions, turnips, and, by late spring, tomatoes, corn, and watermelon. After school and on weekends, I spent hundreds of hours in the garden, watering and excessively weeding. Having had no horticultural interests before, I was thrilled to discover that I really liked gardening. Gardening helped me regain my energy and not get too crazed when Principal MacGyver insisted I take down the Indian chief posters from my classroom wall. After I was fired, though, Linda was offered a teaching job at Crazy Horse High School in Wanblee, about fifty miles east of Kyle. We had to move. The garden was left untended.

ACT THREE

The Great Spirit made us, the Indians, and gave us this land we live in. He gave us the buffalo, the antelope, and the deer for food and clothing. We moved our hunting grounds from the Minnesota to the Platte and from the Mississippi to the great mountains. No one put bounds on us. We were free as the winds, and like the eagle, heard no man's commands.

—CHIEF RED CLOUD, IN HIS
FAREWELL ADDRESS TO THE
LAKOTA PEOPLE, JULY 4, 1903

WHITE THUNDER RANCH

KEEPER OF THE SACRED ARROWS

I don't know the name of the road to White Thunder Ranch; I just know it when I see it. Turn right near the end of town and drive past the odd, weirdly out of place geodesic dome put up by Vista workers when they weren't busy smuggling weapons into Wounded Knee. Originally a meeting place, then a restaurant, then who knows what, it looks deserted, but many people are sitting outside as it is an unusually warm April day—they look up at me as I pass, but no one waves or seems that interested. More of the usual: junked-out old cars; dogs without collars; little girls playing in dirt yards; boys on bicycles, not horses; tall weeds; piles of trash; poverty; a movie theater . . . whoa . . . a movie theater! An awkward-looking corrugated metal building with double doors, no windows, and a marquee—two Indian characters with braids, one smiling, the other frowning, have replaced Thalia and Melpomene on a sign:

TONITE'S MOVIES
NOAH RIO2
FREE POPCORN!

Now I'm getting excited. I haven't seen Vernell in six years. We've talked on the phone, exchanged texts and e-mails, but not seeing him for so long was dreadful. While it may seem silly, we've been "blood brothers" for forty-two years (he was fifteen, I was twenty-four)—a bond that cannot be broken. It came about unexpectedly; I don't think it was meant to be serious, but then, over time, as we joked about it, it gained meaning. On a hot summer day in the Badlands, we were riding bareback on one frightfully powerful stallion Vernell called Thunder Hawk, Vernell in front and me precariously hanging on to him.

"Want to see how we defeated Custer?"

"Sure, why not?"

"AYYY, YA TAY HEY!"

Vernell willed Thunder Hawk to the top of a steep ravine and came to an abrupt stop on a tiny bit of flat land just inches before an impossibly steep drop into the abyss, then shouted out, "Custer had no chance!"

Following this display of Lakota horsemanship, Vernell asked me if I wanted to be his blood brother. Still in shock, I didn't reply, just looked at him dumbfounded as he pulled a penknife out of his pocket, opened it, and stabbed a hole in the tip of my forefinger, then repeated the operation on himself. We intermingled our blood. Vernell claimed this was a traditional Lakota custom, but I think it was something he learned at Waldner's Boy Scout camp.

"Now we are blood brothers."

I don't know when the little three-room house Vernell and Suzy live in became White Thunder Ranch (Wakinyantuwan Tiwahe), with its own Web site promoting horseback-riding lessons, trail rides across the reservation on "beautiful Watogla Lakota ponies," and overnight accommodations in an authentic Lakota teepee, but I do remember the first time I stayed at the "ranch," in 1980, sleeping on Vernell's front room floor under his stunning painting of a male buffalo trudging through a blizzard, with only a thin blanket, my blue jeans rolled up to serve as a pillow. It was late fall, and even though I curled up in front of the little propane stove, it was terribly cold, and it didn't help much that Vernell didn't have hot water. At least there was an indoor toilet. Vernell was living alone while Suzy was in Chadron, Nebraska, studying at the local college to be an IT manager. At that time, White Thunder Ranch was more like a slum bachelor pad: kitchen cluttered with refuse-filled grocery bags, stacks of moldy dishes, half-eaten cans of Dinty Moore beef stew, dozens of empty Perrier bottles. There must have been cockroaches, but I didn't see them, perhaps because it was too damn cold for cockroaches. (All that has changed now. White Thunder Ranch is a now a rustic but charming tourist destination.)

That first morning, Vernell got up before sunrise. I could hear him shuffling about in his bedroom and the bathroom, trying to be quiet so he wouldn't wake me. I got up, went outside with him to feed the horses. Treading carefully so as not to slip on newly hardened ice, I could see our breath, and up ahead, near the barn, the breath of the horses patiently waiting for their morning hay. My hands were stiff and painfully frigid because I had forgotten to bring gloves. Oblivious to the cold, cheerful and alert, Vernell said he had been up since three a.m., reading *The Cherokee Trail* by Louis L'Amour.

"It's all you fault, you know?"

"Why my fault?"

"'Cause I was a dumb happy Indian, and you taught me to read."

As I continue driving, it seems Vernell's ranch is farther south of Kyle than I remember, but then I see a few people mingling on the built-on deck of a trailer house to my right on the far side of a small valley. I must be getting close—I have been here, sat on this very deck with Vernell and his friends, drunk coffee out of tin cups, and listened to them gossip about and tease one another, seamlessly switching back and forth from Lakota to English.

It must be time for *Viva VW* to slow down, as the view of the ranch from here is blocked by a steep, sage-covered ridge; here you have to keep a lookout for the sign, WHITE THUNDER, hand painted on a plywood board. Nailed on a post, it marks the turnoff to a gravel access road over this ridge and down a long, gentle hill into Vernell's sprawling front yard. I worry that I might have already passed by and will end up wasting precious time before I give up and turn around, but at last, there it is! I turn, go up the ridge and over a cattle guard, and see the same little white house, the separate garage, the red barn, the corral, several horses, three horse trailers, four or five cars, a flatbed truck, a couple of pickups, a snowplow, a tractor, a backhoe, and hay wagons, plus a large metal building I don't remember. As I pull up near the front door into an empty spot between vehicles, I wonder if Vernell is home or maybe out in one of his pastures, but before I open the car door, he comes bounding out the screen door and down the steps to greet me. He is wearing the same grease-stained black cowboy hat he's had for twenty-five years, its sides turned up just right; a pink cowboy shirt hanging outside his blue jeans, the sleeves rolled up; and scuffed cowboy boots. He's heavier than when I last saw him, with a few more wrinkles and a few less teeth but the same ironic grin, same distant black BB-pellet eyes. His ruddy face is weatherworn in that handsome way reserved for good-looking older men like Clint Eastwood and Harry Belafonte. Vernell has always been a prime male specimen, a ruggedly beautiful man, testimony I suppose to the superiority of Lakota DNA. He says something I don't want to hear—"You're older"—but everyone is getting older. Tail wagging, his dog, a pure white part-coyote, part–Australian shepherd named Cookie—alarmingly friendly for a rez dog—jumps up to lick my face. We go inside through the front porch, Vernell cautioning me not to fall through the hole in the floor that has always been here, and then through a second door to the living room of his little castle. Everything inside is clean and orderly, a sure sign Suzy must be around . . . and sure enough, she emerges from the kitchen. "Hi, David. Nice to see you after so many years."

As much as I love Vernell, there was a time when I couldn't understand how Suzy could be married to such a wild, untamed man who was happy taking his occasional cold showers outdoors, eating a can of beans for breakfast, another for lunch, and another for dinner—happy as long as he could raise horses and live the life that he calls "playing cowboys and Indians." I sometimes wondered how she could take on all the household and child-rearing responsibilities, serve coffee but stay in the kitchen when Vernell's friends dropped by. But Suzy has a PhD and she is not in the shadows as much as you might think. She shares the hard life with Vernell, cleaning and cooking for a big Indian man on the rez when she could be making good money in Denver. Suzy teaches online college classes, manages most of their tourist business, and behind the scenes has a much bigger voice in family decision-making than either lets on. She grew up here too and loves the rez.

I notice that while the White Thunder kitchen is still barely big enough to turn around in, it has been remodeled, the old tile floor replaced with polished white oak, matching cabinets, new furniture; "A present for Suzy," Vernell says. Otherwise, the rest of the house is the same. Vernell's dramatic painting of a buffalo charging head-on through a blizzard still hangs behind the cozy sofa covered with his grandmother's star quilt—hundreds of diamond-shaped patches of fabric, in tones of blue and white, intricately fashioned into eight-point stars. The little propane stove I fondly remember is still in the corner, and the antler rack for hanging cowboy hats is still above the bedroom door. Vernell motions for me to sit on the sofa; he plops down in an old easy chair. Suzy hangs back in the kitchen; she's boiling water for cowboy coffee.

Vernell wants to know about my family; not the family I live with now, but the first family he remembers: my ex-wife, Linda; my daughters, Mara and Buffy; Linda's mother, Blanche; her sisters . . . where are they living, what's new with them? He also asks about my brother, Roger, who lives in Alliance. Does he still work for the railroad, is he still building dragsters, does he still collect assault weapons? He moves on to my current family, remembers when Jackie was here for the Fourth of July powwow, remembers posing next to her for a photograph while holding up a rattlesnake he had just killed. What about my stepdaughter, Jazz, and my granddaughter? He even asks about our dogs, Charlie and T2. He sees all of us as part of his *tiyospaye*, one big extended family that includes Suzy; their son, Chris, and daughter, Ellen; his brothers, George and Anthony; his dad; his cousins; and if not his dog, most definitely his horses. If we were Lakota and living in the nineteenth century, our tepees would be clustered together along the Niobrara River. At night, we'd feast on newly killed buffalo, share the sweat lodge, and dance around the campfire until dawn.

Vernell called me when his mother died a few years ago—he was very sad; he could hardly talk and said he didn't know what to do. I wanted to drop everything to be with him, but I was leaving the very next day for a conference in New York. He didn't actually ask me to come, but I knew he wanted me to, and I still feel guilty because he was there for me during my times of sadness: my dad's death from a protracted illness, and the unexpected tragic death of my son, Aaron, who was only twenty-six. Vernell and his son, Chris, then a teenager, came to both funerals—my dad's in Alliance and my son's in San Francisco. At each service, they burned sage, played traditional buffalo hand drums, and sang sweet-sad Lakota memorial songs. They were warmly received in San Francisco but met with suspicion in Alliance, where before the service, my brother took me aside to say, "I hope they aren't going to do some mumbo jumbo."

Don't get the impression that Vernell is a saint. He'll tell you he hasn't had a drink in thirty years and that's true, but there were a few rowdy years out of high school when he could have easily become just another drunkard on the path to nowhere. When Vernell first visited me in Albuquerque in 1978, we ended up in a downtown honky-tonk bar on a side street behind the KiMo Theatre. It was the kind of hidden-away place where urban natives like to drink because the cops don't give a shit as long as whatever happens stays out of sight. I bought drinks for the house, we flirted with a gaggle of pretty Navajo girls, may have left with them, but I'm not sure or don't want to remember what all happened—I just know that around sunrise, I somehow ended up in my bed, the room spinning and spinning, no way to make it stop.

Sad to admit, Vernell and I also went drinking in Kyle. Good white teacher man and his prize student copping cheap wine from the local bootlegger, going drunk to the powwow just as Waldner would have imagined it; a blight on my character much worse than Vernell's. I am embarrassed about these things, but when I mention them to Vernell, he only laughs and launches into a story. "One time I was with a couple friends driving through Scenic on our way to Rapid City. We didn't have money for beer, so we stole the front tires of the man who runs the liquor store, took them inside, and traded them to him for a case of beer."

"Vernell, that's crazy. But I want to know about your dad—how is he and can I see him?"

"Oh, I don't know. These days he spends most of his time sitting outside his house, waving to people as they drive by."

"How old is he?"

He laughs. "Eighty-nine going on twenty-nine. We try to get him here for dinner, but it is painful for him to move around much."

I bring up the subject of the missing Crazy Horse memorial sign. What happened? Who took it and why?

"I don't know. Must have been a couple years ago. They took it for the aluminum. They also steal copper wires, rip out the plumbing at the schools, whatever they can sell or trade for drugs and alcohol."

"But that monument was sacred; all they left is a couple steel poles. And now people are leaving litter all over the place."

"No one cares." Vernell shrugs.

"But your dad wrote such great poetry honoring Crazy Horse. Someone needs to raise the money to restore it for future generations."

I can see that my passion moves Vernell, but he says, "What is gone, is gone . . . there's nothing we can do."

"Sad if I don't see him this trip. Remember when I was here last, he drove over in his old Ford pickup truck. He sat in this room, talked for a good hour before he went outside and saddled up one of your horses and took off."

Vernell smiles. "He's more ornery the older he gets."

While Vernell and I talk, I hear Suzy shuffling around the kitchen, setting the table, filling water glasses, opening and closing the refrigerator door; the sound and smell of sizzling meat soon follows. The moment things quiet down, Vernell looks over at her, pushes back his chair, and slaps his hands on his knees as he stands up.

"Lucky dude. You're in time for lunch! Sorry, we ran out of beans, but I can get you some Jack Daniel's for your coffee."

Vernell makes me laugh not because it is particularly funny, but because he has been making jokes about Jack Daniel's since he stopped drinking. He has never fallen off the wagon, but whiskey is constantly on his mind.

We amble into the kitchen, sit at a small wood table. Suzy sits down too, and I'm happy to see this; I would feel uncomfortable if she were just serving us. Lunch is more coffee, hamburger patties, and cottage cheese mixed with chunks of canned pineapple. And considering the probability that this meat came from the Sioux Nation Shopping Center, I am not unhappy that it is well done. Well done and dry. Vernell and I solve this problem by drenching our burgers in Worcestershire sauce.

"Both the Europeans and the natives owe a lot to the Greco-Romans for inventing this fermented sauce," I joke. "You know, if you eat enough of it, it will make you drunk."

"Not like Jack Daniel's." Vernell smiles and rubs his belly. Bemused, Suzy eats her hamburger plain.

Wanting to include her in the conversation, I think of something to ask her. "You have a brother . . . what was his name? I don't remember."

I can barely hear her answer. "Doug. His name is Doug."

"He was too young to be in one of my classes. Does he live nearby?"

I reply, "Few summers ago when I drove through Colorado and Wyoming, I saw hundreds of bikers on the interstate, headed for Sturgis . . . all of them riding Harleys. My brother goes every year."

"Half a million last summer, but we stay away. We don't like the desecration of nearby Bear Mountain—the drinking, drug dealing, and rape that goes on there."

Suzy continues: "Bear Mountain—in Lakota, Mato Paha—is one of the last sacred grounds. Many generations climb it for prayer and fasting—if you go there, you will see prayer cloths hanging from all the trees near the trail.

"There is a secret cave where Maheo, the Spirit Creator, gave the people four sacred arrows. Vernell's great-grandfather, the first Chief White Thunder, was the Keeper of the Arrows."

"So what does it mean that your great-grandfather was Keeper of the Arrows?" I ask Vernell.

"He was the Cheyenne medicine man who guarded them at all times from being touched or seen by anyone except those in a Sacred Arrow ceremony."

Suzy adds, "This is one of the stories Vernell told to Chris and Ellen when they were little."

Vernell takes the cue:

During the "Year of the Starving Winter," around the year 1840, there were very few buffalo—people were hungry and complaining to the warriors. Some of the warriors decided they would ride to the lower Platte River to seek out a Pawnee camp where they could steal food and maybe a few horses. But they were discovered by a bigger group of Pawnee warriors, who trapped them, killed them, and cut their bodies into little pieces, which they threw into the river.

When the murder site was discovered, our people were really angry and wanted revenge, but Chief White Thunder said they should wait one winter, use this time to build up their strength, then move the sacred arrows against the Pawnee. He sent war pipes to headmen of other bands of Lakota and Arapahos, inviting them to join together in one big camp.

The following spring, scouting parties searched for many weeks before they found the Pawnee, and once again, the young warriors wanted to attack right away. My great-grandfather tried to hold them back, saying, "We must first hold a Sacred Arrow ceremony to protect our warriors," but the young men galloped off in defiance, not even taking the arrows with them. Because Maheo forbade White Thunder from carrying the sacred arrows into battle, White Thunder gave them to a fellow medicine man named Bull and told Bull to chase after the warriors. So Bull tied the arrows in a bundle to his lance and followed after.

It was bad luck for us that an old Pawnee decided this was his good day to die. He got off his horse and sat on the ground in the path of our oncoming warriors. When Bull saw him sitting there all alone, he charged to count coup. Bull leaned to the side of his horse to strike the old Pawnee with his lance, but the old Pawnee suddenly reached up with both hands and grabbed it. To keep from falling from his horse, Bull had to let go of the lance. By the time our warriors came back to kill the Pawnee, it was too late—the sacred arrows were lost.

Without telling anyone, my great-grandfather and great-grandmother rode out of camp with a few horses and supplies. It took them ten days to find the Pawnee. Slowly and peacefully they rode straight through the Pawnee camp. People were shocked. They could only look on with respect at this brave act by their old enemy chief.

Chief White Thunder stopped in front of Pawnee chief Big Eagle's lodge, handed the reins of his horse to my great-grandmother, and with no weapons, walked in. Using sign language, he told Big Eagle he wanted to make peace, wanted the sacred arrows back.

You could see the arrows; they were hanging behind Big Eagle in the back of the lodge.

Big Eagle too was impressed with White Thunder's courage. He said, "I will give you one arrow for one hundred horses." Not a great deal, but without at least one sacred arrow, Chief White Thunder knew his people would be unprotected and would go hungry. So he picked out one of the arrows and left. Big Eagle got his horses, but he never returned the other arrows.

Ten years later, in 1850-something, during the month they call "Winter of Stealing Arrows from the Pawnee," a Brulé Lakota warrior named Iron Shell raided a band of Pawnees and luckily captured the other arrows. My great-grandfather wrapped the arrows in a bundle and returned them to the holy cave at Mato Paha. They are still hidden there.

"They want to drill oil at Mato Paha," Suzy says. "The people own the land, but the government manages it and can issue the leases."

"Now you see why I am studying to be lawyer," Vernell exclaims as he again jumps up from his chair and motions to the living room. "Let's move back to my conference room."

As I shuffle behind him into the tiny living room, Vernell mentions that he is taking law classes at Oglala Lakota College, which seems amazing for a fifty-eight-year-old, but at that moment I didn't think he could be really serious about becoming a lawyer.

"Next summer I graduate, then I will have my law degree. I already found somebody to help me study for the bar exam."

"Wow. You could be that far along—how the hell did you get to be so smart?"

"I don't know, but if you had only taught me how to spell, it wouldn't have taken so long."

I was working at a computer company in Albuquerque when Vernell graduated from Crazy Horse High School in Wanblee in 1975. He was offered a scholarship to study at Dartmouth, which in and of itself is mind-boggling, an unheard-of accomplishment. When I asked him how he had managed this, he said, "I don't know. I just filled out the application and mailed it in." He was really excited about Dartmouth until he found out he would need to pay for his own room and board, books, and transportation. Normally the tribe would have helped cover these costs, but post–Wounded Knee, the tribe was broke. Everyone was too distracted by all the disappearances, suspicious fires, and drive-bys to care much about a seventeen-year-old Lakota boy who wanted to become a treaty lawyer.

"Even with a full scholarship, I could not afford to go."

"So if you couldn't follow your dream, what did you do?"

Suzy laughs. "He followed me to Rapid City."

Disillusioned because he couldn't go to Dartmouth, Vernell got a ranch job. He was digging fence posts, breaking horses, living in an unheated bunkhouse when he got a postcard from Suzy. She was leaving Kyle for Rapid City to study at the University of South Dakota and would be gone for a least a year. A few days later, Vernell sold his horse, used the money to buy a '63 Chevy, threw his clothes in the trunk, and drove up to "Rapid," where he easily got a job unloading and loading the semitrucks on the loading dock at Sears & Roebuck. "I lived at a cheap motel, ate bologna sandwiches and drank soda, which I stored in my cooler. That and some Jack Daniel's."

"Don't forget you used my cafeteria card," Suzy says. "It was supposed to last all semester, but I was feeding him, so it went really fast.

"Vernell still has his Sears name tag," she adds.

By now Suzy's chewy coffee has worked its way through my system. I tell Vernell I need to use the bathroom.

"You don't say that here," Vernell says in a semi-stern voice. "Here you say you got to count your money."

"Excuse me, I've got to count my money."

"That's better."

In the bathroom I wonder how long Suzy lived here before Vernell installed hot water for the shower. A couple days . . . or did she tough it out for months or even years? The bathroom, like the rest of the house, is much improved and spotless. I also wonder if as Vernell grows older, he will depend ever more on Suzy, the way Russell Means depended on his wife.

Probably so.

When I come out, Suzy tells me Vernell is outside waiting. "He wants to give you a ride in one of his race cars."

Standing on the front steps, Vernell points to a beautifully restored '57 Ford Fairlane two-door sedan—metallic blue with a creamy white top, creamy leather interior—a hot car powered with a rebuilt V8 and factory supercharger parked in his rutty dirt driveway in the middle of the reservation, and says, "Hop in." I'm not too surprised. The last time I was here, he gave me a ride in a 1931 Ford Phaeton Model A.

"You must have a thing for Fords."

He turns the key just as he answers me—*vroom! vroom!*—so I don't hear him except for something about "cheaper parts." The engine sputters, growls, and emits another *vroom! vroom!* and we head up the hill with ease, out the White Thunder Ranch gate, cruising toward Kyle. I sometimes wonder what people living here think of Vernell. They say it is not acceptable for a Lakota to draw attention to himself, to show off, even though their history is rife with great leaders who did just that—adorned themselves with beads and feathers and war paint and had many wives, many horses, and many followers. Red Cloud was fond of ribbons and eagle feathers; his long, black-bear-greased hair was plaited around the wing bone of an eagle to signal elegance and propriety. You might even say Crazy Horse's minimal style was just a way to be different; his war paint was a simple yellow lightning bolt down one side of his face. No war bonnet, a single feather in his ponytail, a pebble behind one ear—much like Steve Jobs' jeans and black turtleneck, his simple garb made him cool.

Vernell's working cowboy dress, his friendly demeanor, even his laugh are completely ordinary . . . the same as many Lakota men's. But he drives around the reservation in vintage automobiles, has the most beautiful horses, an educated blond wife—tourists from Europe and even Japan come to visit his ranch. I worry that some people are jealous of Vernell and might want to harm him, but nothing like this has happened and I've never seen him get angry with anyone—disappointed, but not angry. Perhaps his eccentricity is overlooked because he is otherwise authentic, about as pure Lakota as anyone could possibly be; he lives the spiritual life, speaks the language, has ridden in every Big Foot Ride, and is one of the last great storytellers—Vernell is a human repository of the rich culture and history of his people.

He slows the Fairlane and points out a newly opened café in a rotting old building with a frontier façade and chipped red paint, which looks like it must have come from the set of *Gunsmoke*. A hand-painted sign announces the name: THE FOOD STOP CAFÉ. It has a drive-up window, but no separate "Order Here" station . . . you stop at the window, tell someone inside what you want, and wait for it to be cooked and handed to you. If there is a car behind you, they have to wait until you drive off before they can order.

"People say they have the best hamburgers on the rez, but I prefer Burger King."

"Yeah, competition must be fierce!"

We both laugh.

"I'd eat Burger King every day if Rapid City were closer."

"Good thing you work so hard or you'd be diabetic."

"Many people here die from diabetes; Norman Underbaggage died from diabetes."

I'm stunned. I was going to ask Vernell about Norman, hoping we might even get the chance to see him. Now I feel even older; I never thought I would outlive my students, students permanently fixed in my mind as teenagers.

"Who else has died?" I ask.

"Calvin and Myron Fire Thunder. They got into a car accident. Francis Harlen, his three sisters. David Black Bear."

We drive on, Vernell now and then revving up his 500-horsepower engine. We pass by the outdoor basketball courts behind Little Wound School, stop to watch a game in progress. It's much faster than the style of ball played by white kids and even by black kids—a visual frenzy, a blur of arms and sneakers, nonstop weaving, head faking, cutting, passing on the run, behind the back, between the legs, three-point shots, blocked shots, follow-up dunks . . . the boys are up and down the court so fast it is like watching a Ping-Pong match, all the while whooping and laughing, their athleticism undeniable.

"Rezball," Vernell says. "That's what we call our style of basketball. When I played in high school, we didn't do all those fancy things, but we always out-hustled the white teams, wore them down. They said it was unfair. Whenever us Indians find an advantage, white people try to change the rules."

One of the boys yells out to Vernell, "Nice wheels," and the other boys stop for a moment. They look over at us, wave. The game continues.

We drive onto an old dirt road that curves down to a body of brackish water, the Kyle Dam, where all too many of Vernell's high school contemporaries took their girlfriends to drink beer and have unprotected sex. Another item in the Lakota litany of woes: the high rate of teenage pregnancy, irresponsible teenage boys, and responsible grandmothers stuck with the consequences.

"We used to fish here," Vernell says with a twinkle in his eyes.

"Yeah, I bet you did."

"Remember that time we got drunk when the Vista workers had movie night, how they terrorized the little kids by showing scary movies? You were trying to hit on that Vista woman with big boobies, no bra. That was funny."

"Fortunately, I do not remember."

I do, however, remember the Vista girl. She was thin, biracial with wild curly hair, wore no bra, was constantly smoking unfiltered cigarettes. Inhaling brought attention to her large breasts. I visualized them filling up with smoke, but I don't remember being particularly attracted to her. Besides, her boyfriend was always hovering about; they argued bitterly.

Changing the subject, I ask Vernell about horses. "Why don't I see horses running free, young boys riding bareback? When I lived here, there were always horses."

"Too many people, too many cars. Back then people drove slower, thirty or forty miles an hour. Now they go much faster."

"This land is no longer free range?"

"No. When it was free range, a tourist from Minnesota killed one of my horses. He wanted me to pay for the damages to his car. I told him as long as a person is a responsible horse owner, he is not the liable party. The man didn't believe me, but his insurance company sent me a check."

As we drive back up the dirt road from the dam to the teacher housing section, we pass by a small section of one-bedroom houses reserved for single teachers.

"Vernell, do you remember Maggie, the pretty young teacher with red hair and freckles who taught seventh grade?"

"Yeah," Vernell says. "All us boys liked her."

"There was a rule against single teachers having an overnight visitor of the opposite sex. When I walked to work one really cold morning—temperature below zero—her boyfriend, who had driven all the way here from Oregon, was sleeping out front in his car."

"So if she was a lesbian and had a girlfriend over, that would have been OK?"

"Even now, I don't think the BIA would admit they have lesbian or gay teachers."

"We always had gay Indians," Vernell says. "We call them '*winkte*.' Some like to do women's work and they like to care for the children. In a naming ceremony, if a *winkte* names your child, it brings good luck and fortune to that child."

Vernell stomps on the gas pedal; the Fairlane's V8 howls, its spinning wheels kick up a massive dust devil, and we peel down the gravel road, rocks spraying every which way. "Spent all last winter working on this baby," Vernell says. "Got to have a little fun with it."

And then he says, "Want to see where I get my spare parts?"

"Sure, Vernell. I would like to see where you get your spare parts."

BOMBING RANGE

WAR BONNET OF THORNS

As we travel east past what Vernell calls the "Kyle city limits," even though there are no city limits, I spot a wooden sign near the edge of the road—the silhouette of an Indian warrior running alongside the silhouette of a running buffalo. The sign says WELCOME TO THE HOME OF TANKA BAR. About a hundred yards down a gravel drive behind the sign, near the Kyle water tower, is a small, industrial-looking brown building with a double-door front entrance, a few small windows, cars parked along the side. I presume it is the Tanka Bar headquarters.

"Wow, I didn't know they made Tanka Bars in Kyle . . . I bought some at Big Bat's."

Vernell is not a fan and complains about a shortage of Lakota people in top management, aside from the CEO, Karlene Hunter.

"Tanka Bars don't even taste good to me," he says.

As there is a certain finality to his pronouncement, I don't ask Vernell anything else about Tanka Bars.

"Here's my turn." Vernell effortlessly twirls the Fairlane steering wheel with one hand, simultaneously stomping on the accelerator. *Vroom! Vroom!* Spitting gravel, we're spinning off the pavement onto a deeply rutted dirt road clearly marked by a new road sign that looks like it belongs in a suburban development, the intersection of BIA Highway 2 and Bombing Range Road.

"What does the bombing range have to do with spare parts?" I ask.

"Have you been there?"

"No. I didn't know you could go there."

"Only if you know the roads. I'm about the only person who comes here."

Vernell stops at a barbed-wire gate, hops out and moves the fence aside, jumps back in the car, tells me he'll put the gate back when we return.

"Some white ranchers lease this land, but we don't care if their cattle get lost."

I have to ask. "Do people steal cows here?"

"Not long ago a rancher was checking on his cattle when he saw several strange lumps on the ground. As he got near these lumps, he could see they were his cows. Rustlers shot them, butchered off the front and hindquarters, left the rest. He was really angry."

"Must be hard for white ranchers around here to get livestock insurance," I joke.

Vernell smiles.

The bombing range is a good twenty miles from this gate, along bumpy tire tracks that branch off in different directions every few hundred yards. The going is slow. Good thing Vernell knows how to navigate the ruts. Bad thing his car has no seat belts.

"Brought some Japanese tourists here once. They were nice people, asked good questions. When we got close to the range, they started crying, really crying, very loudly. I did not realize that the American bombardiers who dropped those atomic bombs got their target practice here."

"That's one of the saddest stories you've ever told me."

"Yeah. Guess I never told you about the years I went to boarding school in Pine Ridge, 1959 through 1961."

"What was it like?" I ask.

Vernell takes a deep breath, slows down but continues to drive on while he looks over at me.

I remember three dates when I was nine years old (that would have been about forty-five years ago). The first was July 4, when my grandfather died; he was ninety-eight. Next was August 7, my birthday, when my parents took me to the clinic to get some shots that hurt; guess I needed them for school. Finally, on September 6, we rode with Leo and his kids to Holy Rosary Indian Mission school in Pine Ridge. They left us with these scary black demons with white faces who took us into the basement, where they shaved our heads and put us under a shower. There was a little bench next to the shower room where they handed you some clothes and you got dressed. Then they marched all of us outside, through a yard, and into the church.

When we sat down inside, I looked up, and there was this man with no clothes, nothing. He was hanging there with his arms stretched out, a war bonnet made of thorns, blood flowing down his face; it looked like someone had pounded nails through his hands and feet. I was scared, wondered if this was what they did to little kids here. I just wanted to run away. At night I could see the stars, so I knew how to get home. But these things play in your head. I was too afraid to run away.

When somebody did something wrong, they punished all of us. Along one of the walls there was a long bench with little hooks above it where kids hung their coats. They made everybody stand up on the bench and face the wall for hours. If some of the little kids cried, we all had to stand there longer. When it was time to get down, everyone was quiet.

When it was time to eat, we had to stand in line and stay perfectly still. Once you got your food and sat down, you couldn't start eating until everyone else was seated. If you did, someone would come behind you and whack you. When the nun up front shook her little bell, we could start eating, but you only had fifteen minutes to eat.

In the mornings we got mush and a piece of toast with a little butter, which was all the butter we ever got. Some kids would save their butter.

The bread was made from wheat the nuns grew themselves. There were husks in the bread, which made it taste like sandpaper, but this was not as bad as the bland tomato soup they gave us for lunch and dinner. We never had traditional Indian foods, meat stews, berries, fry bread. On Sundays, if everyone was good, we got cocoa, the one good thing.

At night, they marched you up three flights of stairs to the dormitory, where there were two rows of bunk beds. In the back, around a corner, was a little section called the wet-the-bed section. Those beds were filled with black rubber. The sheets were cold; there was no heat in the big stone building. No wonder the little kids peed—they were freezing! The rest of us had a sheet and a thin blanket; we were freezing too.

One priest would come in and sit where he could watch us, read the gospel to us. If anyone talked or giggled or did anything wrong, we all had to get down from our beds, line up, pull our pants down, bend over. They used razor strops; everyone got spanked. Another priest had a spooky look that gave me the creeps.

Because I grew up with my grandparents, when I got to Holy Rosary I didn't speak English, only Lakota, but they forbade us from speaking Lakota. Right from the start they said, "English is your language now. You must learn English." If you got caught speaking Lakota, you would get whipped good. Us full-bloods would play way back in the playground where there were no swings, so we could speak to each other. We had to stay away from the half-bloods because they would tell on you. I remember getting spanked quite a bit. The nuns would make you hold your hands palm out and whack you hard with a ruler.

We didn't have to worry about bullies—we had nuns.

After they had spanked you, you had to say, "Thank you, Sister so-and-so, or thank you, Brother so-and-so."

I was there for three years, lived in numbness the whole time. We only got to shower once, on Wednesday, and only then would they give you a

Pfister Hotel: Rushville, Nebraska. The once proud Pfister Hotel, boarded up and sadly abandoned.

White Clay Welcome: White Clay, Nebraska. Welcome to the armpit of Nebraska, unincorporated skid row of the plains.

Four Drunks Across the Road: White Clay, Nebraska.

Inside Big Bat's: Pine Ridge, South Dakota.

Crazy Horse Sign: Pine Ridge Reservation, South Dakota. This sign honoring Crazy Horse is now just blank space, solitary metal sentinels standing skyward.

Mass Grave: Wounded Knee, South Dakota.

Indian Pride: Wounded Knee, South Dakota. Standing underneath the Wounded Knee portal, Ryan raises his fist as a sign of "Indian pride."

Lost Bird: Pine Ridge Reservation, South Dakota. Lost Bird was three months old when they found her under her mother's frozen corpse, frostbitten but still alive.

Big Foot Surrenders: Porcupine, South Dakota. The road sign commemorating the beautiful spot where Chief Big Foot surrendered.

Mato Paha: Spearfish, South Dakota. Many generations climb Mato Paha (Bear Mountain) for prayer and fasting.

Bombing Range: Badlands, South Dakota. Car bodies brought here by helicopter at the start of World War II.

Rezball: Kyle, South Dakota.

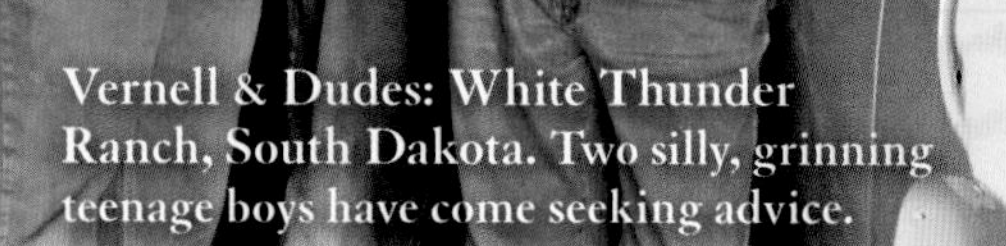

Vernell & Dudes: White Thunder Ranch, South Dakota. Two silly, grinning teenage boys have come seeking advice.

Guy White Thunder: Kyle, South Dakota.

Buffalo: Yellow Bear Canyon, South Dakota.

Indian Ponies: White Thunder Ranch, South Dakota.

Buffalo cooking pots: Kyle, South Dakota. Vernell and his friends have the outdoor cooking pots going for the buffalo stew that will feed several hundred people.

Indian Joe: Kyle, South Dakota.

Riderless Horse: Kyle, South Dakota. Vernell is riding a fine-looking black stallion and leading an equally exquisite black-and-white riderless Indian pony, symbol of the fallen warrior.

Bear-in-the-Lodge Creek: Allen, South Dakota. Standing by himself near the edge of the cemetery as a sign of respect for his father, Vernell must ask the medicine man to cut off his ponytail.

clean set of clothes. All week long you wore the same underwear, same socks, same everything, no matter how dirty they got.

One day I was sitting on the front steps of the building—it must have been a Saturday or Sunday afternoon—when I saw a car coming in the distance. I had a strange feeling about this car. As it got closer, I could see that it was a '59 red-and-black Ford, and I could see that the driver was my grandmother. She pulled up in front, lowered the window, shouted out to me, "Get in, Grandson." As I got in, she said, "You never have to be here again."

I didn't wave good-bye to nobody. I didn't look back. I don't know if my grandmother told them she was going to take me.

"I am so sorry that happened to you. That's some story."

Up ahead I can see dozens of small rust-colored objects; too big to be cow carcasses, they appear to be tangled metal sculptures. As we get closer, I see that they are old cars, or, as it turns out, old car bodies—no wheels, no chassis, no engines—and not just any old car bodies, vintage models, late 1930s up to 1942, when car manufacturers in the United States quit making cars so they could turn their factories over to war production.

Vernell points out a 1941 Ford Coupe, says, "That's my dream car. One of these days, I'm going to haul it out of here."

I'm not a car buff, but I recognize an old Buick with its signature chrome window framing; the detached hood sits on top of the roof, one door is completely mangled, there are dents here and there. It's a strange scene. Wine-colored, rusty car bodies are evenly laid out in a sea of tall, rolling green-and-red prairie grass, spaced about fifteen yards apart. As we walk around admiring them, Vernell points out that they form the shape of a target, a large circle with vertical and horizontal crosshairs. There are 250 car bodies in this one target; there are two more targets just like it. The cars were brought here by helicopter, dropped down in exactly the right spots. They have dents from the bombs, and many of the doors and hoods have been blown off, but they are not marred by bullet holes or graffiti—there are no signs of vandalism.

It's a beautiful sight; it reminds me of Carhenge, only much grander, wonderful except for the story behind it and the reality that there are still unexploded shells and bombs scattered about. The Badlands Bombing Range represents the last major Indian landgrab by the U.S. government: 341,726 acres confiscated from the Oglala tribe by eminent domain, the equivalent of 534 square miles, used throughout the war years for precision bombing exercises as well as air-to-air and air-to-ground gunnery ranges. One day in 1942, over a hundred Lakota families living along nearby Redwater Creek received official notice from the U.S. Army that they had thirty days to pack up and move out. There was no appeal, no monetary compensation, no new housing. Everybody had to be gone, or be arrested and forced out.

Most of these people lived in small one- to three-room cabins. Many kept sacred objects from the old days wrapped up in a trunk or just lying under the bed. Quilted shirts, beaded leggings, ceremonial drums, and the small amulet bags in the shape of turtles or lizards in which every man preserved his umbilical cord. In the turmoil of packing up and pulling out, many of these things got lost. Henry Garnett, the grandson of Crazy Horse's friend Billy Garnett, had a trunk full of precious artifacts that he left behind, thinking it would be safe in the house. After the war, it took his family ten years to get their land back. When the army finally let go, the house was a wreck, the trunk was empty.

"Do you know what was the single most important thing people left behind?" Vernell asks.

"The money they buried in coffee cans out back?"

"No, David. The most important thing was their woodstoves. The shacks families found to move into didn't have heat; they had to sneak back to get their stoves."

"Do you really get car parts from here?"

"Sometimes," Vernell replies, "but mostly I just bring people out because it is part of our history you won't find on the tourist maps."

Now Vernell seems to be a hurry; he revs up his supercharged hot rod just enough to fly over the many dirt ruts in our path and still land soft enough to avoid denting his bumpers. Steering with one hand, he takes a call from someone named Sonny, who is apparently waiting for us at the ranch and wanting to know when we'll be back. "Thirty minutes, sharp," Vernell answers, which seems highly unrealistic considering that it took an hour to get here. I worry about the absence of a seat belt and am somewhat surprised when Vernell dutifully stops to put the barbed-wire gate back in place; from what I can tell, it doesn't look as if any cows escaped. Glancing at the speedometer, I see we are now going seventy miles an hour. Vernell slams on the brakes, and as we spin out on Bombing Range Road and back onto BIA Highway 2, we come to a complete stop. Vernell points his arm out the window at what appears to be an old Sun Dance ground sitting on the bluff just across the creek to our left.

"They do Sun Dances here to make money," he says. "They might have signs saying 'no cameras, no tourists,' but if you look around, you see non-Lakotas taking pictures."

He continues: "We have all these Sun Dances—why aren't people as healthy as they should be? It is supposed to be about healing, but it is all about money and prestige. South Dakota is the biggest tourism state. Many who come here are wannabe Indians. They wanna go to a powwow, learn how to do a powwow dance, pick up a few Lakota expressions, experience the sweat lodge.

"Making money off tourists is just another form of assimilation; it is not who we are. There's good assimilation and bad assimilation."

"What's good assimilation?" I ask.

"Education is good assimilation; that's why I'm back in school."

By now we have driven past Kyle and we're about to turn onto the road to Vernell's ranch. I ask him if he would ever run for tribal office. He laughs and laughs.

"David, if I had the money and staff, there are legal things that could be done, but I don't know yet what I can do. One person cannot do a lot."

Safely parked with no apparent damage to the '57 Ford Fairlane or either of us, we are about to walk up the little steps onto the White Thunder patio when Vernell nudges me to turn around. I look back just as a battered old convertible in a blanket of dust appears at the top of his driveway—it rapidly twists and slides in a smoky descent to within feet of where we are standing. Two grinning teenage boys wave at us as they hoist themselves up and out of the car without opening the doors.

"Hu, Vernell," one says.

"Nineteen-eighty-one Camaro," Vernell replies. "Looking pretty good."

One boy wears a stained brown-and-black Chevy Camaro T-shirt that could very well be as old as the car. I notice that he is taller than Vernell, with thick black hair, rounded shoulders, and a serious demeanor; handsome. Vernell says, "This one is Chet."

The other boy, Sonny, seems more approachable; he is smiling, and even though his eyes are partially hidden behind his tinted horn-rimmed glasses, I can see they are empathetic eyes. His sleeveless black shirt reveals a layer of baby fat and a homemade spiral *S* tattoo on his left shoulder.

Both shake my hand and seem very comfortable, not at all shy about talking shop with Vernell in my presence. They have come seeking advice—how do they go about repairing rust spots on their new baby? Sonny points to an area just behind the top of one of the front doors. He's tried sandpapering the rust away but is finding it very stubborn.

"Let me show you," Vernell says, moving over to the car. "First make sure the area around the spot is clean." Taking a polishing cloth out of his pocket, Vernell buffs the area, and then takes out a pocketknife, opens up a small blade, and uses it to remove the rust that the sandpaper failed to remove.

"Some of this rust is under the paint," Vernell points out. "Dig carefully to make sure you get it all. And you only want to remove the rust, not damage the metal. Auto body putty comes in handy if there is a hole or uneven spot."

The boys look on; they don't just respect Vernell, they admire him. I choke up at the very thought of Vernell becoming a venerable Lakota elder. Like his father, Guy White Thunder, his great-grandfather Chief White Thunder, respected and wise, the old warrior who teaches you how to get the rust out.

The lesson over, Vernell asks the boys if they want to see the car he's working on. We follow him to a metal shed about the size of a standard one-car garage that stands to the side of his house. He unlocks the double wooden doors, swings them open, and there sit the makings of a brightly painted yellow 1938 Ford coupe. The hottest pre–World War II street rod now fitted with a new flathead V8 engine with a custom blue, six-bladed Flex fan and a bright orange Fram oil filter. The hood and front end hang at the back of the building waiting for paint.

"Body of this car was a bit dinged up," Vernell says, giving me a wink, "but I pounded the dents out. It is going to be the fastest car on the rez—from here to Pine Ridge and back in less than an hour."

Chet laughs for the first time; Sonny joins in.

"Not possible," Sonny says. "One-way trip takes longer."

"I know shortcuts," Vernell answers.

Next we follow Vernell across his dirt driveway to a much bigger metal building, a prefab A-frame structure with a footprint at least ten times that of his house. It has an industrial rolling-steel door, a separate entrance door, large windows, and a dirt floor. Inside, covered with a blue tarp, is the '31 Ford Phaeton Model A I rode in the last time I was here. And there's another Ford coupe, this one a 1932 Deuce, the so-called Holy Grail of hot rods. It is painted black with yellowish-orange streaking flames across its sides, and the bright green, hand-painted monogram REZ DOG KRUZER on the hood. At the back of the building, I see a 1960 Ford Galaxie, two-tone, black with a white roof—both the hood and trunk lid are upright; it's a work in progress. Here and there are stacks of tires and wheels, tools, saddles hanging in the rafters, ladders, a lawn mower, halogen floodlights on a yellow lighting stand, and along one wall, a dozen identical long-handled shovels.

Seems odd. "Vernell, why all the shovels?"

"So when I die, they can bury me quick."

Sonny and Chet stroll about, eyes wide, envious, in awe.

"How do you have time for all this?" I ask Vernell.

"David, time is the one thing I have plenty of, especially in the winter. Even if you don't have money, you'd be surprised what you can do with a lot of time."

Back outside I take a quick survey of the other White Thunder vehicles, the ones parked about his yard: a red dual-cab Ford pickup emblazoned with the more subdued hand-painted monogram WHITE THUNDER RANCH; another newer, steel-gray dual-cab Ford pickup; the vintage Ford Fairlane; two fairly new Kia Forte sedans; a forest-green Honda FourTrax Rancher all-terrain vehicle; an old tractor; another Ford pickup truck, this one equipped with a Boss snowplow and floodlights; an old flatbed truck suitable for hauling large amounts of I don't know what; and at least three horse trailers, each big enough for six horses. Some of the cars and pickups have license plates; others don't.

Vernell leans back on the blade of the snowplow, Chet sits on a stack of tires, and Sonny leans against the door of the steel building. They chat about cars, about the upcoming school year, the unseasonably warm weather, about nothing and everything. They chat on until their mini-powwow runs its course, then the boys leap into the Camaro, rev it up, and bust a "u-ey," peeling out of sight in a thermal cloud of gravel and dust.

"Really nice guys," I say.

Vernell shrugs. "Yeah, at least they're not crackheads."

YELLOW BEAR CANYON

BEFORE THE WHITE MAN

I'm craving another cup of Suzy's chewy cowboy coffee. I'm happy that we've taken a few steps toward his little ranch house, toward caffeine nirvana, when Vernell abruptly stops, turns, and bumps into me. "Almost forgot," he says. "I need to check on those crazy *wasicu* survivalists in Yellow Bear—need to make sure they are still surviving. You might want to meet them."

"What about coffee?"

"No time. I'll leave my windows down, and if that doesn't work, I can always kick you."

For this trip, we hop into Vernell's red pickup truck, the one emblazoned with WHITE THUNDER RANCH in bold white letters on the back fenders. This is not one of his carefully restored, souped-up vehicles . . . it's mud splattered, the doors are creaky, the key left in the ignition needs to be turned three or four times before the engine starts. There is much clutter in the cab, empty snack food packages and soda cans, flashlight, gloves, snow chains on the floor, a pocketknife, a hacksaw, and old editions of the *Lakota Country Times* newspaper. The moment the truck sputters to a start, the radio comes on full blast . . . KILI Radio, Voice of the Lakota. More of the old-time country music, the same laid-back, likely stoned announcer we heard earlier on our way back from the bombing range. We rumble up the gravel driveway, over the cattle guard, and turn left onto the main blacktop, where for the first few miles the view out my side window is very beautiful but oddly motionless. I might as well be looking at a landscape painting, perhaps by the great John Mix Stanley—rolling carpet of pumpkin-orange prairie grass; chartreuse knapweeds, their tiny purple buds pushing out like crowning heads of the about to be born; intertwined tentacles of a snarling oak tree, leafless, as are the tangled sagebrush and chokecherry branches. I see a few abandoned vehicles and machines around one-story frame houses in dire need of general repairs, but no children playing in the dirt. No old people sitting outside, smoking. No dogs, no horses. No motion. The road curves this way and that. It is serene, and with my caffeine tank empty it is no that surprise I doze off, start dreaming that I'm driving a shiny red 1947 Ford coupe that Vernell has restored for me across a flat plain of tall grass on a wonderfully warm breezy day when out of the distant sun I spot a squadron of P51 Mustang dive-bombers screaming down upon me. With a tight grip on the steering wheel, I turn sharply down a steep embankment as my eyes open and I realize I may have been dreaming about dive-bombers but the embankment is all too real. Vernell's truck violently descends into Yellow Bear Canyon, a stomach-churning near-vertical plunge on a road that should have but doesn't have switchbacks. Wide awake, I scream for Vernell to SLOW THE FUCK DOWN, but instead of hitting the brakes, he stomps on the gas and hollers, "Hoye! Hoye! Time to wake up, Bunka Dude!"

Luckily, my hands shoot out to brace myself against the dashboard before my soft head smashes into the cold hard metal in a world where there are no neurosurgeons. Vernell, of course, thinks this is funny. When I give him my best evil stare, he only chuckles.

By the time I calm down enough to look out the window, the road has leveled off. I see that Yellow Bear Canyon completely engulfs us and it's an entirely different world, a billowy world of evergreen trees and shrubs, stately lodgepole pines, naked trunks packed together like anxious runners at the beginning of a big-city marathon. But there's very little room overhead for sky, which I find disquieting.

Vernell slows to a crawl. "People call this Yellow Bear Canyon, but its original name is Skokpa, Sh-coke-pah, which means 'down in the valley,' named for the Oglala people who first settled here. Yellow Bears came much later."

Pointing with his left hand out the window, Vernell continues: "That creek along here is called No Flesh. No Flesh was chief of the Cut Off People. He went to Washington with Red Cloud in 1880-something when they tried to explain to us the Dawes Act, how the government was going to divide our lands into individual pieces."

My heart no longer fiercely beating, my vision back to normal, I chime in sarcastically, "We generous white folk are going to give you poor Indians a few acres of the land you already own so you can learn how be farmers, not communists."

Vernell laughs. "Worked out for my grandfather. He built up his land by trading horses for additional allotments—most people ended up with nothing."

"I would say less than nothing."

This time his hands are completely off the steering wheel. Pointing to both sides of the road (hopefully steering with his knees), Vernell says, "Notice how the utility guys mowed the left side but not the right."

Sure enough, I can see that the foliage on the left from the edge of the road up to the barbed wire fence is short. But on the right it is long and wild; you can hardly see the barbed wire.

"I told them not to mow on the right side. The transmission hub for all this area is on my land. I paid for it, so I can shut it down whenever I want, and there is nothing they can do. They send me a royalty check every month for my electricity."

"That would make you the John D. Rockefeller of Pine Ridge."

Vernell either doesn't understand or just ignores my bad joke. "Shortly after No Flesh went to Washington, a white man named Richards married Chief Yellow Bear's two sisters, who then lived in this area. One night, Richards got terribly drunk and beat up his wives. The next day Yellow Bear went over to talk to him, but Richards murdered Yellow Bear with an ax. Most recently a retired white lady schoolteacher sold this land to the people living here now.

"Some developers from Rapid wanted to buy it for a bed-and-breakfast, but I said to them, 'I cannot stop you from buying this land, but I can legally turn off your electricity.' "

When we reach the bottom of the canyon, Vernell veers right where wide tire tracks have forged a pathway through the thicket onto a clearing of muddy ground. There's an old battered Dutchmen trailer parked in front of an immense prefab industrial steel building. Scattered about are the camping and construction tools you might expect to see: sleeping bags, a wheelbarrow, and, most conspicuously, a stone garden sculpture of Mother Mary.

"People living here don't need my electricity," Vernell says. "They live off the grid."

It looks like no one is home: no parked vehicles, no barking dogs, doors and windows shut. Vernell puts the White Thunder pickup in neutral and pulls the emergency brake, leaving the motor running. He opens the driver's door and jumps out. I hear the sharp crunches of his deliberate strides as KILI Radio still blares away; I hear a loud knocking at the door. As this cacophony of human sound goes on, I think I am warming up to this little spot of terra firma, thinking how lovely it might be to live disconnected from the haywire of modern life. You wouldn't know who won the Super Bowl; hell, you wouldn't even know what teams played in the Super Bowl! Rising sea levels might obliterate Manhattan, Bono might become president of the Republic of Ireland, and the Chinese stock market might crash—who cares? I'm easily lost in this fantasy when the front door opens. Vernell turns to look back at me and shouts, "Shut it down! Come inside!"

Stopping for a moment at the doorway before I enter, I can see that this is not a well-lighted place. A small lattice window above the door is the only window on my end of the building; two double-hung windows at the other end are small. A single strand of LED lights runs along the walls near the ceiling like the cheap Christmas decorations you buy at your neighborhood Dollar Store. Vernell vanishes into the darkness. There is something eerie about this shadowy cavern, and I feel apprehensive as my eyes adjust to its dimness. But then a portly man with a fastidiously trimmed beard emerges; he wears a light brown short-sleeved dress shirt, dark brown khakis held up by suspenders. Spooky, but the slightness of his stooped frame makes him less threatening. A funny thought comes to mind: stick a briar pipe in his mouth, add a tweed jacket with patches on the elbows, and he could be a Berkeley professor, someone you might run into while strolling across Sproul Plaza—the Nobel Prize–winning chairperson of the math department. The space behind him slowly comes into focus: an expanse of unadorned concrete, a large wooden table, a few metal chairs, and what looks to be a newly installed kitchen sink and counter; tools and instruction booklets are piled high. In the gloom I spy three other human forms that I think could be teenagers and a child in a playpen. Apparently, we're interrupting a busy day.

Vernell says to no one in particular, "I'd like you to meet David; he was my teacher. He's the reason I can't spell."

The professor laughs a bit too loud for my taste. I'll call him William and change the names of his family members too; he is accompanied by a shy young man looking down at the floor beside him who is six inches shorter and fifty pounds lighter, his teenage son, James. The lovely young woman with a big Kate Hudson smile whom I like instantly is his daughter Eleanor. She is on her knees playing with a darling toddler who giggles and shrieks. William makes a point of telling me that Eleanor's older sister, Helena, is the toddler's mom; at the moment she is out running errands with her husband, Daniel. There's one more member of this pioneering family, William's wife, Deborah, who is in Minneapolis seeing relatives.

"Good day for you to visit. The first day we've had functional electric lights."

William invites Vernell and me to sit with him at the table. I soon learn that he is a geologist from California. Just as we arrived, he finished hooking up the solar-powered generator that runs the LED lights. It will eventually power the refrigerator I saw sitting out in the yard, plus water pumps, power tools, heating, better lights, and, most essential to this enterprise, an Internet connection. If William is to maintain the consulting contracts he has with old-school brick-and-mortar companies on the West Coast, he will have to be online. James, who has been standing stoically at the kitchen counter, raises his head and sputters to life as if there is now enough energy in the room to trigger his programmable memory. "Our family mission is to become energy self-sufficient, raise or otherwise procure all our food, live off the land no matter how harsh the weather, demonstrate to the native people that they can do this too." James's eyes sparkle just like the LED lights, only brighter. "We already have a goat. Tomorrow we are going to buy one of Vernell's horses."

"When it gets warmer," William adds, "we'll get some chickens, a few ducks, and, hopefully, a milk cow. We'll plant a garden. There are many wild strawberries all around here, and my Helena recently shot her first deer."

I am shocked. "Really? She shot a deer?"

Eleanor says she's made goat's-milk yogurt and offers us some, at the same time profusely apologizing for not having any honey or jam to sweeten it. Vernell has zero interest in yogurt, but I happily try a bowl. It's amazingly refreshing and delicious—goat's-milk yogurt on the Pine Ridge!

"When I lived here," I tell them, "I was lucky to get tripe soup at Sally's Cafe." At this point, William is cautiously circumspect and James has returned to his taciturn state, but Eleanor is obviously thrilled to have a little company, happy to tell us about their many adventures. "When we arrived last spring," she says, "four of us slept in a tent;

Helena, Daniel, and the baby stayed in the trailer, where there is heat. For water, we ferried buckets up from No Flesh Creek.

"An early blizzard last October nearly wiped us out. Dad, James, and I were still sleeping in the tent. During the first night, twenty inches of snow fell every hour. When the tent collapsed, Dad woke up to the sound of my screaming. I didn't know what I was pushing and beating at; everything was mixed up in a bad dream."

William jumps back in. "I woke James up, and the two of us were able to rescue Eleanor. We moved into the crowded camper for the rest of the night, and next day we found refuge at Our Lady of Sorrows in Kyle. We lived in the sanctuary until we could move into this building."

I glance over at Vernell, see the top of his water-stained cowboy hat as he is looking down, fidgeting, and crossing and uncrossing his legs. He doesn't appear to be listening, but I know him; he is always listening. Always attuned to the moment . . . very little slips by Vernell White Thunder.

Irrespective of their idiosyncrasy, I am impressed with these survivalists—who wouldn't be?—but there is a long history of white people with good intentions coming to the rez, hoping to save the Indians, show them a new way, lift them out of the morass. Volunteers come every summer—they plant organic gardens, build bunk beds for children, install protective skirting around mobile homes, spay and neuter pets, hold technology workshops. Mostly they do good things, but in terms of making a lasting difference . . . it's dubious.

Vernell stands up, jokingly says, "We got to go milk the buffalo." I shake William's hand, wave good-bye to James and Eleanor; tell them I might be back this way one of these days, say perhaps I'll drop in to see how they are doing. William walks us to the door, and we return to the White Thunder Ranch pickup. As soon as we are out of earshot, I ask Vernell what he thinks about white people thinking they can teach the Lakota how to be self-sufficient.

"He is skeptical and doesn't approve of their self-imposed hardships. He worries for their safety."

Turning the key, angrily revving up the engine, Vernell slips the clutch so that the wheels of his truck ominously kick up a vast splodge of dirt, much like a Lakota war pony might do before charging into an early morning camp of the hated Pawnee. "Let me show you where I grew up with my grandpa and grandma. You will understand how we Lakota were self-sufficient."

As we spin out, I take one last look at this unlikely modern sod house, chuckle at the thought that these homesteaders settled here 150 years too late. The sun begins to dip behind the mysteriously steep hills; I begin to feel a chill, am thankful we don't go far.

Vernell turns off KILI Radio, slows his truck to an idle, turns left off the ungroomed side of the road, drives across a shallow gully, a nearly hidden creek, over a thick bed of ferns to a broad clearing nestled in a cradle of hills, bare-branched cottonwoods, sweet grass, and sage. What a splendid womb of nature! Much larger than the barren survival camp, it is, I can see, protected from howling winds, blowing snow, the searing heat of summer.

Coasting to a stop, Vernell shuts down the motor. "Here is where my story begins. Let's get out and take a look around."

The one-room log house where Vernell spent the first eight years of his life is no longer standing, but he points out chunks of concrete that once made up its foundation. In back of the house, dug into a hillside, is what remains of the corral where Vernell's grandfather kept the wagon team horses.

We walk down the other side of the hill to the bed of a small but fast-moving creek. "Right about here," Vernell says, "we had a wooden box where you could keep butter, milk, whatever needed to stay cool. Grandma also dried a lot of meat, stored it in canvas bags—you never see that today.

"We had a huge garden—tomatoes, corn, and green beans, some of which my grandmother preserved in clay jars. We stored potatoes and turnips over there in our root cellar, and we had goats . . . there was always goat milk, but no goat cheese or goat yogurt; only *wasicu* eat these things."

Walking along, Vernell kicks up pebbles with the scuffed toes of the Apache boots he's been wearing for as long as I can remember, and with each kick, he uncovers old memories, memories as numerous as the pebbles.

"David, we were rich compared to others. When my grandfather butchered a cow, neighbors came for a feast; everyone went home with *something*. Grandfather used to say, 'Grandson, there are spirits watching over our food, making sure it is good and plentiful. If you share, they stay. If you don't, they get angry and leave.' "

Vernell was only two months old when his parents brought him to this very spot, left him to be raised by his mother's parents, George and Emma Poor Thunder. It was late August 1954, Moon When the Chokecherries Are Ripe. Vernell is not sure why his parents abandoned him, nor does he seem bitter about it. "Perhaps with three other children," he says, "taking care of me was too much for them." Already in his eighties, Vernell's grandfather was a legendary horse breeder and traditional medicine man, and his grandmother was the granddaughter of the great chief American Horse.

Before moving to Yellow Bear Canyon, George Poor Thunder lived on the Rosebud reservation, where he was one of the last breeders of highly prized Appaloosas, the remarkable spotted-coat war ponies of the Nez Percé.

"Appaloosas would be forever extinct if my grandfather hadn't understood Nez Percé breeding practices."

"What were those?"

"I wish I knew them all, but gelding inferior male horses was part of it."

"Wonderful."

"Whenever a white man came to Grandfather and wanted to buy a saddle-broken Appaloosa," Vernell said, "Grandfather would tell him the price was two hundred dollars a head. Most would angrily say it was too high and leave, only to come back in a day or two with cash in hand because there was nowhere else to buy horses like these. 'That was yesterday's price,' Grandfather would tell them. 'Now it will cost you two hundred and fifty.' "

After marrying Vernell's grandmother Emma in 1908, Poor Thunder moved to Yellow Bear Canyon in a buckboard wagon with his wife and children, including Vernell's mother, Mary. They were leading two hundred head of the most beautiful horses in the world.

Only twelve at the time, ninety-two-year-old Guy Dull Knife, interviewed by Pulitzer Prize–nominated writer Joe Starita, remembered the spectacle of Poor Thunder's arrival, and more interestingly, his appearance: "Poor Thunder had long gray hair and wore a full-length overcoat, two pistols stuck in the waistband. His lower lip came up over his upper lip, making him the scariest-looking man I ever saw, but my father admired many of his good-looking horses. After Poor Thunder had settled, they became good friends."

Already revered among traditional Lakota as an old-style medicine man, Poor Thunder began to take charge of the spiritual ceremonies held around Yellow Bear. In the summer of 1911 he presided over a large Sun Dance held in a secret location in the nearby hills, attended by many friends and relatives. People remember his long graying braids and the traditional way he draped his blue medicine blanket about his body, which presented a picture of power and dignity. The Sun Dance was illegal, but the local Lakota policeman who knew about it was not going to make any arrests. He rode up to the Sun Dance lodge just before the painted dancers marched in with their sacred buffalo skulls. Poor Thunder told him, "If we lose the Sun Dance, we will no longer be a people. We will be something else, but no longer Lakota."

The policeman stayed to listen to the drummers and their songs, which recalled the thundering buffalo herds that once were so plentiful, but he had to leave before Poor Thunder skewered the dancers' chest muscles with the razor-sharp sticks known as *chawakha*. He dared not witness this torture nor watch as the dancers frantically flung themselves backwards for hours and hours until the *chawakha* ripped away, leaving ragged bits of flesh to be trimmed away with a ceremonial knife and then laid on a bed of sage as an offering to the sun. To see this would make the policeman complicit in what the agency considered a serious crime. He would lose the job that gave him prestige and many privileges.

Hands in his pockets, Vernell briskly strides up the hill behind the dugout where his grandparents once kept the team horses. Because he's never told me such stories before, I don't want to miss anything he says, so I struggle to stay abreast of him.

Grandfather was very powerful. People came to visit him because he was one of the last yuwipi *men. He presided over this traditional ceremony where you ask for help from the spirits to cure a sickness. The missionaries called* yuwipi *"devil worship," so we had to be very careful.*

Before the yuwipi, *they would put all the furniture outside, cover the doors and windows with heavy tarps nailed to the wall so no light could get in. One time my uncle Daniel left the plate of food for the spirits on the roof while he assisted my grandmother.*

We had little kittens then, and they were under her feet, getting in the way. She said to me, 'Grandson, please take these kittens outside.' I threw them on the roof so they would not chase me back inside.

Uncle Daniel and the other helpers prepared the sacred altar in the center of the room. Four coffee cans filled with dirt were placed on the floor to form a square, each containing a colored piece of cloth representing one of the four directions—white for north, red for east, yellow for south, and black for west.

They connected the cans with strings of tobacco ties, small squares of colored cloth filled with a pinch of tobacco representing the spirit helpers my grandfather would need. Sometimes there would be four hundred of these ties. Grandfather placed his sacred objects on a bed of sage: the eagle bone whistle, his pipe and pipe bag, rattles, and other things. Before sealing the door, Daniel went back outside to retrieve the spirit food, but when he took the plate down, it was empty. Everyone thought the spirits had eaten the food! They went "Aawe! Aawe!" *Everyone but Grandmother—she gave me a stern look and said,* "Shilasica!" *which means "bad little boy."*

Having reached the top of the hill behind where the log house once stood, Vernell stops. "Here is where the garden stretched all the way back alongside this ridge. Corn on this side, cabbage and lettuce over there, and rhubarb along the back. My job was to bring the water up from the creek, sprinkle it all across the garden, and pull out the weeds."

"That must have been some garden, but I would really like to know more about the *yuwipi*."

"Some of these things are private," Vernell says.

"I heard many things about *yuwipi* when I lived here. I just want to know what it was like for you."

"I will tell you parts. Maybe when I feel closer to the call to the Spirit World I will tell you everything, but not now."

"OK."

"*Yuwipi* ceremonies would last all night. The helpers bound Grandfather's arms behind his back and bundled him in a star quilt tied by a long rope. Laying on a bed of sage, he would sing the songs of the *yuwipi*, use his sacred objects and powers to contact the spirits, talk to them in a mumbling voice, ask how he might cure the sickness. When I stayed awake, I could hear spirits entering and leaving the darkness, and I sometimes saw flashes of light. It was really scary when the floors and windows began to shake.

"One time I was still awake after they had sung the last song and turned on the lamp. Grandfather was sitting alone in the center of the room; the bindings and star quilt in a pile on the floor. His hands and arms were free."

"Did Poor Thunder always agree to perform a *yuwipi*? it seems like such a major commitment of time and energy."

"Not always. I remember when our neighbor Seymour Rouillard was nearly killed by lightning. His family brought him to us in a wagon for a *yuwipi*, but my grandfather said they had to take him back to the top of the hill where the lightning had struck him. 'Once you are there, dig a hole in the ground, and you will find something very unusual; bring it back to me.' When they dug the hole, they found a large ball of ice, which they brought back. Grandfather boiled it in some water with magic herbs from his medicine bag, gave it to Rouillard to drink. It healed him right away. We had a celebratory feast, and the family went home."

Sensing my discomfort standing all this time in the same spot, Vernell motions toward the stump of a fallen tree. "Sit. This may take a while." And then he continues:

"As Grandfather might say, all these memories fill my mind like a tobacco pouch at the beginning of a long journey. I have told you too much, but I need to share some things with somebody or I'll go crazy."

Walking back and forth in front of me, Vernell's eyes seem to be focused far away but he does not stumble. Something I haven't seen from him before, he gestures excitedly with his arms and hands as if he is drawing pictures in the air around him.

Every morning I would wake up when it was still dark, but my grandparents would already be sitting there talking, drinking coffee. After breakfast, Grandfather and I went to get the team horses, hitch them to the wagon. We came to Kyle many times in that team and wagon. On hot days, sitting in the back, I would pull a tarp over my head to stay cool. We stopped under chokecherry bushes. Grandmother stood up on the wagon seat and picked them. She always let me eat as many as I could.

We'd be coming by No Flesh Creek, getting close to the Broken Rope camp; someone would shout out "George!" We would go over there, and they would feed us, give us coffee. At Little White Man's camp, it was the same thing. Two Crows's as well. By the time we got to Kyle, we were stuffed like white people on Thanksgiving. Sometimes at these stops we would pick up kerosene jars to get filled at the store in Kyle. We'd drop them off and go to my mom's house. Before we went back, we'd pick up the full jugs so we could return them. When we got home, Grandmother would go into the house, light the lamp, cook something. Our job was to take care of the horses, come back to the house, eat, go to bed.

Pointing now to where the log house once stood, Vernell says, "Grandfather's bed was on the side of the house, right about there. Above his bed on a windowsill he had an old set of ceremonial drums. Sometimes he would take one down and sing to us. He also told stories, not short stories like the *iktomi* [spider] stories you probably know; these were very long stories—buffalo hunts, war parties, and creation stories.

"Like Grandpa, I tried singing the old songs, telling stories to my children. Sometimes they listened, but not always. No one tells stories today; they are being lost. Today kids watch TV, play video games . . . they cannot be still long enough to hear an old story."

"Vernell, you were lucky to have lived with your grandparents, learn about the old ways. But it is too bad Poor Thunder died when you were so young."

"Well, I was young, but he was ninety-eight."

"Do you remember when he died?"

"My little brother, Anthony, and I came to Kyle with Grandfather on a brown-and-white Paint horse named Happy Jack. We were going to the store for kerosene. On the way back, my grandfather and Anthony got on the horse. It was my turn, but for some reason, I did not want to. When I finally did, Happy Jack bucked all three of us off. Anthony and I were OK, but Grandfather got hurt. He had internal injuries from this fall.

"Everybody was mad at Happy Jack, but not Grandpa. He said it could not have been the horse's fault. He was right. When my uncle Norman took the saddle off, there was a nail stuck in it that must have poked the horse. The nail caused it to buck."

Vernell pauses for a moment to fish out a small pocketknife from his blue jeans; he opens it and starts digging out some of the tar-like dirt from under what's left of his obsessively chewed fingernails.

"I take it you got him home, Vernell. What happened next?"

It was the night before the Fourth of July, and people knew that Grandfather might not recover. My stepsister Theda came to stay with us. The Broken Rope and Dull Knife families camped next to this house. Us kids were throwing those popper things in the campfire. I remember hearing him getting up before dawn to go to the bathroom, and then he went back to bed. A little while later, Grandmother got up, and then my sister got up; they were crying. My sister came over to me. "Wake up, brother," she said. "Grandpa is dead."

Someone made a coffin out of some lumber. First, they put blankets and sage in the box, and then my grandfather. Next, they moved all the furniture out of the house and put a whole tub of ice under the window where he had slept. They put the coffin on top of the ice to keep him cool. All this time more and more people were coming. My mom and dad came, and I was mad at them because they were drunk. The elder women sat in the house with my grandmother. The men were all outside. Everyone was wailing and weeping; this went on for four days.

I remember us kids would steal the ice.

Our little dog, Mickey, laid next to Grandfather and did not move except once when he stretched and made a whiny sound like dogs do. The women jumped up and in Lakota said, "He's alive! He's alive!" They ran out the door. When we realized it was the dog, everyone started laughing.

Next morning, they took Grandpa by wagon to be buried in Norris, near where he was born on the Rosebud. I did not get to go, but plenty of people stayed around the house. That night we sat at the campfire. It was the first time I ever ate roasted marshmallows. I remember throwing some over the hill to feed the spirits. My grandfather would have wanted me to do this.

A few days later, my parents brought me back to Kyle while my grandmother and her friends were burning my grandfather's possessions so that they would travel with him to the spirit world. A few days later my parents burned down the house for the same reason, a practice that is seldom done today. Grandmother moved to Kyle, and you already know the rest. Soon they took me to boarding school.

Before we get back into the White Thunder Ranch pickup, Vernell reaches down to pull a few sprigs of a plant with small brown flowers that I recognize as ragweed. It is still dry and brittle because there has not yet been enough spring weather to bring it back to life. As he pulls a stem between his thumb and forefinger and rubs the dry leaves into a powder, Vernell says, "We even had our very own Lakota pharmacy. This plant we called *poipiye*, which means 'to cure the swelling.' You put some crushed leaves into a small amount of hot water to form a paste to reduce inflammation. I used it recently when I twisted my ankle jumping off a horse. Pregnant women make tea out of *poipiye* to stop them from vomiting. They say you can even use this for diarrhea, but then it has a different name, *canhlogan onzipakinte*, which means 'weed to wipe the rear.'"

"You must be kidding!"

"Not kidding, and if we had more time I could show you many other plants we use for traditional healing. But we should go—there is one more place I want to take you before darkness comes."

I am reluctant to leave this little spot of land in Yellow Bear Canyon, this unexploited Lakota habitat, safely wrapped as it is in the hills and ridges, the arms of Mother Earth. A return visit unlikely, I want to sit here quietly, feel the presence of Poor Thunder, the comfort of his peaceful, contented spirit. Vernell's grandfather lived much as he would have if Anglo-Europeans had never invaded his lands, never discovered gold in He Sapa. Ignoring the admonishments and laws of missionaries and agency officials, he ministered to the physical and spiritual health of his people according to the traditional ways as they were practiced by his forbearers.

What a far richer world this would be if my ancestors had only had the wisdom to honor the treaties, the foresight to let native people live their lives as they had been living them. What lessons we could have learned! How ironic to have destroyed their ability to live freely off the land, and then complain about lazy Indians on food stamps. How blind not to have appreciated the pageantry of their rituals, the poetry of their songs, the rhythm of their dancing, the exquisiteness of their craftsmanship and their artistry, the power of Tunkashila. How crazy not to have visualized a thriving partnership instead of this lopsided domination. How ignorant to not have understood the will and inevitable triumph of a people who have survived every imaginable deprivation. The Sacred Hoop is no longer broken. The revenge of the red man is coming, I swear it is, and hopefully I will be alive to welcome it.

But we are on the road again, headed back in the direction of White Thunder Ranch.

RETURN OF THE BUFFALO

DANCING WITH JANE FONDA

As we rumble along the crunchy asphalt road, the soft breeze is fragrant with the sweetness of early spring wildflowers, there's a mellow country ballad on KILI Radio, and both of Vernell's powerful hands grip the steering wheel, his eagle eyes steady ahead, an easy smile on his face. I think he enjoyed our time in Yellow Bear Canyon, the storytelling, and memories of when life for him was less complicated. I'm happy too, daydreaming about his grandfather, the *yuwipi* ceremonies, when across the unmowed side of the road I catch sight of mountainous dark forms looming through the bare branches of dying pine trees and a stand of chokecherry bushes—not deer or antelope or cattle but buffalo, mighty humpbacked *Bison americanus*, with their huge walnut-shaped heads, short but lethal hooked horns, and penetrating, protuberant eyes. They have not yet molted, the luxurious thickness of their dark nappy coats a sure sign there is still cold weather to come.

These buffalo know no fear because nothing threatens them. Fiercely painted warriors no longer charge up on horseback to unleash the deadly sharp spears and arrows that once sliced through their heavy carcasses, and they are no longer slaughtered by the thousands from great distances by the bone-shattering bullets of hidden white buffalo hunters firing large-caliber rifles. Imperturbable, these buffalo deliberately saunter up the hill. All but one. He looks back at me, and from his size, I can tell he is a bull.

"Over there, Vernell, are those your buffalo?"

"Yes. I've had buffalo since you and I went into business. Do you remember that?"

"My God, how could I ever forget?"

My mind snaps back to a bicycle ride I took one cheery Sunday in the early 1990s during a happy time when my publishing ventures were throwing off cash faster than I could spend it. Mindlessly riding through San Francisco's Golden Gate Park, I glided past the Victorian aggregate of wood and glass known as the Conservatory of Flowers, the Roman gladiator statue near the historic band shell where both Pavarotti and the Grateful Dead once performed, and onto John F. Kennedy Drive, closed that day to vehicular traffic. Near Spreckels Lake, distracted by attractive rollerblading girls with ponytails, I spotted something out of the corner of my eye that nearly caused me to crash into a curb. Standing in a fenced-off meadow as if their presence were no more peculiar than a sighting of the Sisters of Perpetual Indulgence on Castro Street, was a small herd of shaggy buffalo.

Buffalo in San Francisco! I saw no sign explaining why, and there was no park ranger to ask. The buffalo were just hanging around chewing their cud like so many cows in an Iowa cornfield; only they were much bigger than cows, magnificent and regal. Straddling my bike, I stood watching them. How had they gotten there? Why did I not know about them? While living on the reservation in the early 1970s, I never saw a single buffalo. Plenty of buffalo skulls, beautifully painted buffalo hides, a few robes and artifacts made from parts of buffalo, but no live, breathing *tatanka*.

Believing that strange encounters happen for a reason, I instantly became obsessed with these particular buffalo and buffalo in general. Like a doped-up cyclist in the Tour de France, I madly pedaled back through the park, up the Panhandle and Fell Street to the Civic

Center, where I parked in front of the Main Library. It didn't take me long to find what I was looking for. I knew, of course, that buffalo had been vital to the Native American ecosystem, that most had disappeared, but I did not know that their numbers were rebounding. Sitting at a large oak library table behind a pile of books and magazine articles, I discovered that buffalo are technically not buffalo at all; they are bison, as distinguished from water buffalo that live in Africa and Asia. However, the word "buffalo" has been misused so often to describe them, the two terms are interchangeable.

Similar to indigenous people, bison wandered to North America from Asia about ten thousand years ago, crossing the land bridge that once connected Siberia to Alaska. Weighing up to five thousand pounds with horns that spanned more than six feet, the first to arrive must have been scary as hell. The little herd in Golden Gate Park and larger herds in Yellowstone Park and Custer Park had become major tourist attractions. A handful of ranchers in Wyoming and South Dakota were raising bison instead of cattle for food, and the prospects looked very promising because their meat tastes similar to beef but has less saturated fat. The more I read, the more excited I got. It was early in this game, and with Vernell's help, I figured we could raise buffalo and, as entrepreneurs like myself liked to say in those halcyon days, "catch the wave." We could be part of something transformational, hasten the return of the American bison, and perhaps get rich at the same time.

Having no change in my pocket for the pay phone in the lobby (cell phones had not yet been invented), I had to wait until I got home to call Vernell. Luckily, he was in his house and not out in one of his pastures. I breathlessly asked him if we could raise buffalo on his ranch. As inscrutable then as he is now, he answered my question with silence, and after waiting a long time I was about to hang up, thinking the line was dead, when Vernell finally replied, "We'll have to build a nine-foot-high fence around my pasture."

"A nine-foot-high fence! Why nine feet?"

"Buffalo may look like clumsy defensive linemen," he replied, "but they run and jump like champion wide receivers."

"What do you mean?"

"A two-thousand-pound buffalo can run forty miles an hour and jump eight feet in the air. If we put them in my pasture without a taller fence, they'll be gone by morning. I'll be spending all my time chasing after them."

"OK, let's build a fence."

I came up with the funds, and once Vernell had the fence in place, we purchased a dozen buffalo from a rancher who lived near Pierre, South Dakota. Ten cows and two bulls, which Vernell promptly named Jimi Hendrix and Dennis Rodman because, like Hendrix and Rodman, they sported impressive Afros.

I don't know why we needed *two* bulls, but this turned out to be our first major mistake. Our buffalo liked their new home—they made no attempt to knock down the fence, didn't get nervous around people or horses, and required very little of Vernell's attention. That is, until mating season, around mid-July, when Hendrix and Rodman started knocking the shit out of each other. For two weeks, instead of humping the cows, our testosterone-crazed bulls spent all their time viciously head-butting. Vernell suspected that Jimi Hendrix had a broken rib, but he couldn't get close enough to be sure. When the mating season ended, the boys calmed down, but there would be no calves the following April. We would have to get rid of one of them, which turned out to be Dennis Rodman. We shipped him off to be butchered, and donated his meat to the tribe for an upcoming powwow.

Not nearly as bad, but amusing, we also missed the spectacle of buffaloes having sex. According to an article I had read at the San Francisco Library, when a bull ejaculates, his abdominal muscles flex so violently that his back hooves lift completely off the ground, causing his whole body to come to rest on the haunches of the receptive female. "If you're not here when this happens," Vernell had said, "I'll take a photo and send it to you for your scrapbook."

When I told my California friends I was now in the buffalo-raising business, that I had visions of repopulating the Great American Prairie with buffalo, they looked at me like they had known all along that I lived in my very own, uniquely distorted reality. Undaunted, I calmly explained to them that there were once fifty million to a hundred million buffalo in this country and that buffalo were the most numerous large mammals to *ever* exist on the face of the earth; the only phenomenon in today's world that comes close to the sight of the thundering herds of bison that once blackened the plains is the Masai Mara wildebeest migration. Traveling in huge herds, buffalo dominated much of North America from the Missouri River to the Rocky Mountains, from Mexico to Saskatchewan. If my friends were still listening or at least pretending to listen, I would tell them about a letter that a soldier named George Anderson sent to his sweetheart in 1871 describing a buffalo herd he saw in Kansas. "I am safe in calling this a single herd," Anderson wrote, "but it is impossible to approximate the millions that composed it. It took me six days on horseback to ride through it." It's hard for us to imagine now, but buffalo were once in such abundance that they could literally drink a river dry.

Plains Indians considered the buffalo a gift from the Great Spirit. They dreamed of buffalo, prayed to them, created myths about them, saw much of their world in buffalo terms. Using the buffalo hide as a measurement, they described trees as one-robe, two-robe, or three-robe—however many would stretch about a trunk; likewise they measured tepees in terms of how many robes sewed together created each one. Most whites, however, saw buffalo as pests who fouled the water, knocked down telegraph poles, blocked wagon trails, and held up the trains. To them, the very word "buffalo" was derogatory. If you were tricked or cheated, you were "buffaloed."

When I asked Vernell why he agreed to join me in this risky venture, he replied, "Buffalo were the basis of our life. We ate all the meat, the humps, tongue, heart, marrow. Some even ate the testicles and fetuses. We used the hides for making moccasins, tepee covers, robes, and leggings. We used buffalo hair for ropes, sinew for bowstrings, horns for spoons and cups, hoofs for rattles, teeth for ornaments, the bladder for a container. We even used the dung for fuel; with buffalo dung you could keep a fire going for days."

He paused for a moment, and then added, "The U.S. Army defeated us by killing off the buffalo."

How sadly true, I thought. The army promoted buffalo hunting for stated good reasons: to provide jobs for out-of-work Civil War veterans, to supply meat to feed railroad workers, to make it easier for ranchers to raise cattle, etc. But the one true real reason was to eliminate buffalo as a food source for the so-called hostile tribes who refused to give up their nomadic freedom for the idle life on a reservation. Without buffalo, they could surrender or starve. "Buffalo hunters are doing their patriotic duty," General Philip Sheridan, commander of the Military Division of the Missouri, said, "by depleting the Indians' shaggy commissary."

Armed with surplus Springfield rifles, thousands of buffalo hunters roamed the plains in search of the dwindling herds. From a distance of a few hundred yards, they could kill up to 250 in a single day. Millions of buffalo robes were shipped back East to companies like John Jacob Astor's American Fur Company to be used for coats and lap robes that were tucked around the legs of those riding in sleighs and carriages. A new trading center for hides sprang up in Leavenworth, Kansas, where tanneries found more uses for the material, including drive belts for industrial machines. Buffalo tongue became a delicacy in fine restaurants throughout the country, but the rest of the carcass was left to rot until a new market developed for buffalo bones. The extreme heat and cold, wind and sun of the plains caused the remaining buffalo flesh to dry up quickly. It disintegrated into dust, leaving the bones of entire skeletons as clean and bare as if some powerful chemical agents had processed them.

Once it was discovered that these bones could be converted into carbon for use in refining cane sugar, the gathering and shipping of buffalo bones became a new industry. In 1873, the Atchison, Topeka and Santa Fe Railway shipped 2,743,000 pounds, and in 1874 it handled 6,914,950 pounds. The Northern Pacific Railway shipped even larger quantities. As late as 1886, overland travelers saw immense heaps of buffalo bones lying alongside the tracks waiting for shipment at stations throughout South and North Dakota, Nebraska, and Kansas. This trade continued until the bones were gleaned so far back from the tracks that it was no longer profitable to seek them.

Obsessed with reaching a "final solution" for the buffalo, the army routinely outfitted civilian hunting expeditions to destroy as many as possible. In 1872, General Sheridan organized a grand buffalo hunt for the Russian czar's son Grand Duke Alexis, who was visiting America to celebrate his twenty-second birthday. Sheridan met Alexis in Omaha with two companies of infantry; two more companies of cavalry; a regimental band; three wagons of provisions including caviar, Champagne, and royal spirits; and a complement of teamsters, night herders, couriers, cooks, and civilian merchants called sutlers. There was even a trailing group of friendly Indians led by Chief Spotted Tail to provide entertainment in the form of a mock Indian battle and an evening "war dance." Buffalo Bill Cody was hired to be the guide, and among the other soldiers was Colonel George Armstrong Custer. Loaded onto a special train provided by the Union Pacific Railroad, the merry hunting party chugged off for North Platte, Nebraska, where in five days of glorious indulgence they managed to slaughter hundreds of buffalo. Most were shot with large-caliber rifles, though Alexis is said to have killed one old cow at close range with his revolver.

Train companies offered passengers the opportunity to shoot buffalo from the windows of the coaches. The Northern Pacific advertised that Montana passengers could "either from the window or platforms of the moving train test the accuracy of their six-shooters by firing at the retreating herd." Much like today's Napa Valley Wine Train, buffalo-shooting excursions were promoted as "gala outings" with a complimentary gourmet lunch and Champagne. E. N. Andrews, a correspondent for *Frank Leslie's Illustrated Newspaper*, described the moment when his touring train pulled to a stop alongside a small buffalo herd near Ellsworth, Nebraska. "In an instant a hundred car windows were thrown up, and the left of our train bristled with two hundred guns." Unfortunately, from his perspective, most of the buffaloes got away except for two immense bulls that "were seen to stagger and fall." Their tour guide, "the irrepressible Mr. Catts," jumped down from the train, ran over to the largest bull, and "disemboweled him in but a few moments." A rope was attached to the bull's horns, and while the train's band played "Yankee Doodle," he was "dragged bodily into the front car and hoisted aboard," to be embalmed and mounted once they returned to their starting point in Lawrence, Kansas. The celebratory passengers "christened" the bull Maximilian.

At the conclusion of his article, Andrews wrote that for him this outing was more educational than a trip to Europe, "to enlarge the conceptions of creation, and to give the peculiar tone of novelty, especially when for the first and perhaps last time one finds himself among the princely buffalo." Inspired by articles such as these, hundreds of rich Americans and European noblemen traveled by rail from New York City to Omaha, Nebraska, or St. Louis, Missouri, a new rifle in one hand and a bottle of Champagne in the other, not just to shoot buffalo from train windows but to make brave safari among the herds and to bivouac among the cottonwood trees.

And, of course, it had to happen—there were buffalo killing contests. The record, set by a Kansas homesteader, was 120 killed in just forty minutes. The most famous match was between William Frederick Cody and Billy Comstock, who shot it out for five hundred dollars and the right to the title "Buffalo Bill." Early on a chilly morning in 1868, with snow and ice on the ground, a gathering of trappers, hunters, wolf-poisoners, soldiers, and some of the soldiers' ladies from nearby Fort Wallace, Kansas, excitedly waited for the showdown to begin. At precisely eight a.m., mutual friend and stakeholder Carson Rivers raised his pistol and fired a shot to signify the start. Comstock jumped on his horse, galloped straight into the nearby peacefully grazing buffalo, and began chasing them down and killing them with his fast-shooting Henry repeating rifle. Cody took a different approach. Riding at a leisurely trot, he went clear around to the front of the herd, dismounted, squatted down on one knee, and began knocking them off from a distance with his larger-caliber Springfield Model 1863 rifle. He later named this rifle Lucretia Borgia after the legendary beautiful but ruthless Italian aristocrat who was the subject of a then-popular play by Victor Hugo. At four p.m., Rivers again fired his pistol to signal the end of the contest. Cody had won hands down, 69 to 46. The buffalo heads were delivered to the Kansas Pacific Railroad to be mounted and displayed around the country as part of a promotional campaign. The remains of the 115 carcasses were left on the frozen ground. Albeit headless, they would stay intact until the spring sun warmed them and the smell of chokecherry and wild rose blossom mingled with their stench to make a summer odor that was all too common on the plains—the odor of thousands of rotting buffalo carcasses.

Realizing that total extinction was close at hand, Cody and others began to favor new laws to protect the few buffaloes left standing. However, when Cody lobbied the Texas legislature to outlaw buffalo poaching on Indian lands, General Sheridan, who requested the opportunity to address the lawmakers, thwarted his change of heart. "For the sake of lasting peace," Sheridan pleaded, "let the buffalo hunters kill, skin, and sell until the buffalo are exterminated. The Indians will forever cease to be a threat, and your prairies will be covered with speckled cattle." The bill was defeated.

By 1890, the buffalo holocaust was over. Just one wild herd of twenty-three survived in a remote valley in Yellowstone Park, and, no surprise, Wyoming ranchers wanted to finish them off so they would not escape park grounds and somehow threaten their cattle. A coalition of naturalists and conservationists including Rubin Lloyd, the superintendent of San Francisco's Golden Gate Park, backed by Teddy Roosevelt, lobbied Congress and blocked their efforts. Today the Yellowstone herd, numbering thirty-five hundred, is the world's only continuous bison herd. Two of the Yellowstone bison were shipped to San Francisco as an acknowledgment of Superintendent Lloyd's support. They were named Sarah Bernhardt, after the famous stage actress who had appeared in San Francisco at the Baldwin Theatre a few years before, and Ben Harrison, after the then president of the United States. Fortunately, they procreated, and the Golden Gate herd grew to one hundred. Two little herds of bison in public parks were all that remained of the millions that had roamed the plains only a few years earlier.

When Vernell and I acquired our first buffalo, their total population was still under five thousand. I was proud to be part owner of such majestic animals and marveled at their rugged independence. As might be expected from creatures that so dominated North America without human interference, our buffalo were perfectly suited for the environs of Vernell's pasture. We didn't have to feed them hay; they were perfectly happy eating prairie grass, which they chewed for hours, regurgitated, and chewed again. Impervious to bad weather, they didn't need the shelter of a barn during heat waves or blizzards. When there was snow on the ground, they used their powerful front hooves to dig through it for the underlying brittle winter scrub and copper-colored grass. If the creek was frozen, they broke through its hard surface only if necessary, as they were otherwise content to get their water from eating snow. In early spring, they calved on their own and never required antibiotics or growth hormones to stay healthy and reach full size.

While balancing the vagaries and vicissitudes of my business life, I traveled to the rez as much as I could because it was such great fun to hang out with Vernell and see the buffalo. We would stand at the tall fence and just watch for what seemed like hours, and if they were too far out in the pasture, we would go through the gate and walk up to them, but not too close.

"If Jimi Hendrix looks at us and raises his tail," Vernell would advise, "turn around and run for your life!"

And now, many years later, idling in Vernell's pickup alongside the road, we are watching buffalo again as the last of the cows and calves saunter over the hill. The bull stands his ground, motionlessly staring, and I wonder if he feels challenged by us or perhaps by the pickup truck, but then he turns his back and follows in the path of his harem, leaving the land undisturbed. Vernell pushes the gearshift forward and we are on the road again. He looks over at me and says, "Do you remember when we went to that buffalo conference in La Crosse, Wisconsin?"

"Yeah! The first International Bison Conference. You danced with Jane Fonda."

"No, you danced with her."

"Well, one of us did."

The day I discovered there was such a thing as the National Bison Association and that they were having a big event, I signed up Vernell; my wife, Jackie; and myself. I called Vernell and told him, "We've got to go. There's no way around this," and for once he immediately shared my enthusiasm. He didn't pause to marvel as he often did at the fatuity of the white man; he too saw this as a potentially significant development. A few days later, Jackie and I flew from San Francisco to Denver, where we met up with Vernell in the airport and flew on to La Crosse.

Held at a downtown convention hall, the conference was one of those groundbreaking occasions that sometimes define the beginning of an industry. For me, it was like being at the first personal computer show. You could see, almost taste, the excitement felt by several hundred attendees, mostly ranchers from across the Midwest seeking a better way to make money than raising cattle. In the exhibit hall, people were selling a surprising array of bison-derived products: buffalo jerky and sausages, polished buffalo skulls, mounted heads, wallets, gloves, hats, handbags, robes, and jewelry. They were even taking orders for mail-order steaks packaged with dry ice. There was a two-day program of workshops and panels on nuts-and-bolts topics such as bison husbandry, disease management, marketing, and humane slaughtering practices. Everywhere I looked I saw charts forecasting future market growth, which in retrospect were ridiculously optimistic.

The major buzz that had everyone talking, however, had nothing to do with buffalo; it had to do with the presence of media mogul Ted Turner and his wife, Jane Fonda. Ted was fifty-five and Jane fifty-six; both looked glamorous but out of place dressed in much-too-stylish urban cowboy and cowgirl outfits in a crowd of down-home folks, men with scuffed boots, old Levi's jeans, and misshapen hats, women in grandmotherly calico dresses and excessive turquoise jewelry. Still, Ted and Jane were a wondrous sight. Ted, with his trademark pencil mustache, full head of finger-combed alabaster hair, wry smile, and impish eyes, was easily the tallest man there; and Jane, whom I had thought of as anorexic, looked more like a healthy country girl with her ripe apricot complexion and a big, genuine smile that showcased her perfect teeth. Looking at her, I couldn't help but think of Barbarella floating nude in weightless space.

Ted had recently purchased his third ranch, the 113,613-acre Flying D Ranch in Montana, which he was populating with buffalo. Scheduled to be the keynote speaker at the concluding banquet, he still came early, spent a great deal of time in the various workshops, walked around the convention hall shooting the breeze with the men. Jane too was very accessible, talking to everyone who wanted to meet her.

Turner always had a knack for contrary opinions, was known for his outrageous but memorable proclamations, and it was obvious that he loved having a beautiful, adoring actress for a spouse, but I doubt if he was prepared for the added layer of controversy Jane Fonda brought into his life. There was the tomahawk chop, for example. When the fans of his baseball team, the Atlanta Braves, adopted the Florida State Seminole war chant and chop, no one thought much of it until Jane was seen on national television standing alongside Ted making the chopping motion in unison with him and most of the fans. Then it became a big deal.

The regional director of the American Indian Movement, Aaron Two Elk of Atlanta, who grew up on the Pine Ridge Indian Reservation, called the tomahawk chop "dehumanizing, derogatory and very unethical." Tonya Gonella Frichner, president of the American Indian Law Alliance, simply could not believe that "Miss Progressive Jane Fonda" could sit there doing the chop. As far back as 1970, she could be counted upon to support native causes. That year Jane was the only non-Indian to join a hundred protesters from the Puyallup and Colville Confederated Tribes who occupied an unused army post in Seattle's Magnolia neighborhood called Fort Lawton. After prolonged conflict and negotiations, aided by the international media attention Jane brought to the cause when she was arrested, an agreement was reached whereby half the land became an environmental sanctuary called Discovery Park and the other half an Indian cultural center managed by the United Indians of All Tribes. Shortly after Fort Lawton, Jane showed up on Alcatraz Island during an even bigger occupation that was not so successful but which galvanized many Native Americans. Plus, she was at Wounded Knee!

And now she was doing the tomahawk chop alongside Ted Turner.

Two Elk and dozens of native activists staged a noisy protest outside Minnesota's Metrodome before the first game of the 1991 Atlanta-Minnesota World Series, carrying STOP THE CHOP and SHAME ON JANE placards. Perhaps as a statement of journalistic integrity, the protest was broadcast live on Ted's CNN, which also carried an interview with American Indian Movement leader Clyde Bellecourt, who growled, "America is scholastically retarded about Indian culture and history. . . . It is pure ignorance." And now, here in little ol' La Crosse, population less than fifty thousand, hundreds of animal rights protesters stood outside the La Crosse Center with blown-up photographs of bloody buffalo carcasses. I distinctly remember one of the signs. It read, BUFFALO AREN'T FONDA JANE. Getting past the demonstrators was a bit like crossing a picket line—lots of chanting and evil stares, but no one tried to block our way. When striking janitors and maids stood in front of downtown San Francisco hotels, I refused to enter no matter what business I had inside, but this was different. Jackie and I found it amusing, but Vernell seemed confused. He had never known people to not eat meat or to find doing so offensive. "There's no end to the craziness of white people," he commented.

At the end of the first day, we walked five blocks up Front Street alongside the Mississippi River to a restaurant recommended to us for its prime rib. Called the Freighthouse Restaurant, it was in a historic, three-story cream-brick Italianate building built in 1880 by the Chicago, Milwaukee, St. Paul and Pacific Railroad. Its rows of tall, narrow, red-framed arched windows made it easily the grandest structure we saw in La Crosse, and the prime rib was as good as you might find at Lawry's on La Cienega Boulevard in LA at half the price. The wine list was inferior, but Jackie and I easily put away a bottle or two as we debriefed each other on what we had learned that day and how it might apply to our business ambitions. Vernell was not drinking—he had gone cold turkey a few years earlier—but if you had been sitting at the next table, you might have thought otherwise. He was unusually loud and gregarious; my worries that I might be dragging him reluctantly into this adventure evaporated. He went on and on about the opportunity we had to revive the economy of the whole reservation. We would bring the people back from hopelessness and restore their pride by providing them with jobs not dependent upon the government. "Once our herd reaches fifty or more," he said, "I'll have to hire some local wranglers, and when we get even bigger, I'll need to lease more land." He visualized a buffalo-processing plant in Pine Ridge and a meat distribution company. "We might need a brand—Lakota Meats, perhaps?"

"How about White Thunder Bison?" I suggested, and he replied, "I'm not sure my ancestors would go for this unless we gave it all away."

After dinner, with Vernell driving the rental car, we went back to the motel and congregated in his room to catch the local evening news. A camera crew had been on the convention floor, and one of the reporters had interviewed Vernell, who was conspicuous because he was nearly as handsome as Ted Turner and the only Native American in attendance. We were excited to see this and curious about what they would say about the conference, and I guess I should have known. The local broadcast focused solely on the animal rights protest. They didn't show the interview with Vernell, and there was no coverage of the conference itself. The only person interviewed was a young man wearing a *Meat Sucks* T-shirt. I was too upset to remember what he said, or care.

The next evening at the awards banquet, the president of the National Bison Association introduced Jane Fonda and asked her to introduce her husband. She began with a pointed remark aimed at the animal rights advocates. "To some it is perhaps wrong," she said, "but to save the buffalo, you have eat them; otherwise ranchers will have no incentive." Jane clearly explained this simple concept, said she was thrilled to be part of a historic event and had no movie acting plans, and in a stentorian voice shouted out, "Ladies and gentlemen, I'm proud to introduce you to AMERICA'S BIGGEST BULLSHIPPER!"

All of us, Ted included, had a good laugh at that line.

"When I brought Jane to the Flying D Ranch in Montana," Ted began, "I worried she might have the wrong idea, might not realize my ranch is a workin' ranch, not some dude ranch. But when I woke up the first morning, she was already outside, rounding up the horses with a couple of my ranch hands. God love her, Jane's a natural cowgirl!"

Turner was first attracted to bison as a boy because he liked how they looked on nickels. In 1938, the year of his birth, they stopped making buffalo nickels, but there were still plenty in circulation. He had read a book about bison, how close they came to extinction, and came to regard this as one of America's greatest tragedies, "right up there with Pearl Harbor and the Great Depression." Starting with three bison, which he bought in 1989 and kept on his farm in South Carolina, Turner had grown his herd to be the largest in America, just over one thousand head, and he was aiming to have many more.

"Buffalo are not only good to eat," he said, "but they are much easier on the environment [than cattle]. Their manure and urine supply nutrients for plant cover, their hoofs stir the soil, help to bury seeds, create small pockets to capture moisture. As they graze, bison don't damage the soil because they roam about. Damn cows stay in one place until they eat the grass down to the root."

Looking back, Ted Turner has been true to his convictions. Today he still owns the most bison, fifty-five thousand out of approximately five hundred thousand total, and he is the second-largest individual landowner in North America, with twenty million acres, including seventeen large ranches. When Turner found it challenging to get restaurants to buy his buffalo meat, he opened Ted's Montana Grill in Columbus, Ohio, and now has fifty-seven locations in nineteen states. Items on his menus include bison nachos, buffalo chili, bison steaks, and hamburgers.

Sadly, however, he is no longer married to Jane Fonda.

When Ted said he had over one thousand bison, I turned to look at Vernell, who shrugged. Our ambition to own the biggest herd was an unrealistic pipe dream, but I did not care. A couple of years later when we had one hundred buffalo, I relinquished my half to Vernell and went on to other entrepreneurial adventures. Vernell is still hanging in there, and I am proud to have played a small part in the return of the American buffalo.

"Vernell, you're right," I say. "I was the one who danced with Jane Fonda. It was at the 'barn dance' following the banquet. We both talked to her. I probably had a little too much to drink, and you weren't drinking then. I asked her to dance; she thought it was funny."

"Jackie was jealous," Vernell said.

"I don't think so; I think she had her eyes on Ted."

Vernell told me he had recently gone to a buffalo sale in Rapid City, looking for a new bull to replace Jimi Hendrix, who had fathered hundreds of offspring before dying of old age.

"You wouldn't believe it, David. One bull sold for over seven thousand, and females are now selling for twelve hundred. A few years ago

I couldn't give them away for four hundred. Cost me four thousand for my new bull."

He paused, looking thoughtful. "I like buffalo; learned to deal with them the hard way, understand their temperament. Like horses, they are part of my life; I just like having them around."

All across the reservation today, buffalo are around. The Oglala tribe maintains a herd of three hundred and wants to have many more. To make this happen, they are evicting white ranchers from land they leased years ago for raising cattle. Plans call for turning sixty thousand acres of currently leased tribal grassland located on the southern edge of the Badlands into a huge buffalo pasture that will support a thousand head. Today when someone dies, the tribe provides thirty pounds of buffalo meat for the traditional community meal after the memorial service. The tribe also sells buffalo meat to local schools and to Sun Dance organizers. Dozens of tribal members, like Vernell, are raising smaller herds on their private lands, often donating calves to the tribe. A native organization called the Knife Chief Buffalo Nation, located near Russell Means's boyhood town of Porcupine, has donated thousands of pounds of buffalo meat to elders across the reservation.

"Our deity is of the buffalo," says Vernell. "They're a source of spiritual power as well as a source of food. We received our sacred pipe from the Buffalo Calf Woman. It is even more necessary now to have them."

HORSE PASTURE

A FIVE-THOUSAND-ACRE INDIAN

Rumbling down Vernell's driveway, I see a middle-aged white man and his younger female companion sitting on the front steps, petting the dog. From the big waves and enthusiastic smiles, I gather they are Vernell's tourist friends, and when we pull up, Vernell jumps out of the cab, again without bothering to turn the engine off.

"*Grüezi*!" he exclaims. "Happy to see you."

He turns to me. "David, meet my good friends from Switzerland, Reto and Lillian."

Reto has a graying ponytail but otherwise is clean shaven; his face is thin with long, thin eyebrows and blue eyes. Right away Lillian strikes me as one of those women who could be truly glamorous if she cared to be—flowing hair, oval face, sparkling eyes, sweet smile, but no makeup. When they stand up to shake my hand, I see that both are tall and athletic, fitting for people from one of the healthiest countries on earth.

"What brings you to the reservation?" I ask.

"Been here many times," Reto answers, and Lillian adds, "I think we lost count."

Married without children, Reto is a software engineer and Lillian teaches high school. A few years ago they found themselves visiting so often, they bought a camper trailer and permanently parked it near the pond behind Vernell's house. "We save up to come here when we have vacation time," Lillian says.

"Sounds incredible," I tell them as we walk into the house, where Suzy is heating up the coffee and making herbal tea for Lillian. Everyone sits, and I am content to just listen as they reminisce about horseback rides in the Badlands, misadventures in Rapid City, muddy roads, going to the Pine Ridge Sun Dance, and their times together in the sweat lodge.

"You remember 'Old Wooden Eagle,' don't you?" Vernell says. "The man from England who wanted to get a photo of an eagle, so I stopped the car on the gravel road through the Badlands, told him there was an eagle up there on that fence post and if he walked quietly, he might get close enough to take a picture. From where we stopped, the eagle was about the size of a hummingbird. The man crouched, walked cautiously toward it. Amazingly, the eagle did not move. When he got close, he realized it was a wooden eagle someone had carved out of the top of the fencepost. He turned around and waved his arms—he was really mad—but when he saw we were all laughing, he started to laugh too. I told him, 'From now on your name is Old Wooden Eagle.' "

I enjoy Reto and Lillian but would much rather spend my time with Vernell, so I'm happy when Lillian says they need to go to their trailer and get some rest. It is none of my business, but after they walk out, I ask Vernell how much he charges them to stay at his ranch.

"Oh, nothing," he answers. "When people become my friends, I can no longer charge them.

"Last summer, we had over a hundred visitors, from Europe but also Japan and Australia. Most are respectful, want to know about my life, our history, and even spiritual things. Two guys from Russia spoke fluent Lakota."

"How could that be possible?"

"They had language tapes, talked Lakota for an hour a day. Said they started a year before their trip."

"Wow. You can't even get most Lakota people to learn to speak Lakota, at least not fluently."

"Two gay guys from Australia, very nice men, come here every summer. They also speak Lakota."

"And you charge these people?"

"Except for the seminarians from Pennsylvania who come to broaden their spiritual perspective. I cannot charge for anything spiritual."

"Considering your experience with the Catholic boarding school, I would think you would charge them double."

"No, no, never. Do you want to come with me to check on my horses?"

I grab my camera thinking he means the few horses in the nearby corral. But once outside, he points to a green all-terrain vehicle near the side of his house, says it belongs to Suzy, motions for me to get in.

"Different wheels for every occasion?" I remark.

As with the other vehicles parked in front of Vernell's little three-room estate, the keys are in the ignition. Suzy comes out on the porch, and Vernell says, "I hope you don't mind if we borrow your little green monster."

She smiles as if she is in on the joke—I rather doubt if she has ever driven this thing, but Suzy is full of surprises. With me hanging on tight to the roll bar, we take off with a sudden start, swing around the corral, and head down a hill to where No Flesh Creek meanders from the Kyle Dam toward Yellow Bear Canyon. Then we zoom up a barren, bumpy hill, back down a step impression, and then up again to a sudden stop in front of a barbed-wire fence.

"Help me open this gate," Vernell says.

We hop out of the still-running ATV. Vernell pushes the fence post while I pull up the strand of wire that serves as the top latch to the gate, which is just a section of fence. Elegant engineering—two posts held together by two strands of wire, one on the bottom, the other on top. Vernell moves the gate section of the fence out of the way and lays it on the ground. We jump back in the ATV and take off, leaving the gate open, as he did on the bombing range.

"Now for the fun part," Vernell says. "Hang on tight."

"I know you, Vernell White Thunder," I answer.

We ascend at an unsafe speed, straight up—never mind the rocks, the ruts, clumps of thistle and sage, hardened mounds of horse dung. This thing has seat belts, but of course, like the ones in his Ford Fairlane and his truck, they don't function. I hang on for dear life to the roll bar, my butt bouncing hard up and down. I look at the ground. It is a blur. Mercifully, Vernell brings us to a jarring stop at the top of the hill.

I look out at the endless expanse of early spring grass, patches of golden brown, clumps of wildflowers in front of me, literally miles and miles of undulating hills stretching to the distant horizon. I don't see any fences or trees, just a few chokecherry and buffalo berry bushes in the gullies, no signs of human life. My God, it must have looked exactly like this when Oglala warriors on horseback stopped at this very spot, scanned the horizon for marauding herds of deer, buffalo, or other wild game.

"My biggest holding is on the Rosebud, and I have many small parcels. I tried to get the tribe to swap bits of land with me, but they won't do it. I tore up the hundred-and-ninety-thousand-dollar check they sent for my small parcels, told them, 'You can have the parcels only if you give me equivalent land next to my other land.' "

Stunning me, Vernell adds, "My children don't want to live here. Chris has his life in Denver, and Ellen hers in Memphis. I tried to get them interested in carrying on. Maybe I'll create some foundation."

"Well, you'll be a lawyer," I remind him. "You can fill out the paperwork yourself, file it with the court."

"This is true, David."

I take a few photos, wondering if the Happy Hunting Grounds look something like what I am seeing through my camera lens. Vernell doesn't like to sit still, but he patiently waits as I click away. It must seem odd to him how we white people are always taking photographs. Many of the great chiefs—Red Cloud, Sitting Bull, Standing Bear, American Horse, Vernell's great-grandfather White Thunder—dressed up in their finest Indian regalia to pose for photographs. Crazy Horse was a famous exception. He refused to let the white man capture his shadow, as did Vernell's maternal grandfather, the medicine man Poor Thunder.

Back in the ATV, Vernell guns the engine, we turn right, head straight down, bounce off the bottom, then up again, and my baseball cap flies off. I tell Vernell it is not important, but he makes a wide circle and picks it off the ground without slowing down. We are on our merry way, my stomach in my throat, Vernell grinning, laughing.

Suddenly we stop again.

"Look over there!" Vernell points to a far hill, where I see a dozen Hereford cows and two white men on horseback.

"Aren't they trespassing on your land? You should shoot their asses."

He ignores my comment. "The land on the far side of my pasture is leased to some white dudes who run cattle, but they don't take good care of the fences—their cows are always getting in my pasture. When I see them, I make sure they see me. Just look at the sad cow ponies they ride. If you look behind you, you'll see some real ponies."

I swing my head around to a magnificent sight. Headed in our direction are about twenty Indian ponies—American Paints—magnificent horses galloping, manes flying and tails swishing, kicking up dust, no two the same, splashes of white on black canvas, brown canvas . . . chestnut, sorrel, tobiano, overo, and a single speckled gray Appaloosa.

We chase after them. Shouting over the roar of the ATV engine and pointing wildly, Vernell says, "Little Crow is the black-and-white one, the chestnut one is Billy Bow, Fry Bread is running up the hill, and Lunch Meat is the funny speckled horse. I call him that because when

I tried to break him, he bucked me off, so I told him, 'If you buck me off again, you are going to be lunch meat.' I have names for all my horses."

Vernell lets up on the gas and coasts to a stop, as do the horses when they realize we are no longer chasing them . . . serenity settles back in on this little piece of the prairie paradise.

"Sometimes," Vernell says, "I meet people who think they know all about horses, but I come to find out they only have one or two horses, a little corral alongside their house. They look at my muddy boots, old jeans, my hat, and they say, 'You must be a cowboy.' But I'm not a one-acre cowboy, I'm a five-thousand-acre Indian."

I swear if you tell a Lakota that once they had no horses, that they relied on dogs to pull their travois, they will look at you like you are fucking nuts, even if they know this is true. Tepees were much smaller; you might point out that this was because dogs couldn't carry such heavy loads. You hunted buffalo by stampeding them over a cliff, you tell them. Such insulting thoughts—only a white man would think like this.

Spaniards brought horses to the New World in the 1500s, but these weren't ordinary horses; a mixture of Arabian and Andalusian blood, they were the best horses in the world. Because he had such horses, Cortés made mincemeat of the Aztec. You might wonder why the Spanish were so foolish as to lose possession of their horses, let them get into the hands of the very natives they were trying to suppress. In the early years of the Spanish invasion, they declared it illegal for an Indian to own a horse, but America's plains and deserts are gigantic—the Pampas and Los Llanos of South America, the Great Plains and southwest desert of North America, the coastal plains of Mexico—rich in prairie grass, meandering streams and rivers. It took only a handful of stray horses, three or four lost on the trail, to form the kernel of an enormous herd of wild horses that even today overruns much of the Western U.S. rangelands, decimating grass and water resources.

Over fifty thousand descendants of American Indian horses, which in turn are descendants of Spanish horses, run wild on federal land. The Bureau of Land Management holds another fifty thousand in a system of private ranches and feedlots. In 1900, there were one million wild horses in the United States. We largely looked the other way while all but a thousand were hunted down, shot, butchered for pet food. Their total extinction was averted in 1971 when Richard Nixon signed a bill making it a crime to kill a wild horse on federal land.

Not every tribe saw the potential of this hefty, omnipotent, dog-like creature. The Mandan, who lived in dome-shaped earth lodges along the Missouri River in what is now called North Dakota, traded horses to other tribes but never took to the equestrian life themselves. Some speculate that this is why they were wiped out by smallpox, as smallpox is more deadly to sedentary communities.

The Lakota immediately saw the horse as a gift from the Great Spirit, Wakan Tanka, which is why they called horses Sunka Wakan, meaning holy dogs. In partnership with Sunka Wakan, Lakota territory quadrupled, and then quadrupled again and yet again. Horses tipped the balance of power in favor of mounted warriors. It was easier to hunt buffalo. Warriors could travel hundreds of miles to steal horses from enemy tribes. They made life for women easier too, because unlike dogs, horses could lug heavy loads from camp to camp.

These big dogs were low maintenance. You didn't have to feed them meat, they ate grass, and during the winter snows when grass was unavailable, they survived on cottonwood bark. Owning many horses became a sign of wealth. When a young warrior picked out a potential bride, he tied one of his finest horses outside the tepee of the parents of his bride-to-be as a gift and sign of his intentions. Many religious ceremonies came to be based on Sunka Wakan and its contribution to Lakota life; there even evolved a horse medicine cult that was practiced by a dance with imitation horses. And, of course, medicine men like Poor Thunder performed the Horse Dance ceremony.

Young boys grew up obsessively practicing horsemanship skills. They learned how to maneuver galloping horses from side to side so that they could ride in the middle of stampeding buffalo without being trampled or so they could avoid oncoming arrows or bullets from an enemy. They practiced shooting arrows riding full speed, hanging from one side, aiming at targets on the other side by leaning low to the ground beneath the horse's neck. More skilled riders leaped from one galloping horse to another. They could pull a horse up short, slide off, take a few running strides, swing up onto another horse, and gallop away, only to do it again. These skills as much as anything explain how the Lakota and their allies defeated the U.S. Army.

Today Vernell has twenty-seven horses, but at times he's had over a hundred. There isn't much money in buying, raising, and selling horses, but part of his summer business involves taking visitors on scenic horseback rides. Some are brief one- or two-hour trips; others are much more involved. One example is a six-day excursion to Pine Ridge promoted by a London-based adventure travel agency called Spirit Trails, three days of which involve four- to six-hour horseback rides with "famed Lakota horseman" Vernell White Thunder.

Nowhere in the Spirit Trails brochure or Web site does it mention that for gringos, riding a horse for more than an hour or two at a time can give you a profoundly sore butt, that bowlegged cowboys are bowlegged for a reason. The day after I rode with Vernell through the Badlands, I could barely walk; no way could I have gone on another ride. When I ask him about this, he shrugs his shoulders and says, "But they do it.

"David, it is easy to be romantic about horses, but if I am lying in bed and it's thirty below, I know the horses are thirsty but can't drink water because there is ice on the creek. So I haul myself up, go out to the creek, and break a hole in the ice. I am not in it for money; for me it is way of life. I have respect and admiration for my horses. My horses have souls; their souls absorb everything we are feeling. When the soldiers killed our horses, they killed our souls."

Incapable of defeating the Lakota warriors on the battlefield, the U.S. Army resorted to search-and-destroy tactics, early morning surprise attacks on sleepy villages where the operational goal was to kill as many Indians as possible—women and children included—burn all the tepees, destroy food supplies, tools, clothing, and weapons, saving the horses for last. In 1876, after routing an encampment of Comanche and Cheyenne, Colonel Ranald Mackenzie ordered his men to shoot fourteen hundred horses left behind when people fled on foot. The troopers roped the crazed horses and led them to the firing squads, where they were killed twenty at a time. The massive piles of dead horses rotted to the bones, which lay bleaching in the sun for many years.

"When you decided to marry Suzy, did you give her mom a horse?" I ask.

Vernell laughs. "No, but later I gave one to her brother."

As Vernell recklessly drives me back to his ranch house, bouncing up and down, I realize that my butt can get just as sore in his ATV as on one of his horses. At least my hat is now pulled tightly on my head and I'm hanging on with two hands instead of just one. We suddenly stop to secure the gate. Vernell jumps out, yanks up the section lying on the ground into its proper position, jumps back in, and we are off before I can catch my breath. Down the gully, as we splash across No Flesh Creek, I look up a dirt embankment, where I see Reto standing in front of his trailer house in boxer shorts.

Vernell slows down, yells out, "I'll turn on the water for you."

We whip down another gully, ricochet, bounce into the air, and stop suddenly in front of a quaint little log house that I know nothing about. Hidden in a scenic spot behind his ranch house, it is his guest cabin, Vernell says; he built it himself. Another surprise.

"Look around while I turn on the water," he says.

Spanning the front of the cabin is a finely crafted, covered wooden porch. Sturdy tree trunks support the roof; there's a gas grill on one end, an easy chair, logs to sit on. The cabin has dark-red-painted vertical wooden slats, windows, door. It looks very homey. If a person wanted to get away from the hustle bustle of city life for a few days, a week or two, this could be the ideal place. Inside I discover a polished knotty pine interior, a double bed, a single bed that doubles as a sofa, a kitchen table, a dresser, and plenty of natural light.

"Can I stay here next time I come up?" I ask Vernell.

"You might want to wait until I finish building a bathroom and shower, and there's no electricity."

The sun is low in the sky. It hides behind a cluster of stratus clouds near the western horizon, glowing brightly on top, pure orange on the bottom. Not as spectacular as the sunsets I once experienced in New Mexico, but still a glorious end to a holy day, Good Friday on the rez. I want to stay here. I have thoughts of moving back to Kyle, perhaps teaching again at Little Wound School if they will have me, horseback riding with Vernell, participating in the Chief Big Foot Memorial Ride, Native American Day at Wounded Knee, *yuwipi* ceremonies. Purifying myself in the sweat lodge, attaining oneness and harmony with all forms of life. I thank Tunkashila for the four directions, Sun Dance sacrifices, the Giving of the Gifts, the Rabbit Dance, vision quest, Rezball, the spirit of Crazy Horse, Buffalo Calf Woman, sage and sweet grass smudging, staring into the sun, piercing, fancy dancing, the Sacred Pipe, Pahá Sápa, Mato Paha.

I want to stay, but I am not an Indian, not a wannabe, just your average aging white man, and there is a family gathering tomorrow in Alliance that I must attend. Vernell has offered to take me to a nearby sweat lodge, and while this is tempting, the last time I did a sweat lodge with Vernell, the heat made me so dizzy that I had to lie down for a couple of hours before I could go anywhere. I politely decline.

I reluctantly say good-bye to Vernell, Suzy, Reto, and Lillian. They stand out front as I get into *Villa VW.*

"Guess I should get out of here so Vernell can work on his paper for law school."

"Eat more meat," Vernell proclaims.

"And you eat your veggies."

"Next time I'll arm wrestle you; we'll see which makes you stronger, meat or lettuce."

ACT FOUR

They were a great people, these old buffalo-hunting Sioux, and some day their greatness will reach full flowering again in their children as they walk the hard new road of the white man.

—MARI SANDOZ, *CRAZY HORSE: THE STRANGE MAN OF THE OGLALAS*

GORDON

SOME WHITE BOYS ROUGHED HIM UP

I've had an incredible day and would love to get to Alliance before Ken and Dales closes at eleven p.m. Perhaps I'll make it, but there is one more thing I must do. Driving up the hill from White Thunder Ranch to the main road, I turn left. Instead of going back through Kyle, I head south toward Yellow Bear Canyon, determined to take the same sixty-two-mile route Raymond Yellow Thunder took dozens of times as he went back and forth from Kyle to Gordon, Nebraska, where he worked as a ranch hand.

Unwittingly, Yellow Thunder became one of the most significant figures in Native American history. His tragic murder in 1972 was the spark that set off a series of events ending in the occupation of Wounded Knee, and a new native assertiveness that has in turn led to many good things. Vernell was just sixteen, Yellow Thunder fifty-one, when the killing took place; they never met, but they are related. Raymond's mother, Jennie, was one of the daughters of the great chief American Horse, and Vernell's mom, Mary, was one of his granddaughters.

Born in 1921, Raymond had an impressive lineage, but his family was dirt poor. He lived with his parents and six brothers and sisters in a one-room log house just outside Kyle on American Horse Creek. His father, Andrew, was a sober, hardworking man who disdained the traditional ways. He made his sons cut their hair short, do daily chores on their meager farm and horse ranch, and go to the day school in Kyle. They spoke English and were taught to be obedient and work hard. On Sundays, Raymond's mom made sure all seven children were scrubbed and wearing their best clothes for services at Kyle's Episcopal Church of the Mediator.

The coming darkness turns the hills one-dimensional as *Villa VW* descends to the bottom of the canyon, past the survivalist camp, before winding its way up again. A few more hills and curves later, I am on the far side of Yellow Bear, where there is still enough light to see a couple of farmhouses, barns, tractors, cows, gigantic rolls of hay immobile in fallow fields; a sprawling pancake boredom that extends to Gordon and just beyond before you enter the majestic Sandhills of Mari Sandoz's *Old Jules*. The road itself is empty: no rez cars, pickups, semitrailers, dogs, or horses; no Raymond Yellow Thunders thumbing a ride into town. It's just *Villa VW*, the great American desert, KILI Radio, and me.

Like Vernell, Raymond Yellow Thunder loved horses, excelled as a basketball player, and was a superb artist. However, he had no aptitude for study; quitting school before the ninth grade, he found work doing odd jobs for neighboring ranchers. Thanks to the influence of his father, Raymond always showed up, kept all his promises, and never got into a single fight. A loving uncle, he drew pictures for his nieces and nephews while they pulled his hair and crawled over him. Unlike their parents and the teachers, he never raised his voice. At his memorial service, his brother Russell said of him, "If Raymond had any enemy in the world, it was the bottle."

After a failed marriage and the death of his parents, Yellow Thunder started drinking heavily on weekends or whenever he didn't have a job or family matters to attend to. Still, his talent for working with livestock and willingness to do any job required on a ranch or farm made him very much in demand. In the early 1950s he landed a cowhand job with rancher Harold Rucker, just a few miles south of Gordon, which was to last eighteen years. He lived in the Rucker bunkhouse, and except for cheap wine that he bought on the weekends and a few changes of clothes, all his money went toward buying groceries for his sisters' families and gifts for the little ones.

The Yellow Bear Canyon Road, aka Allen Road, aka BIA Highway 4, ends at Highway 18. From there it is a ten-mile drive west toward Pine Ridge before you head south again on Nebraska Highway 27 straight into Gordon. I slow down, take my time; you never know what hazard will be just in front of you at night on these roads—perhaps a deer or a cow, a stalled car, a staggering drunk, a wild turkey, an old buffalo . . . or a boy on a bicycle. The turn onto Highway 27 comes as a relief because I will soon be off the reservation, which I foolishly imagine is more dangerous at night than Highway 27. More miles of monotony, except for the strangely located Dohse Auto Sales lot that pops up out of nowhere. I imagine that the good folks at Dohse sell respectable clunkers to Indians who have just gotten a tribal check for their remaining little spot of land, land that's been in the family since the 1887 Dawes Act.

Never having owned a car, Yellow Thunder was adept at hitching rides. One fateful Saturday night (February 12, 1972), he asked Bucky Rucker, his employer's teenage son, for a ride into town to buy some new blue jeans (plus there was the temptation of the Sheridan Lounge). Bucky was reluctant—his friend Jerry had just stopped by—but Yellow Thunder knew just what to say: "I'll buy you and Jerry a half-case of beer."

It was an offer Bucky and Jerry could never refuse. "Hell yes, Big Chief, let's get us some beers."

With Raymond in the back, they sped off for Gordon, and after a pit stop at Wagon Wheel Liquors on the edge of town, the boys dropped Raymond off on Main Street. It was early evening, but the temperature had dropped into the mid-twenties, and it felt like a winter storm was on the way. Yellow Thunder went to Saul's Discount Department Store, where he bought his jeans, and then he hiked up to the Sheridan Lounge for a few boilermakers. He was well known at the bar, the old quiet Indian who drew sketches and always paid up, never caused any trouble. Not much better than a Whiteclay liquor store, the Sheridan Lounge was perfectly suited for out-of-luck cowboys and invisible Indians who were welcome as long as they paid for each drink as it was served to them.

"Sorry, Injun," the bartender would say. "Only white guys can run a tab here."

Gordon is a little town of about 1,544 people (in 2013), dumbly named after John Gordon, whose claim to fame is that he was the first white man to sneak a party of miners into the Black Hills after Lieutenant Colonel Custer's 1874 gold-discovering expedition.

Investors in Sioux City, Iowa, saw an opportunity to outfit and organize trips to the Black Hills for miners and wannabe miners. You might think of this as the original adventure travel agency. Everyone knew the risks. If they were caught by Lakota warriors, the clients would be gleefully burned alive. If they were captured by the soldiers, their wagons and supplies would be destroyed, and they would be confined for trial at the nearest military post. Fueled by irresponsible newspaper headlines and shameless promotions about the instant fortunes to be made, the rush for gold was on—there were plenty of fools willing to fork over the three-hundred-dollar deposit.

There was just one thing missing: a tour guide. Enter John Gordon, the only applicant for the job ballsy enough to claim that he had extensive knowledge of the Black Hills and knew how to drive oxen. Truth was, Gordon had never been to the Black Hills, and his experience with oxen was dubious.

After secretly assembling wagons and supplies three miles outside

Sioux City, Gordon led his tour group of twenty-six men, all wannabe miners, on a zigzag course through the Sandhills. At night he posted sentries and allowed no fires. Miraculously, they made it into the Black Hills without seeing a single Indian or soldier. Emboldened by Gordon's success, the Sioux City investors organized a much bigger trip. This time there were 150 fools, and not all were miners—they included merchants, Civil War veterans, immigrants who could barely speak English, blacksmiths, cowboys, railroad workers, and one determined woman fleeing from an abusive relationship with the strongbox of money her husband had hidden under their bed in Kansas City.

Five weeks later, his party having traveled hundreds of miles, Gordon's luck ran out; the army caught up with them. At sunrise, Gordon and his sleepy followers woke to find themselves surrounded by sixty heavily armed U.S. cavalrymen under the command of Captain Anson Mills. Two Gatling guns had been set up on top of nearby ridges. After arresting Gordon, Captain Mills sent a few of the wagons down a ravine and had them set ablaze. The other wagons were pushed on top, creating a gigantic bonfire that would have dwarfed those at the biggest college football pep rallies.

News of the Gordon party's fate caused a sensation in the nation's newspapers and only encouraged thousands more gold seekers to invade Lakota land. The army caught a few and handed them over to civilian courts, but they were freed, and many went right back to their Black Hills claims. By the end of 1875, the U.S. Army had given up trying to hold back the tide. When a group of Methodist settlers from Indiana built a town twenty miles from where Captain Mills had burned his wagon train, they named it Gordon.

While Yellow Thunder quietly drank his beer at the Sheridan Lounge, Les Hare, age twenty-eight, his younger brother Pat, and friends Toby Bayliss and Butch Lutter tossed back a few on the front porch of his dad Dean's house a mile or two west of Gordon. Les's girlfriend, Jeannette

Thompson, just eighteen, was there but not drinking. Les, Pat, and Butch had been coyote hunting—a despicable sport—that day, Butch flying an airplane overhead spotting coyotes; Les, Pat, and Dean chasing after them in Dean's extended-cab pickup; three killer dogs poised to leap from the bed of the truck and take down any coyotes by their back legs, flip them over, and kill them by ripping open their throats. Lucky for the coyotes, the hunting was not good that day. Unlucky for Raymond Yellow Thunder, the boys were frustrated, anxious to stir up some shit—not just because they had failed at coyote hunting but also because there was a big USO benefit that night at the American Legion Hall, and everyone would be there except Les and Pat, who had been eighty-sixed by the "dumbfuck manager" Bernard Sandage. Earlier that day, they had been told never to come back because they refused to take off their cowboy hats and because Les was caught patting an older waitress named Thelma on her fanny.

"We was just having a little fun. Shucks."

Suddenly I'm in Gordon, so lost in thought I didn't notice the last few miles roll by. Highway 27 turns into a four-lane Main Street, which could very well be the boulevard of a bigger city except there is little traffic. I pass several blocks of tidy post–World War II suburban tract homes, the Jack & Jill Food Market, a Dollar General store, vacant lots leading to a downtown of solid-looking brick-façade buildings. Unlike those in Rushville or Hay Springs, none are boarded up. Beyond downtown loom three towering white grain elevators, multi-silo behemoths, the tallest buildings in Western Nebraska—bigger than the stinky sugar beet factory in Scottsbluff. They so dominate Gordon's skyline it is hard not to get distracted, but then on my right, just past Stockmen's Drug, of all things, I spot the sign for a sweet little coffee shop: COFFEE NOOK & GIFTS. I park *Villa VW* and go inside. The display racks in front are crammed with handcrafted ceramic cups and saucers, jars of homemade jams and gourmet mustards, popcorn, and Dark Canyon brand coffee beans. There are cute signs to hang in your kitchen, one of which reads BELIEVE IN THE POSSIBILITY; decorative dragonfly sculptures; *Bless this Home* pillows; patchwork quilts, and tons of Nebraska Cornhusker football merchandise: caps, T-shirts, sweatshirts, jerseys, shot glasses, banners, ashtrays, coffee mugs, decals, game-day blankets, and fanny packs emblazoned with a big red *N* or *Huskers*.

Hidden in back of the merchandise is the coffee counter, and next to it are a few iron-rod tables and chairs occupied by a clique of blue-haired ladies who appear to be drinking coffee and eating cake—Gordon's female aristocrats holding court; their husbands night be dead, or perhaps it's poker night at the Hacienda Lounge out on old Highway 20. The middle-aged barista has her back to me as she whips up a peppermint mocha, which I see by a nearby sign is the Good Friday special. When she finishes, she turns to me, and I order a small latte with an extra shot of espresso.

She asks what to me is a very strange question: "Do you want any flavorings?"

On the shelf behind her I see dozens of bottles, DaVinci brand syrups. There's orange, lime, cookies and cream, cherry, cheesecake, hazelnut, chocolate, watermelon, raspberry, root beer, pumpkin pie, and, of course, peppermint.

"No, thanks. I'm trying to avoid sugar."

"Well then, cowboy," she says, "how 'bout some whipped cream?"

Giving in, I go for the whipped cream. While the barista finishes my drink, I mention to her that I was in Rushville this morning and that the Gordon downtown area seems to be much more alive than downtown Rushville. "You're lucky," I say. "Most businesses there are boarded up."

"That may be so," she says, "but there are some good people in Rushville, working hard to keep it going."

I ask her if she knows anything about the old Hotel Pfister, the pawnshop lady who had the fabulous collection of Indian artifacts. Surprisingly, she knows quite a bit. "It was a sad ending," she says. "Helen was sick for many years, and when she died, there was a court battle over her estate. Her collection was sold off to pay legal bills. Nothing is left."

"Dirty shame," I say. "Helen said it was going to be her 'retirement.' I guess she didn't live long enough to retire."

"Frail bird, she was. Smoked like a chimney."

I learn that the barista's name is Barb Haller. She grew up in Gordon, moved to Santa Monica in her twenties, came back, has owned the Coffee Nook for a couple of years, loves it here, will never leave again. Walking out the door, I taste the latte. It's yucky sweet thanks to the artificial cream, but I don't care; it will keep me awake all the way to Alliance. Looking back up the street, I am surprised to see that the Sheridan Lounge is still there, still open, still serving drinks, I presume, to falling-down drunks—cowboys and Indians alike.

Raymond Yellow Thunder stumbled out of the Sheridan at around ten thirty that fatal night in 1972. He was headed north toward Borman Chevrolet so he could sleep in an old panel truck parked in the back lot—something he did when he was too drunk to sleep on the sofa at Arlene Lamont's house. Arlene always welcomed him, but Arlene was close to his sisters who lived on the rez, and she might tell them how drunk he was, which would be embarrassing.

The Hare brothers, Les and Pat; their friends Toby and Butch; and Les's girlfriend, Jeannette, were still driving around Gordon in Toby's newly painted blue Ford. Earlier that evening they had stopped at the Wagon Wheel liquor store to stock up on liquid refreshments. Les liked Schlitz, which came in bottles, and Pat liked Budweiser, which came in cans, so they bought a case of each. Toby and Butch didn't give a shit—they would drink anything as long as it got them blasted—and Jeannette was not drinking. When one of the boys finished a beer, the empty can or bottle was tossed out the car window, mostly onto the lawns of people they despised: churchgoing, uptight Gordonites. When a glass bottle shattered, everyone laughed, and someone would shout, "Fuckin' A!"

Les was the first to spot Yellow Thunder. "Look at that goddamn Indian! Let's get him!"

On cue, Toby whipped his car over the curb onto the sidewalk in front of Yellow Thunder. Before it came to a complete stop, Les jumped out, ran up to Yellow Thunder, slugged him as hard as he could on the side of the head, knocking him down, and hopped back in the car.

As they sped away, he hollered, "I got him good!"

Others were cruising about Gordon that night, mostly teenagers with nothing better to do; it was a standard activity in small Nebraska towns—get away from the adults, socialize, drink beer. Still, the gang had to be careful; no one cared if an Indian got his ass kicked, but the cops were fed up with the Hare brothers and their antics. The cops would love to find an excuse to put them in the same slammer with the same Indians they harassed, throw away the key, and watch the fun.

And damn if they weren't out of beer again—one more trip to the Wagon Wheel and this time just one case: half Schlitz, half Bud, and maybe a pint of Old Crow.

By now they were so drunk on their collective asses that when Toby accidently stepped on the back of Pat's heel as they came out of the liquor store, both went tumbling to the ground and remained there for a few moments, hysterically laughing. No one remembers who came up with the plan for what they should do next; Les said it was Toby, who said it was Pat. The brilliant idea went like this: *Let's find that goddamn Indian, stomp him some more, take off his pants, haul him over to the Legion, and throw him inside. It will be funnier than hell. Dumbfuck Sandage will call the cops, and the cops will shut down the dance; they'll send people home.*

"Hell, Sandage might even lose his bullshit job."

"But where is that Indian?"

A few moments later, Raymond Yellow Thunder would have been safely tucked inside the panel truck where he had stashed a blanket for such occasions, but as he staggered into the Borman used car lot, Les caught sight of him.

It didn't take long for Les to reach Yellow Thunder. He grabbed his arm, yanked him to the ground, and yelled out: "Yeah! I got the son of a bitch."

As Toby came running, he saw that Les was hanging on to the truck for leverage, that he was violently hopping up and down on Yellow Thunder's face and torso, kicking him in between hops.

"I'm stomping him," Les said.

Toby reached down, grabbed Yellow Thunder by his hair, lifted his head, and punched him hard in the mouth, twice for good measure.

"Come on, Butch, this is hella fun," Toby yelled out.

To his credit, I suppose, Butch was horrified and did not want any part of this, but he did nothing to stop it. Pat too declined to join in the beating. He stood watching, not sure what to do until his brother turned to him and said, "C'mon, damn it, help me get his pants off."

Pat followed his brother's instructions; they stripped Yellow Thunder of his shoes, pants, and underwear, leaving him only his socks from the waist down. While Les and Pat carried him toward the car, Toby jogged ahead to open the trunk.

Toby hollered back at the brothers, "Ain't no way that stinking Indian rides in front."

Les and Pat stuffed the dazed but still conscious Yellow Thunder into the trunk as Jeannette watched passively from the front seat. After Toby slammed the lid shut, the four men piled back into the car and sped off, leaving Yellow Thunder's shoes, pants, and underwear piled on the ground.

Next stop: the American Legion Hall.

It was around midnight. The parking lot at the Legion Hall was crammed; there were people coming and going, and it was obviously not the right time for pulling off a prank without being detected. Toby drove by without stopping, went back to cruising up and down Main Street. They would return when things died down, but first there was more serious drinking to do. More empties to throw onto the lawns of the local bourgeois.

"Hey, Les," Butch said. "That stinking Indian is as drunk as we are. Suppose he might like a beer."

"Hell, no. Ain't going to waste no brewski on no goddamn Indian."

"I just hope he ain't barfing in my trunk," Toby said to no one in particular.

About an hour later, down to one last beer apiece, they decided to give their scheme one more try. "If it doesn't work this time, we'll take Geronimo back to the car lot before his nuts freeze off."

The Legion was still busy, but now everyone was inside except for some dude sitting in his car near the front door, his motor running, lights on. Right away, they recognized Max Anderson, one of Jeannette's friends from high school. Too young to go into the Legion, Max was waiting for his two older buddies to score some beer before they continued on their merry way. Jeannette volunteered to talk to him. She walked up to the car, motioned to Max to roll down the side window, and said, "Hey Max, ain't I your friend?"

Max smiled at her. "You always have been."

"Can you turn your lights off? We got this drunk Indian in the trunk with his pants off, and my friends are gonna throw him into the dance."

Max did as he was asked, just as if it were just another ordinary Saturday night in Gordon, Nebraska.

Afraid to struggle or cry out, Yellow Thunder was relieved just to be out of the trunk. He went along willingly when Pat said, "Hang on, Chief. We're going to take you inside where it's warm." Pat and Butch guided their victim up the steps, through the foyer, and into the ballroom, where they gave him a stiff shove, nearly knocking him over, and ran back outside, making sure to shut the doors tightly behind them.

Woozy from the beating and bouncing up and down inside the

trunk, not to mention the boilermakers he'd had at the Sheridan Lounge, Yellow Thunder was stunned by the bright lights, the loud twang of a steel guitar, banging drums, thumping cowboy boots, whirling ladies with billowing dresses, farmers dancing the country two-step. Embarrassed, he grabbed the front of his shirttail, pulled it down to cover himself, and frantically looked for the door, a way out. The dancers stopped and stared at him for what seemed like an eternity. Disheveled, bruised, his forehead caked with dirt and blood, eyes bloodshot, half naked, and an Indian—*Indians aren't allowed in the Legion!* When someone finally acted, it was the pharmacist, Marvin Wheeler, sitting in a nearby booth with his wife, Virginia. Grabbing his jacket from the coatrack, he tried to cover up the poor Indian, but Legion manager Sandage intervened with his bartender, Bob Buchan. Pushing Wheeler and his coat aside, they guided Yellow Thunder to the front door and outside into the freezing night.

"What the fuck is going on here?" Sandage asked.

"Some white boys roughed me up," Yellow Thunder replied.

When Buchan asked Yellow Thunder if he wanted them to call the police, Yellow Thunder shook his head and said, "Just let me go." He trotted back into the bitterly cold night toward the highway, crossing the gravel parking lot with only socks between his feet and the frozen ground, as Buchan and Sandage testified. Rumors have been circulating for years that people inside the Legion thought that Yellow Thunder's sudden appearance—drunk without pants—was hysterically funny. Making him dance "Indian style," they pushed him around the dance floor, whooping like drunken warriors themselves, and only when they tired of this frivolity did they push him outside—so the story goes. None of this was proven.

What did happen is bad enough. The good white folks of Gordon did not give a whit for Yellow Thunder's welfare. They left him outside in below-freezing weather wearing no pants, underwear, or shoes.

Guilt is a strange thing. Les Hare got to thinking how cold it was, decided they should find the goddamn Indian and take him to retrieve his shoes and pants. So for a third time, they drove around looking for Yellow Thunder, found him past the railroad tracks, east of the grain elevators, coaxed or forced him into the trunk, and drove off to get his stuff. This final task accomplished, Les broke down and offered Yellow Thunder a beer for being such a good sport.

Once he had his pants and a can of beer, he was free to go—and the very same Raymond Yellow Thunder who at the Legion Hall didn't want anyone to call the police went directly to the police station. He told the cops about the white boys beating him up, about being thrown into the Legion Hall, and asked them if he could have a sleepover in one of the vacant cells. The Gordon police were very familiar with Raymond, liked him because he was quiet and never caused a bit of trouble. Granting his request, they noted what had happened to him but did not bother to investigate. It was no big deal, just some whacked-out cowboys, probably the Hare brothers, having a little too much fun. Happened all the time.

While Yellow Thunder checked into his cell, Les and his gang moved their rolling party to a late-night café on the edge of town with the odd name Seger Oil Company. As on most Saturdays after midnight, the place was packed. Seger had great steak and eggs and chicken and waffles and acceptable coffee. Many of the customers had been at the dance and were buzzing about what they'd seen, wondering how the hell that naked Indian ended up on the dance floor. Jazzed up, Les foolishly began to brag in a very loud, drunken voice. Everyone heard him.

"We pushed that naked Indian right into the Legion dance," he said over and over. Toby thought Les was hilarious; he couldn't stop laughing. Butch, Pat, and Jeannette were grinning but not so sure they wanted everyone in town to know they'd been involved in such a childish prank.

"Should have seen the look on his face when we stuffed his ass in the trunk and slammed the lid shut. Scared him shitless. And I'm not kidding. Look here, I have shit on my hands," Les said, turning his palms up to show Jeannette.

More than most young women, Jeannette had a high tolerance for brutishness, seemed to find it amusing, but this was where she finally drew the line.

"Jesus Christ, Les," she said angrily. "Go into the fucking bathroom and wash your hands!"

A few years later the Seger's Oil Company was rechristened Western Café. The menu was changed to Chinese cuisine, drawing much derision from local folk who thought that if they were going to serve "Chink" food, the name should have been changed to the Eastern Café. Looking out the window of *Villa VW* at the corner of Highway 27 and Highway 20, I see there is still a café; it looks like the same building. These days it is the Antelope Creek Cafe, featuring Gordon home-style cooking—tuna casserole, meat loaf, chicken cutlet sandwiches, hot plates with real mashed potatoes. Tempting, perhaps, but the thought of Les Hare washing shit off his hands in the bathroom sink is more than enough to keep me from venturing inside.

Just east of the Antelope Creek Cafe is the old American Legion Hall, a sprawling, ugly green metal building with no windows. The American flag is fluttering atop a disproportionately tall flagpole. The same gravel parking lot Yellow Thunder once traversed in his stocking feet is still there. And most notable, on the corner near the highway is a Vietnam-era Bell HueyCobra attack helicopter with what I assume are deactivated M75 grenade launchers. I am amazed that American Indian Movement activists never burned down this hateful place, never trashed the helicopters.

Head pounding, Raymond Yellow Thunder woke up in his cell the following morning with no appetite, declined to eat the instant cereal offered him, and left the jail looking for the one thing that might relieve his aching head, a bottle of cheap wine. A few hours later, on his way to his janitorial job at the First National Bank, fifteen-year-old George Ghost Dog spotted Raymond when he cut through the Borman back lot. He caught a glimpse of a head poking through the window in an old panel truck and recognized one of his mother's cousins, the nice man who liked to draw pictures and hand out quarters to Indian kids.

Thinking it would be fun to give Yellow Thunder a little surprise, he crept up to the passenger door, flung it open, and hollered, "Wake up, old man!"

Yellow Thunder didn't jump up as expected. He stirred slowly; it looked like someone had beaten him pretty bad. He had two black eyes, a fat lip, scratches, a big bruise on his forehead, blood on his shirt.

"Hey, Uncle, what happened to you?"

"Four white guys beat me, but I just need sleep."

Satisfied that his uncle would be fine, George Ghost Dog went on to his job at the bank. He would be the last person to see Raymond Yellow Thunder alive.

When Yellow Thunder failed to show at the Rucker Ranch Monday morning, Harold Rucker was worried. He knew about Raymond's drinking, but somehow he always pulled himself together, always turned up, got the job done. Figuring Raymond might have gone back to Kyle to see his sisters, he called Annie Eagle Fox. "Have you seen Raymond? He didn't come to work today." Annie called her sister Amelia Comes Last and brother-in-law Albert Crazy Bear in Porcupine. They had no idea where Raymond was, so she called Arlene Lamont in Gordon. "Did Raymond come over to your place this weekend?"

Alarmed, knowing that Yellow Thunder was sometimes busted for public drunkenness, Arlene went to the police station and found out that Raymond had slept there Saturday night but left Sunday morning. The cop on duty, Officer John Paul, should have known that Yellow Thunder needed medical attention, but he just saw him as another drunk Indian. The cuts and bruises, the unsteadiness, meant nothing to him.

Officer Paul knew that intoxicated Indians often slept in old vehicles behind Borman Chevrolet, but he said nothing about this to Arlene. He only said, "Haven't seen him since he left Sunday morning." Shockingly, Officer Paul knew one more thing—he knew that Yellow Thunder had been the brunt of a horrible prank—but even this wasn't worth mentioning. Arlene would find out in due course. Perhaps she would have the good sense to let sleeping dogs lie.

Five days later, some white kids playing touch football in the street in front of Borman Chevrolet's back lot discovered Yellow Thunder's body in an old panel truck.

Unobstructed light from a trillion stars and a nearly full moon lights up the sky as I drive south from Gordon through Mirage Flats on the north edge of the Sandhills, where Jules Sandoz, a Swiss doctor seeking happiness and freedom in the new world, parked his ox-drawn wagon, built a dugout starter house, and began to establish his little empire that no one would remember if his oldest child hadn't grown up to be one of Nebraska's greatest writers. Even though it's past seven p.m., I can see that the Sandhills look very much as Mari Sandoz once described them in her book *Old Jules*: "A storm-tossed sea, caught and held forever in naked, wind-pocked knobs."

When Arlene Lamont heard that Raymond Yellow Thunder was dead and learned the circumstances of his death, she was furious. What kind of person or persons would strip a man half naked on a freezing cold night and push him into the Legion Hall? Arlene's father, Albert Crazy Bear, who worked as a mechanic at Borman Chevrolet, was a full-blood Lakota. She knew that nudity is taboo to Lakota men; they don't even like undressing in front of their doctors. Arlene could not imagine the humiliation Raymond must have felt. One of the few accomplished Native Americans in town, Arlene had graduated from Gordon High School, attended Chadron State College, and become a Head Start teacher; she had recently been appointed director of the Head Start program. One of her white friends, Michael Smith, sat on the Head Start board of directors, and he happened to be the Sheridan County attorney.

Arlene hopped in her car, sped over to Smith's Main Street office, barged past his secretary into his private office, and demanded he investigate the murder of Raymond Yellow Thunder. Arlene was persuasive. And unlike in most of the cases where Indians were found dead in Gordon, there were plenty of witnesses and plenty of reasons not to like the Hare brothers.

As there was no professional coroner in Gordon, Smith asked the coroner from Scottsbluff to perform the autopsy. And because he had little faith in the Gordon cops, he turned to Max Ibach, the tough-minded lead detective from the Nebraska State Patrol, to head the investigation. The coroner found that Yellow Thunder had died from a subdural hematoma (brain hemorrhage) caused by a heavy blow to his head. The cause of death, he ruled, was murder. Following the coroner's report, it took Ibach all of twenty-four hours to determine who the perpetrators were. On the morning of February 25, 1972, just four days after Raymond's body was discovered, County Attorney Smith signed warrants for the arrest of Les Hare, Pat Hare, Butch Lutter, and Toby Bayliss.

As I casually drive along these dark, windy Sandhills roads outside Gordon, it strikes me that while change normally unfolds slowly, sometimes events happen very fast. *Bang, bang, bang.* At six a.m. the day after County Attorney Smith signed the warrants, Russell Means was rudely awakened from a deep sleep in his motel room in Omaha, Nebraska, where the American Indian Movement was holding a conference. Standing at his door was a large Lakota man wearing wire-rim glasses and a heavily stained white cowboy hat. Means recognized him as Severt Young Bear, an old acquaintance from Porcupine, his home village on Pine Ridge. Young Bear had driven seven straight hours in the night to deliver a message to Means from two of Porcupine's most respected elders, Young Bear's aunties Annie Eagle Fox and Amelia Comes Last. White racist cowboys in Gordon had killed their brother Raymond Yellow Thunder, and they wanted AIM's help to prevent the killers from going free. Impulsively, Young Bear jumped into his unlicensed rez car, borrowed gas money from a friend, and gunned it for Omaha.

Means invited Young Bear into his room, listened intently to his account, and then left the room to wake up fellow AIM leaders Dennis Banks and Vernon Bellecourt. He said to them, "A defenseless Lakota man has been mutilated and killed in the racist border town called Gordon. We must immediately go to the Pine Ridge. His killers are walking free! We must go. The elders have asked for our help."

Many natives criticized AIM, which was based in Minneapolis, for being an urban Indian movement with few roots on the reservations. Here was an opportunity to change that perception.

By seven a.m. Young Bear was down in the lobby getting a cup of coffee at the café that had just opened, while the three AIM leaders hurriedly walked about the motel waking up the others, about fifty total. Before Young Bear could finish his coffee, they were standing around him, ready to leave. Bellecourt took the wheel of Young Bear's car so he could sleep in the backseat. There were two other AIM members in the car; the trunk was loaded up with shotguns, rifles, and ammunition.

By seven thirty a.m., a caravan of crazed, radical Indians was on the road, headed for Pine Ridge. They took a circuitous route: 82 miles north on Route 77 to the Omaha Reservation, 20 more miles to the Winnebago Reservation, 87 miles west on Highway 20 to the Santee Reservation, up Highway 18 270 miles to the Rosebud Reservation, then on to Pine Ridge—480 miles total. At each stop, they recruited more followers until there were well over fifty cars and pickups, each with three or more passengers. They arrived in Pine Ridge in plenty of time for a raucous emergency meeting at seven thirty that very night at Billy Mills Hall. Two days later, fifteen hundred Indians from many different tribes marched on Gordon, Nebraska.

I laugh so hard thinking how the terrified citizens of Gordon must have visualized themselves in Lakota cooking pots, I nearly run off the road, and decide to pull over for a few minutes to catch my breath. Turning off the lights, I get out of the car, look up at the glorious sky. A meteorite streaks across the far horizon. I can see the constellation Orion, low in the western sky; I mentally draw a straight line from the three stars making up the Great Hunter's belt through the Hyades star cluster onto the small Pleiades cluster, seven stars commonly referred to as the Seven Sisters. Vernell's grandmother taught him how to navigate home to Yellow Bear Canyon by first determining the position of Pleiades. He could have used this to run away from the boarding school, but he didn't, and I imagine he was afraid they would only send him back. Just a young boy, Vernell had been taught to be obedient, wasn't about to defy his parents or grandparents. *Defiance doesn't come easy for many natives*, I think. *Perhaps it took the white man to make them defiant.*

For sure, the good white folk in Gordon weren't used to rebellious Indians. Much like black people in the Jim Crow South, Gordon's Indians were expected to keep their heads down—do what they were told, never talk back. But when AIM came to town with fifteen hundred friends and fellow warriors, suddenly it was the white people who were subservient. AIM wanted food to feed the protesters. Gordon provided it. AIM wanted all fourteen Indians currently in Gordon's city jail released. They were released. AIM wanted the use of the Neighborhood Center to hold what they called a red-feather grand jury. It was made available. Fueled by rumors that Raymond Yellow Thunder had been tortured and castrated, AIM demanded a second autopsy by a coroner of their choosing. A few days later, Raymond Yellow Thunder's body was dug up from his unmarked grave near Porcupine and transported to Rapid City for the autopsy. This second autopsy witnessed by AIM representatives found no signs of mutilation and confirmed the original findings.

The day he arrived in the town, Russell Means said, "We came today to put Gordon on the map. If our demands are not met, we will come back to take Gordon off the map."

AMONG THE DOG EATERS

RACISTS CONVICTING RACISTS

Among the Dog Eaters

My *kola* from *Pejuta* Haka* called
two weeks ago tuned tightly and fired up.
"It's the same on most reservations," he said.
"These white men come in
and steal our women . . .
They become Indians by insertion! Instant
experts on redskin culture. Once they dip their wicks
they start speaking of Indians as . . . *us!*
When Indian men spit on these squawmen,
the squawmen lick the spit and get stiff dicks.
The result is novels by white poets who label
themselves *Native Americans*, anthropological

---

* My friend from Kyle Adrian C. Louis teaches at the Oglala Lakota College. He is recipient of several book and poetry awards and an enrolled member of the Paiute Indian tribe.

monographs by liberal assholes,
and more breeds like you."

—Adrian C. Louis

Starving, eager for real food, since I've eaten only a few nuts and dried apricots since lunch with Suzy and Vernell, I urgently drive on. It's lonely at night in the Sandhills on old Highway 27, the Mari Sandoz Trail. I must be in the middle of the magnificent Spade Ranch; at a half million acres with sixty thousand head of cattle, it was once the biggest ranch in America.

Founded by Bartlett Richards, the son of a Congregational Church pastor, the Spade Ranch owes its existence to the Homestead Act, and the discovery that cattle can not only survive but thrive during Sandhill winters. To build up his holdings, Richards took full advantage of the federal government's open range policy, which allowed ranchers to run cattle on land not claimed by homesteaders. To further protect his land from these very settlers, Richards paid Civil War veterans, or their widows, to make land claims, and then transfer the leases to the ranch—hundreds did so, but not enough to meet his ever-growing need for additional grassland. Rationalizing that the Sandhills were unsuitable for farming (most homesteaders abandoned their claims after a year or two), Richards fenced off huge chunks of unclaimed federal land, and like the railroad and mining monopolies in the east, he created a Spade Ranch company town, Ellsworth, Nebraska. Here, Richards built a private railhead for shipping cattle to the big packing plants in Kansas City and Denver. A three-story building, rare in these parts, served as ranch headquarters. There was a Spade hotel and large brick houses for the ranch foreman, business partners, and the Richards family, who also had homes in Chicago and Coronado, California. Ellsworth had a blacksmith's shop, a post office, and a general store stocked with groceries, Western clothing, saddles, fishing gear, and hunting rifles. Richards created his own Ranch Telephone Company, strung up phone lines from Ellsworth to Gordon, Rushville, and Chadron.

Life was opulent for Richards and his family and close associates. During the winter months, they went on shopping sprees to Omaha and Denver. Opera companies, dance troupes, and other entertainers traveled from the four corners of the world to Ellsworth in luxurious, private Spade railcars. If there had been a *Forbes* magazine in those days, Bartlett Richards would have been on their annual list of richest Americans. But in 1905, Richards' world began to unravel when, spurred on by Jules Sandoz and other indigent homesteaders, federal prosecutors filed felony charges against him and his business partner, William Comstock, for illegally fencing 212,000 acres of federal land. Initially, the men received a ridiculously light sentence—six hours' jail time and a three-hundred-dollar fine—but the government wasn't finished. The United States Secret Service spent the next thirteen months investigating and compiling more evidence, taking affidavits from 600 interested parties, issuing 165 subpoenas, and calling up 132 witnesses for a new trial beginning November 12, 1906. This time, the charges were grave: conspiracy to defraud the government of the title and use of public lands, subornation of perjury, and conspiracy to suborn perjury. This time, in spite of their immense resources and team of top lawyers, the partners were found guilty on thirty-five of thirty-eight counts and sentenced to eight months in a not very pleasant jail in Hastings, Nebraska; six months later, Richards was excused from confinement in Hastings to go to the Mayo Clinic, where he died two days later from complications following gallstone surgery. Remarkable as it may seem, the day after his death, President William Taft commuted Comstock's sentence so he could attend Richards' funeral in San Diego.

Much smaller today, the Spade Ranch still exists. There still is an Ellsworth, a few buildings and houses, the vacated railhead, and the general store. In fact, I'm approaching it now. Lights on the veranda are just bright enough that I can see a life-sized ceramic horse pulling an old buggy wagon; and I can read the sign: OLD SPADE RANCH STORE, ESTABLISHED 1898.

Richards' empire fell into the hands of crafty New York bankers Ed Brass and Ed Meyers, the "two Eds," who wisely hired Richards' former foreman, Lawrence Bixby, to manage what was left: forty square miles—sizable, but much smaller than the two thousand square miles it once occupied. Over the next twenty years, Bixby bought or was awarded chunks of the ranch here and there until he became the de facto new owner. Bixby turned out to be one of Nebraska's outstanding entrepreneurs—to protect the land from wind erosion and enhance its beauty, he planted fifty thousand trees; he built a ranch airstrip and hangar for his planes, restored the grand Richards family house, and was always adding buildings: corrals, horse barns, calving barns, bunkhouses, cookhouses, feed storage facilities, feedlots, industrial livestock scales, cattle dipping vats. He converted the Spade herd from Herefords to Black Angus and built up a reputation for producing the best beef in Nebraska.

Bixby admired his old boss man Bartlett Richards. The homesteaders, he claimed, would have starved to death if Richards hadn't loaned them milk cows and horses, let them charge stuff at his ranch store. He thought Richards had gotten a raw deal from the Feds, who didn't relate to the vicissitudes of life in the Sandhills. Richards had only fenced federal land to keep his cows from eating themselves to death in the cornfields and wheat fields of adjacent tableland. In 1939, Bixby's lobbying efforts got Bartlett Richards inducted, posthumously, into the National Cowboy Hall of Fame.

As I come to the end of Highway 27, I recall that it was Lawrence Bixby himself who donated the money to have this very highway paved. Otherwise, there simply are not enough people living here to justify such a project. I turn right on Highway 2, a publicly funded road, and head west for Alliance, now just thirty miles away.

Oddly enough, the last chapter of the Raymond Yellow Thunder story unfolded in Alliance, where the Hare brothers were put on trial for false imprisonment and manslaughter. In his eighties, the lawyer defending them, Charles Fisher, was an old-fashioned, brilliant impresario of an attorney; you might say he was the wannabe Melvin Belli of western Nebraska. His white hair long and flowing, he wore rumpled suits with white socks and had an unquenchable thirst for lawyering, good bourbon, and beautiful women. Plus, he was willing to represent the most despicable defendants.

At the first hearing, Fisher motioned for a change of venue. "Les and Pat can't get a fair trial in Gordon," he argued. "Too many people here are afraid of Indians. They imagine the most unmentionable things, and they are afraid if my clients aren't convicted, the Indians, especially outside agitators from AIM, will burn down their town."

Knowing it would be hard to find unbiased jurors in Gordon, Sheridan County Attorney Michael Smith didn't object; he figured the jury pool in Alliance was at least bigger. The presiding judge, Robert Moran, lived in Alliance and wasn't too keen on traveling back and forth to Gordon, so it was a no-brainer; he granted the motion.

Alliance's most prominent Indian, Mark Monroe, who was to play an important role in the events that followed, wasn't so sure it was possible to obtain a conviction in his hometown.

Because of his last name, people thought Mark was only part Indian, but his mother was full-blooded Oglala, and his father full-blooded Cheyenne. Like Vernell White Thunder and Raymond Yellow Thunder, he was born on the Pine Ridge reservation in a log house. His great-grandfather Sleeps Long Time traveled across Europe with Buffalo Bill's Wild West Show in the late 1880s and grew tired of being teased about his name; thus he took the name Monroe after the fifth U.S. president. Curious choice, but he probably did not realize that President Monroe had waged war against the Seminoles in Spanish Florida—that he was no friend of Native Americans.

In 1968, fully recovered from years of alcoholism, Monroe found himself living a normal if mundane life with his wife, Emma, and their five children, all of whom were in school, determined to graduate and build successful lives for themselves. Tragedy struck, however, when an older white man kidnapped and raped his sixteen-year-old daughter, who was on her way home from school. Monroe was furious. He reported the crime, insisted the police knew who committed it, but feared they cared little about crimes committed against Indians. A few weeks earlier, an underage boy had run over an Indian pedestrian while driving his inebriated parents home late one night from the Elks Club. The victim was a Chippewa from Wisconsin named Fred Pahlow who was in Alliance visiting relatives. Profusely bleeding from head wounds, Pahlow was in obvious need of medical attention, but the Alliance cops determined he was drunk, arrested him, threw his ass in jail, and escorted the nice white family home. Following brain surgery, Pahlow died a few days later in a Denver hospital. The boy was never charged.

Alliance police chief Verlin Hutton explained to Mark that the "situation" with his daughter was one of those unproveable he-said, she-said encounters.

Monroe wasn't about to go away quietly. Wanting to protect his daughter and prevent similar tragedies from happening to other Lakota families, Mark founded the American Indian Council. Using the teachings of Mahatma Gandhi, which Monroe studied during the long days of his rehab in an army hospital recovering from wounds he suffered in the Korean War (his left hand and leg were shattered by machine gun bullets near Ma-Jon), Monroe's council would provide services to local Indians and use nonviolent resistance tactics to assert their rights.

Monroe's first action as chairman of the new organization was to face down three farmers on the school board of a one-room schoolhouse in Berea, Nebraska, ten miles north of Alliance. A white boy was taunting an Indian boy, and when the white boy called him a nigger, the Indian boy shoved the older boy, knocking him to the classroom floor. The teacher punished the Indian boy by spanking him with a yardstick. Mark threatened legal action. He made it very clear to the Berea School Board that a civil lawsuit would be filed in state court in Lincoln if they did not suspend the white boy and reprimand the teacher and make her apologize to the Indian boy. Surprisingly, the farmers capitulated.

Emboldened, Monroe took a giant leap when he filed to run for Alliance City Magistrate & Justice of the Peace in an upcoming election, challenging longtime judge Nell "Nellie" Johnstone, who had been a fixture in county and city courts since 1925. Over and over and over again, Judge Johnstone sentenced the same Indians to the Box Butte County jail for intoxication, never considering that there might be better ways to reduce public drunkenness.

During the campaign, Mark got threatening phone calls, and someone tried to firebomb his house, but he made a good showing. He lost the election but got six hundred votes, more than half of Judge Johnstone's tally. Most important, the sheer dignity of how he campaigned gained him respect from some of the more tolerant white citizens, and from that moment on, Mark Monroe became the "go-to Indian" in Alliance, the liaison between two cultures. The city fathers provided Mark a building for his organization, an old barracks left in Alliance after the U.S. Army abandoned the airbase, which they moved to south Alliance for him. From this new headquarters, Monroe sponsored a Native American Alcoholics Anonymous program, an Indian Boy Scout troop, a native arts club, and a medical screening service. He also started a community garden, bus service to the hospital in Pine Ridge, and a meals program, and built a sunshade for powwows.

With his crew cut, old-fashioned horn-rimmed glasses, clean-shaven face, dress shirt, and tie, Mark Monroe hardly projected the image of a radical activist. He preferred to work within the system, having faith that over time he could warm the white man's heart. But the brutal killing of Raymond Yellow Thunder shook him to his very soul—some whites were apparently so evil, he figured their hearts had calcified; nothing could change this. Mark worried that Yellow Thunder's killers would never be convicted in Alliance, where Indians died like flies in the city jail and no one seemed to care. While Monroe knew the risks when he invited AIM leaders to meet with him at his American Indian Center to plan a protest strategy, something had to be done.

Five days before the start of the trial, on May 19, 1972, Russell Means, Dennis Banks, and Vernon Bellecourt, with their entourage of long-haired big-city Indians, some with revolvers tucked in the waistbands of their blue jeans, descended upon Monroe's sedate community center. They drank coffee and devoured the big platter of doughnuts he brought in from the local bakery where he worked the night shift. Sitting in chairs, on desktops, and even on the floor, they began the meeting as if he weren't present. Dumbfounded, Monroe listened as the AIM militants said they were going to demand that Alliance provide food and indoor shelter for up to two thousand protesters expected to arrive the following day. They wanted the use of a city facility for meetings and press conferences, and were going to demand that Alliance close the liquor stores during the trial. Most bizarre, they were going to demand the right to address students and parents at the Alliance High School graduation, coming up in just two days at the school football field, called Bulldog Stadium.

Mark was impressed with AIM's audacity, but he was not amused by their boisterousness, misplaced irreverence, and contempt . . . and especially their disrespect for him. He began to think it had been a mistake to invite them. AIM would bring violence, and the cause for dignity for Indian citizens in Alliance could be set back years. Mark kept his objections to himself, but he was to break with AIM before the trial was over.

The following day, the AIM leaders walked into Mayor Glen Worley's office with their list of demands. No one had told them that in Alliance, the position of mayor was largely ceremonial, as most decision-making powers rested with the city manager. Not surprisingly, Mayor Worley was a bit confused as to how to handle these types of requests, but he agreed to get back to the leaders by three p.m., which he did. The city denied the demand for food and shelter and suggested that AIM ask the local churches. It was OK for AIM to use the Alliance City Auditorium, an old basketball court with a small stage at one end, floor and balcony seating, and a hallway in front. It would be available for meetings and press conferences only, not for cooking or sleeping. AIM members and their followers were free to set up a camp in Bower Field, the baseball park near the train tracks and the local Indian neighborhood. And the city said they would set up a Human Relations Board to better the understanding between Indians and white citizens in Alliance.

If the city fathers thought these decisions would be well received and would lower tension, they were dead wrong. AIM felt insulted, especially about the campsite. Dennis Banks complained, "They got us down in the slums, in what the *honkies* call Indian Park." At this point, the ranks of the protesters had grown to about five hundred. Still not the two thousand Banks had projected, but sizeable, easily the largest demonstration Alliance had ever seen—five hundred Indians beating their drums, singing, yelling out slogans as they leisurely marched from the auditorium up the brick street to Box Butte Avenue, past Gibson's Discount Center, the Newberry Hardware Company, Art & Jerry's Boot Shop, the candy store, and the theater playing *J. W. Coop*, a modern-day cowboy movie directed by and starring Cliff Robertson. An unnerving sight to the few Alliance citizens not hiding out in their basements—all those strong-looking young Indian men, defiant, unafraid. Indian women too, with their braided hair, beautifully beaded earrings and necklaces, confident, equally proud. Whatever happened to those nice, docile Indians Alliance was used to seeing?

Once the protesters arrived at the neoclassical citadel that serves as the Box Butte County courthouse, easily the grandest building in Alliance, they broke into two groups. One group carried a large buffalo-skin powwow drum through the front doors into the expansive courthouse foyer, where they set it up on the floor on top of the mosaic tile Great Seal of the State of Nebraska. They began drumming and singing war songs. Their piercing, shrill voices and the booming of the drum bounced off the marble walls and up the two flights of stairs, vibrated frosted windows on office and courtroom doors. It was a primeval euphony that scared the bejesus out of the old-lady county librarian, freaked out the clerks in the Veterans Affairs office, even spooked the lawyers and judges. A court officer locked the door to his office and hid behind his desk. Out on the courthouse lawn, the other protesters headed for the tall flagpole and brazenly lowered the American flag. They raised their own blue, yellow, white, and red–striped AIM flag and turned the American flag upside down, flying it below the AIM flag. The county sheriff, Don Underwood, and his deputies dared not interfere; they stood nearby, helplessly watching, taking photos. The protesters stayed a few hours, listened to speeches, announced that they would be back in bigger numbers the following day, the first day of jury selection.

The part of Highway 2 I am on now is nearly as desolate as the Mari Sandoz Trail, too far away from Alliance for me to see the city lights. With no other cars on the road, it is so dark that the beams of my headlights extend only a few feet before being completely absorbed, until a long coal train headed east breaks up the blackness—but only for a minute or two, as it is traveling very fast. In a few miles, I'll be near the old army airbase. During World War II, my dad was in France with the 86th Infantry, so my mom moved to Denver, where she lived with her sister and worked in an airplane factory. Consequently, I didn't hear much about what Alliance was like during those years, but I've always been curious. Nearly all the local young men were fighting distant battles while their wives and girlfriends were mostly left to fend for themselves. Meanwhile, thousands of other young men were stationed five miles outside of town learning how to jump safely out of airplanes. I imagine they got weekend passes. There must have been quite a party scene in Alliance, with all those horny young men and lonely young women.

Counting himself one of Mark Monroe's friends, my dad was one of the few citizens sympathetic to the Lakota—he was interested in their history, and tried to understand their struggles. When Monroe needed funding for his mobile health van service, Dad wrote letters on Mark's behalf to the governor and the Nebraska legislature. In his newspaper columns, he advocated treatment for Indian alcoholics instead of jail time and encouraged school officials to shut down the "Opportunity Room" at Grandview Elementary School, where Indian students were warehoused without a teacher, just a lowly paid supervisor. Here, they spent their days drawing, coloring, reading comics, and marking on the chalkboard. It was the Alliance school system's way of obeying the state law that required all children, including Native Americans, to stay in school until age sixteen. Still, Dad was defensive about Alliance's racism; he thought most of its citizens were fair-minded, and he did not like it when Russell Means called Alliance "the most racist town in the number one racist state in America." Seeing the American flag flying upside down was also offensive to him, as it was to most people in Alliance, including Monroe. No one bought the explanation that this was a symbol of distress—this was a clear provocation that would not win AIM any friends. My dad stayed as neutral as he could, covered the events of the day, got to know most of the AIM leaders. He sat through every minute of the trial, providing his readers thorough and remarkably unbiased commentary.

The day before the trial, I was in Alliance, having driven down in the morning from Kyle with Linda and our daughter. After leaving them with Linda's mother, I went to the courthouse, arriving shortly after AIM hoisted their flag above the upside-down American flag, in time to hear Russell Means speak to a crowd of several hundred AIM protesters, local Indians, and a few sympathetic whites. Convinced that the Hare brothers would never be convicted, he called upon AIM supporters across the country to come to Alliance, to occupy the courthouse once the "not guilty" verdicts came in, to effectively shut down the town.

"Racists don't convict racists," Means said. "Not in Mississippi, not in South Dakota, and certainly not in the number one racist state, Nebraska."

That night I went with my dad to Bulldog Stadium for the high school graduation. It was a perfect spring evening; a few parents wore suits, the students had their caps and gowns, but most of the spectators, who sat on the concrete bleachers built into the side of a hill, were in shirtsleeves. The 166 graduating seniors were on the field in folding chairs. In full regalia, the marching band was positioned behind them, as was the high school choir, standing on risers. Dad and I sat in the front row, in a section reserved for the press—usually a reporter from the *Times-Herald* and another from Alliance's KCOW radio station. On this occasion, however, there were also correspondents from the *Scottsbluff Star-Herald*, the *Omaha World-Herald*, and the *Kansas City Star.* They were in town to cover the trial and had heard there might be a demonstration or disruption at the ceremony.

As at graduations taking place all across America, the evening began with a processional. First the band marched in, followed by the choir, and then the seniors. I got comfortable on my bleacher seat, settling in for what I feared would be a long, boring evening. About midway through the drawn-out diploma presentations, Dad and I walked down to the cinder track that circled the football field, then over to the front entrance gate. A crowd of AIM supporters stood just outside, held back by a small contingent of cops and sheriff's deputies. The Alliance school superintendent, Harold Petersen, was huddled with the mayor, a group of school officials, and school board members, discussing what they should do. One of the board members, Keith Sorum, said to my dad, "That Bellecourt guy wants to address the crowd. We don't think graduation is an appropriate place for such a speech."

"Maybe so," my dad advised, "but there are enough protesters here to keep people from leaving by blocking the gate."

"What do you think we should do?"

"I think you should tell the crowd that the Indians want to speak to them. Tell them they are free to stay or free to go."

Much to my surprise, Sorum agreed. He discussed the idea with Petersen and the others, and they were on board. I was proud of my dad. He maneuvered the reluctant city leaders to do the right thing, preventing an ugly scene that could have easily turned violent.

AIM's minister of information, Vernon Bellecourt, wearing a deerskin cape, his strong facial features tempered by dominating dark aviator glasses, the ends of his braids tied with rabbit pelts and eagle feathers, resolutely strolled up to the speaker's platform. The others followed behind him, standing or sitting in the grass—they looked serious, dignified. Dad mentioned to me that none of the protesters were drunk or seemed to be drinking, which he thought for Indians was remarkable. This very piece of turf they were standing upon had once been their land, and if the treaty laws were ever enforced, it could conceivably revert to them. Sadly, most of the students filed out before Bellecourt could begin. The trickle of people headed for the exit soon turned into a stream. However, this did not deter him.

"You have prospered," he said, "but the Indians living in Alliance live in terrible poverty. Two Indian students graduated here tonight . . . finally, but for all the years before, you did not have a single Indian graduate. We are not a violent people. We are the sovereign people of this land. We are not here for confrontation. We have been asked to come here by your Indian citizens because there is a trial going on that is important to them. The American characteristic we oppose is the one that brought about the massacre at Sand Creek in Colorado and Wounded Knee in South Dakota. Sadly, it is the same characteristic that still lives today, most recently responsible for the My Lai massacre, and unfortunately for the death of our brother Raymond Yellow Thunder.

"The same Great Spirit places us all on this earth, and he wants us to live in peace. Peace and justice is all we ask."

Bellecourt ended his talk by thanking all who had stayed, saying they gave him the feeling that there was hope for America in treating his people justly. Those remaining clapped, a few even cheered; there were no catcalls. As Bellecourt was leaving, he motioned my dad to come over, shook his hand, and talked to him in a quiet voice so others couldn't hear. Of course, as soon as I could, I asked Dad what he had said.

"He said, 'Good thing it was me talking and not Russell Means or Dennis Banks; you'd have a riot on your hands.' "

At last *Villa VW* and I are in Alliance; it has been a long day, with too much driving. On top of the Third Street overpass, I see multiple train tracks stretching for miles in both directions; huge flat railroad switching yards eerily lit up by powerful floodlights on top of towering steel poles, similar to those you might find at a Major League baseball park. Chuckling to myself, I think, *So this is what energy independence looks like.* The railroad boom is revitalizing small-town America; it's an efficient way to transport oil and coal; why do we need pipelines?

Once I'm back at street level, it is a straight shot to Ken and Dales, just seven blocks from here. I visualize a nice, cozy stool for myself at the bar, away from the front door and near the TV, tuned to an NBA playoff game or at least ESPN *SportsCenter*. Ken and Dales holds a special place in my psyche, much like the Holiday Inn Express. When I'm in Alliance, if I'm not enjoying some over-the-top Lebanese food at my former mother-in-law's house, I go to Ken and Dales. I go there for down-home comfort food, breakfast, lunch, and dinner. It's not exactly Le Bernardin; Chef Ripert would gag on the French-fried shrimp, obviously frozen, and the waiters at Smith & Wollensky would be extremely apologetic if they had to bring you one of Ken and Dales rib eyes. But name a fancy New York restaurant that offers you the choice of three outstanding side dishes with every entree. Ken and Dales is a quaint little place in an old square brick building, the kind of place Guy Fieri might feature on *Diners, Drive-Ins and Dives* if he ever gets to western Nebraska. Sitting at the bar, drinking a perfectly shaken-not-stirred Grey Goose martini, even though I haven't been here in eight years, I again order the shrimp.

As there is no NBA game, my mind wanders back to the trial, that first chaotic day of jury selection. The AIM followers were back, and again they put their powwow drum on top of the Great Seal, took down the American flag, started drumming and singing the Lakota national anthem. The old courthouse had no air-conditioning and temperatures were in the mid-eighties, so the windows in the third-floor courtroom had to be left open. The noise coming from the foyer and from outside was deafening. AIM leaders had planned to add to the pressure by packing the courtroom with their followers, but there was one little problem: they were ten minutes late. Having little appreciation for "Indian time," Judge Moran pounded his gavel against the sounding block; no one would get into his courtroom until the next recess.

Box Butte County Sheriff Underwood and Alliance cop Glen Jenkins stood guard outside the courtroom door. Deputy Sheriff Leonard Benze and Nebraska trooper Phil Kuenle, beefy men who were once Cornhusker football teammates, were shoulder to shoulder half a flight down the staircase, blocking AIM leaders and about thirty of their followers. Leaning over the banister, Sheriff Underwood got into a shouting match with Dennis Banks. "Dennis, cut the goddamn racket. You can send in a delegation of four people at next recess. That's the best I can do."

"Bullshit," Banks replied. "The outcome of this sham trial has already been decided."

Some of the women protesters near the foot of the staircase egged the men on, urging them to force their way past the cops and into the courtroom. Violence seemed imminent, but at the last moment, Banks turned his back to the officers and signaled his followers to march back down the stairs. Friends with Yippie movement founder Abbie Hoffman, he was no stranger to the concept of guerrilla street theater, the power of manipulating the media, scaring people into giving in to your demands. Besides, Banks had been to jail on more than one occasion and knew the futility of trying to accomplish anything while locked up. The Indians continued their drumming, singing, chants, and war whoops.

Defense attorney Fisher discovered an easy way to dismiss prospective jurors. All he had to do was ask, "Are you afraid of the demonstrators?" When the first dozen or so answered, "Yes," the judge promptly dismissed them. As the pool was only seventy, the odds of having a jury seemed to be slipping away, and Prosecuting Attorney Mike Smith was losing his cool. Dressed in a mod blue-denim leisure suit and polka dot tie, his long sideburns neatly trimmed, Smith took pride in his dispassionate courtroom demeanor, but beads of sweat poured down his forehead; he wanted to shout out, *What kind of fucking circus is this?* Instead, he asked to approach the bench. "Judge Moran," Smith whispered, "can't you please do something about these noisy demonstrators?" The judge agreed to ban them from banging on their powwow drum in the foyer but said he couldn't stop the AIM people from congregating outside on the lawn. Wisely, he called for a recess. Because this recess allowed AIM to send four people into the courtroom, they readily agreed to move their powwow drum outside.

Jury selection continued with a bit less commotion. A few more prospective jurors declared that they were afraid of the demonstrators and were sent home. Judge Moran also dismissed the seven Native Americans in the pool. Smith was biting his nails when it came time to question retired schoolteacher Ruth Dempsey. When Fisher asked her if she was afraid of the demonstrators, she said she was "*decidedly* not intimidated" and could render an unbiased verdict. Her courage seemed to buoy up those who followed. Determined to have a jury, Judge Moran pushed the process to the peremptory challenge stage, where the state and the defense were allowed to eliminate jurors one at a time down to twelve plus one alternate. Fisher and Smith crossed names off a typed list that they handed back and forth to the clerk, Susan Dyer. By two o'clock that afternoon, there was a jury, which included a cross section of white Alliance: retired railroader, housewife, auto mechanic, beautician, farmer, president of the Jaycees, candy-store clerk, pharmacist—plus the alternate, Ms. Dempsey.

At 3:05 p.m., with the jury seated, attorney Mike Smith made his opening statement. "Eyewitnesses," he said, "will provide proof beyond any reasonable doubt that Raymond Yellow Thunder was murdered by the Hare brothers and their accomplices. About midnight on February 12, 1972, the door of the American Legion Hall in Gordon, Nebraska, flew open. An Indian man without pants or shoes, Raymond Yellow Thunder, tumbled onto the dance floor. Earlier that night, five people, including the defendants, were driving around Gordon in a 1966 Ford sedan, excessively drinking beer they purchased at the Wagon Wheel liquor store. Upon spotting Raymond Yellow Thunder, one of the five, defendant Les Hare, jumped out of the car and brutally attacked him. He slugged Yellow Thunder in the head, and when he fell to the ground, kicked him with his heavy cowboy boots. Later that evening when they again spotted Yellow Thunder, who was going into a used car lot, they got out of their car to search for him. Shoving him onto the dance floor was their sick idea of fun; they were having a good ol' time at the expense of this poor Indian man. Yellow Thunder came to the Gordon police station at one thirty a.m. and talked to a policeman on duty who will testify that Yellow Thunder had a large bruise and cut on his right forehead. Five days later, a group of boys playing baseball in an adjacent street discovered his body in the cab of the panel truck at the same used car lot."

As Attorney Fisher countered with his opening statement, the strategy for the defense became absurdly clear. Raymond Yellow Thunder had voluntarily gotten into the trunk of Toby Bayliss's car, which was equipped with a special lever so it could be opened from the inside, and for this reason, Yellow Thunder had not been imprisoned. The defendants had never struck Yellow Thunder. If a blow to his forehead caused his death, it could have been an accident or come from someone else; there were many other people driving about Gordon that night. Taking his pants off and pushing him into the American Legion was a prank—immature, ill advised, for sure, but just a joke. Besides, the defendants figured the American Legion manager would call the police and Yellow Thunder would go to jail, where he would be safe and warm.

Sitting with their attorneys, the Hare brothers didn't look like the gruff, macho cowboys who'd abducted Yellow Thunder; they were clean shaven with fresh haircuts, nicely dressed in brown business suits, white dress shirts, blue ties. Instead of scruffy cowboy boots, each wore brightly polished black dress shoes. Throughout the trial, they listened attentively, made eye contact with the jurors, and seemed like nice young men, college graduates who perhaps worked as part-time assistant managers at the local bank.

The shrimp having arrived, I take a break from my musings and marvel at how big, perfectly fried, and scrumptious they are, just as I remembered them. I order a glass of Stella Artois on tap; it's incredible to me that I can get such wonderful brew in Alliance—when I lived here, we had only Budweiser, Pabst Blue Ribbon, and Schlitz. No Coors, even though the brewery is nearby in Golden, Colorado, less than a four-hour drive away. In 1873, the German immigrants Adolph Coors and Jacob Schueler planned to build their Coors brewery right here. They found the artesian water coming from the Ogallala Aquifer better than the water from the Rocky Mountains. So that the brewmasters and other workers would have a place to stay, Coors built the Alliance Hotel near the rail terminal. But alas, local members of the Temperance Society, pointing out that Alliance already had more than twenty bars, launched a campaign against the brewery that was ultimately successful. Under tremendous pressure from their wives, the city councilmen voted not to approve the permit. Furious, Coors and Schueler banned the distribution of Coors beer in Nebraska, a ban that was to last more than a hundred years.

"Ridiculous," I mutter to myself. "Just ridiculous."

The young man sitting near me, a nice-looking boy with engaging brown eyes, a ponytail, and hip John Lennon glasses, who ordered Jameson on the rocks and a chef's salad, says, "What's ridiculous?"

I look over at him, slightly annoyed at the interruption, but reply, "Alliance. Alliance is ridiculous. Did you know we could have had the largest brewery in the world here?"

His name is Pearce. He's interested that I once lived here, enjoys hearing my tale about Adolph Coors. I learn that Pearce grew up in Kansas City; went to Rockhurst University, where he majored in electrical engineering; and came here to work on the railroad. He likes it in Alliance. "There are a lot of young people here," he says. "They come from all across the country. Most didn't go to college, but they have good-paying jobs thanks to Burlington Northern."

I ask him if he's been to the rez, expecting he'll say he doesn't know what I'm talking about, but much to my surprise he answers, "Yeah, man, of course. I ride my Harley up there all the time; beautiful country."

"But have you been to Big Bat's?" I ask.

"Oh, yeah. Love the burgers there."

"Do you know who Raymond Yellow Thunder was?" I ask.

"No, never heard of him."

I tell Pearce about Raymond Yellow Thunder, the events in Gordon, his killers, the fact that the trial was right here in Alliance. Again he surprises me; he is actually interested, says he is part Indian himself, his father Irish, his mother Choctaw; she grew up near Muskogee, Oklahoma. I ask him, "Do you know the song?"

"Yeah, I know the song."

Spontaneously, not caring what the twenty or so other patrons at Ken and Dales might think, we start singing: "I'm proud to be an Okie from Muskogee, a place where even squares can have a ball. . . ."

We laugh. Ken, who is standing in the kitchen, and Dale at the front counter join in the laughter, as do some of the customers, and right then

I realize that Alliance is changing. Like me, it seems to have mellowed out, doesn't take itself so goddamn seriously.

I ask Pearce, "Do you want to know why the Hare brothers got convicted?"

"Sure," he says. "Why did they get convicted?"

"Two reasons. First, the jury was intimidated by AIM, all the drumming, singing, shouting out on the courthouse lawn. Every second during the trial, even during the deliberations, the jurors could hear the pounding noise. It scared the holy fuck out of them."

"And the second reason?"

"The defense attorney, Fisher, was too clever for his own good. He called the younger, more believable of the two brothers, Pat, to the stand as his last, surprise witness. Might have worked, but the story they concocted was such a whopper, not even the local yahoos on the jury could swallow it. Would you believe, he referred to Yellow Thunder as the 'Indian gentleman.' 'This "Indian gentleman," Pat said, 'was obviously drunk, walking down the street on a very cold night. We worried he might freeze to death, so we asked him if he would like a ride.' Only when they realized how stinky the 'Indian gentleman' was did they asked him if wouldn't mind riding in the trunk. Yellow Thunder was agreeable. He climbed in all by himself. Someone started closing the trunk, and Les told the 'Indian gentleman' to look out for his fingers!"

Pearce and I laugh loudly; I notice that a few old-timers in one of the booths behind us are looking over their shoulders at us. They are not amused; too many strangers in Alliance these days.

Pearce asks, "So why did they shove him into the Legion dance?"

"Well, you see, we were all so fucked-up drunk" Pat said, "we figured if we went to the police station, we would all be arrested. So we decided to take him to the Legion. Once we pushed him into the dance without his pants and shoes, the manager would call the cops. The cops would take Yellow Thunder to jail, where he would be safe and warm.

"Prosecutor Smith had a field day with this bullshit. On cross-examination, he sarcastically said to Pat Hare, 'So you were being a

Good Samaritan? So you took his pants off to *refresh* him? Your acts were *humanitarian?* You explained to him how to open the trunk, how he could get out, *in all his naked glory*, while you drove down the street?

"'YOU GAVE HIM A BEER for his troubles?'"

I explain to Pearce that as far as I'm concerned, it was a proud moment for Alliance that while Judge Moran gave the jurors the option of finding one or both Hare brothers guilty of the lesser charge of assault and battery, after only five hours of deliberation, they found both guilty—guilty as charged—of manslaughter and false imprisonment.

AIM was so convinced that the brothers would get off, a few had conspired to attack the judge, the Hare brothers, the jurors, and the police officials. They managed to grab about a dozen seats in the courtroom for the verdict. Each protester had a predetermined target. As soon as the "not guilty" verdict was read out, Russell Means would charge the bench to beat up Judge Moran. Others would take down the Hare brothers.

"So what did the Indians do?" Pearce asks.

"Hell, they had a party outside on the courthouse lawn, banging away on their drums, singing, dancing all night long."

By now, Pearce and I are both drinking shots of Jameson and it's near closing time—Ken and Dale are anxiously waiting for us to leave so they can close up. Using our cell phones, we exchange contact info, and I tell Pearce if he's ever in California he should look me up. He's already my best buddy in Alliance.

Outside, it is getting cold; the unusual early spring weather is coming to an end. I carefully drive up Third Street, conscious that the days when Alliance cops arrested only Indians for drinking are over, and wouldn't it be ironic to find my ass in the drunk tank, perhaps the very same one where Chillo Whirlwind hung himself. I try not to drive too slowly either. Somehow *Viva VW*, like one of Vernell's Indian ponies, finds its way back to the Holiday Inn Express. I get out and look up. Orion, no longer low in the sky, is high overhead. Again I try to trace a straight line from the three stars making up the Great Hunter's belt through the Hyades star cluster and on to the Pleiades, but I cannot see either one as the lights of my hometown obliterate the brilliance of the night sky. Here, Vernell would not have been able to find his way back to the little log house in Yellow Bear Canyon. I wonder what percentage of the world's people look up at the stars but miss the vastness of the universe.

My phone buzzes. It is a message from Vernell: *U must b in Alliance.*

I return the text: *Home but lost.*

FINALE

DEATH OF A CHIEF

On the first Sunday of Advent, Chief Guy White Thunder slowly rises with the morning sun. He puts on his tattered housecoat and ambles into the kitchen next to his bedroom, not an easy trek for an eighty-nine-year-old man with aging hips, strong hands from years of hard labor, aging knees, and frail ankles. He puts a pot of water on the stove to boil, sits down at the old Formica kitchen table. Guy's long, gnarly fingers gingerly roll a cigarette from the Bugler tobacco Suzy White Thunder brought to him. He's lucky to have such a thoughtful daughter-in-law; he must remember to thank her again for being so respectful to elders. Deeply inhaling the sweet smoke, he thinks about his many accomplishments, how he stopped the uranium miners, brought solar energy to the reservation, organized the Grey Eagle Society, fought for the return of Páha Sápa, advocated speaking Lakota at all the council meetings, worked with the United Nations on international treaty rights. He remembers his travels to New York, Washington, D.C., Germany, and Switzerland. *I've fought the good fight*, he thinks, *but I'm too tired, too old to fight anymore.*

By now his fifty-seven-year-old youngest son, Anthony, is up, putting coffee into the boiling water, rolling his cigarette. He asks Guy if he wants coffee. Guy mumbles incoherently, which Anthony interprets as a yes. He pours. The two men sit smoking, sipping coffee; they look out the kitchen window through the thin, nicotine-stained curtains Mary White Thunder hung years ago, one of the few signs a woman once lived in this house. The sun is bright; perhaps the snow on the ground will melt today.

Guy stands up tall, squares his shoulders like those of a much younger man. In a clear voice, he says, "I've got to go now."

Anthony thinks little of this as his dad walks back into the bedroom. Perhaps he needs more sleep. Guy White Thunder closes the door and walks over to the old rocking chair; he sits down, closes his eyes, and takes one last breath. A few hours later, I receive an e-mail from Vernell. A one-liner, it reads: "My father passed into the spirit world today."

This message brings tears to my eyes. I tell my wife, Jackie, "I'm going back to the reservation. The Chief of the Chiefs, Vernell's dad, has died. I must go." The full draft of this book is nearly finished, but it will have to wait.

Like a president lying in state, Chief White Thunder is placed in an open casket in a community hall behind the Our Lady of Sorrows Catholic church in Kyle. Beside him is his Eagle Staff, wrapped in soft buffalo hide, eagle feathers attached to the red banner down its length, signifying his honor as an *akicita*, a leader who has earned distinction. Resting atop the curvature of the staff is his chief's war bonnet with its stunning black-tipped eagle feathers and extraordinary beadwork and quillwork. Directly behind him is a large honorary banner from the Oglala Lakota Nation. It depicts a circle of nine tepees representing the nine districts of the Pine Ridge reservation; across the top are the words GUY HOBART WHITE THUNDER, and on one side, CHIEF, COUNCIL OF ELDERS. Hung across the back wall are dozens of beautiful handmade star quilts of every color imaginable. Resting on tables in front of these quilts on equally beautiful blankets are framed photographs of Chief White Thunder on horseback, with friends and family, with tribal officials. Also sympathy cards, flowers, candles, newspaper and magazine articles, citations, more star quilts, boxes of decorated cakes like those you might find at a birthday or anniversary party. The frosting design on one cake depicts a black buffalo standing in front of two crisscrossing peace pipes, with lettering that says: "In Memory of Uncle Guy." I can't help but notice that the label on the cake box indicates that it is from the Whiteclay Grocery & Cake Shop; at least they sell something in Whiteclay besides beer. There are six of these cakes.

Chief White Thunder's body lies serenely in state for two days and two nights. Thousands come to bid him farewell, express their condolences to his family. Fellow warriors, elders, their faces wrinkled and spotted with age, missing teeth, some with tears in their eyes, many using canes and walking sticks. Grandmothers, their strides noticeably short. Some need walkers; at least one is in a wheelchair. They watch over young children who fidget and want to run about but are told to stand or sit still. Rugged middle-aged men with headscarves, hunting caps, dust-stained cowboy hats, one of which has a headband with the name *Indian Joe*. Young men with tattoos, buzz cuts, and ponytails, Tupac T-shirts, unbuttoned long-sleeved Western shirts hanging outside their pants, some wearing hoodies, basketball shoes, and work boots. Mothers with sad faces and beaded chokers, many wearing warm jackets, as the air is chilly inside this hall. They come and keep on coming. Some stay a short while, others sit for a long time in one of the folding chairs, meditating or quietly talking to one another. The tribal president drops by; many of the council members too. All acknowledge Guy's greatness, how kind he was, how they will miss him. Some stand up to say a few public words. One is the great medicine man Crow Dog; even with his walking stick, he needs help getting to the front, where he recites a prayer over White Thunder's body and then turns to address the people present. Most of his teeth are missing, yet he speaks loud and clear. His message is in Lakota, but I can tell it is well received; there are many *hau*s and much nodding of heads.

During all this time, Suzy and her few helpers are in the kitchen, chopping vegetables; stirring pots of beef broth; making white-bread-and-bologna sandwiches, endless pots of coffee, and Kool-Aid for the kids; baking cookies in the oven. Everyone hungry must be fed. The women scurry back and forth into the main hall with plates of food, stacks of paper plates, napkins, and Styrofoam cups. I ask her if she needs help. She smiles, thanks me, but says it won't be necessary. I get the message; men are out of place in Lakota kitchens. Still, I make myself useful, taking empty plates to the trash and driving Vernell on numerous errands, one to a meat locker behind someone's house where he picks up eighty pounds of frozen buffalo meat for Friday's post-funeral feast. Another to the border town of Interior, South Dakota, past Cowboy Corner gas station to the Badland's Grocery store, arguably a misnomer as they sell no fruits, vegetables, or dairy products. He's on friendly terms with the pleasant chain-smoking owner, a blond lady named Carrie; he jokes with her and buys more star quilts, as if there aren't enough already. Each quilt is four hundred dollars; he pays for them with cash from a big roll of twenties. "Have to make sure all the old people are warm this winter," he says.

Driving across the Badlands back to Kyle, Vernell tells me that Carrie and her husband are nice to him because he leases land to them for raising cattle. "I like them," he says, "so I give them favorable terms." It's none of my business, but I say to him, "What's with all those twenty-dollar bills?"

"Had to pick up some money from the bank in Martin," he replies. "They gave me nine thousand dollars in twenties."

"And what did you use for collateral?"

"Oh, nothing," Vernell says. "I just call up the bank president when I need money and go visit him in his office. I tell him a joke or two, and he gives me the money. The interest is only two percent; I always pay it back."

"That's amazing, Vernell. I wish I could do that."

"Helps to have an eight-point-five credit score," he says. "I am one of the few Indians who knows how to manage his money—all of five bucks."

On Friday morning, the day of the funeral, I leave the Prairie Ranch Resort, where I am staying, at around eight a.m. and head straight for the Community Hall. The day is bright and clear—it will probably warm up by afternoon. The service is not for a few hours, but I want to be there if Vernell or Suzy needs help. As I drive up, I see that Vernell and two of his friends already have the outdoor cooking pots going for the buffalo stew that will feed several hundred people. They are laughing; I assume Vernell has told them one of his jokes. While he is terribly sad that his father has walked on to the spirit world, he makes irreverent comments such as "I'm glad to get rid of him—he was always up to no good."

There are twenty or so cars parked out front; several young men stand around quietly talking. An older woman dressed in black, wearing sunglasses, is on the front deck smoking a cigarette; she looks drunk, but maybe she's just sad. The man I recognize as Indian Joe is forlorn; he stands with his hands in his pockets, blankly staring out onto the road. I notice the gaping holes in his red-and-gray plaid shirt, the black smudges on his old insulated winter vest, wonder if he's here because he was one of Guy White Thunder's friends or if he's just hungry for food and companionship. Excusing myself, I walk past him through the door. I have a sense that today there will be more sadness than yesterday. As the hour draws near for people to say a final goodbye to the old chief, the mood will get heavier, not just for his loss but for the passing of another generation—the links to the old ways are ever more tenuous.

Inside, Suzy is talking to her daughter, Ellen White Thunder, a stunningly attractive young woman whom I have not seen since she was a little girl. I'm thrilled that she is here along with her brother, Chris White Thunder; I'm hopeful there will be an opportunity for them to reconnect with Vernell, smooth over whatever was keeping them apart. "Ellen," I remark, "is that you?" and even while a tear rolls down her cheek, she gives me a hug, says, "It is nice to see you," and asks me about Jackie.

"Jackie," she says, "had a big influence on me. She taught me that women can be elegant, took me for lunch in downtown San Francisco, where I had my first bottle of mineral water."

"That's wonderful. She will be happy to hear that."

Chris is across the room; a gorgeous young man with movie-star looks (such genetics these White Thunders have!), he lives in a Denver suburb, works as a race-car mechanic, and is very active in the Stronghold Society, a Native American nonprofit that builds skateboard parks on the reservations, including one in Pine Ridge. Chris married a woman named Estella, who also grew up in Kyle; they have three children, a teenage girl and boy from Estella's previous marriage and a four-year-old daughter named Autumn Wind.

Ellen and Chris have strong feelings for the reservation; both are glad they grew up here. Ellen says she would move back if she could pursue her career as an architectural engineer here, but that is unlikely. Chris says he just cannot tolerate the harsh weather.

I am surprised at how quickly the hall fills up. They say Indians are always late, and it has been my experience that this is true. Powwows, parades, football games, meetings—no one bothers showing up until at least forty-five minutes past the starting time, but today is different. People arrive early. Many quietly take their seats; others hug Suzy, touch Vernell on the shoulder, file past the coffin, look at the photographs, the array of star quilts. Every hour, it seems, another donated star quilt arrives.

Rooted in tradition, Guy White Thunder never missed a powwow or Sun Dance. He spoke fluent Lakota and believed in the values of the traditional ways, and yet, like many of his generation, he also went to a Christian church. He was Catholic, as was the great chief Red Cloud. Vernell tells me his father once sought to be a deacon. This is a strange testament, I think, to the ineffectiveness of the church's efforts to stamp out native culture; people come, they kneel on the kneeling benches, recite the Lord's Prayer, take communion, confess, and then go home in time for a *yuwipi* ceremony. Over time, as has happened in many places, the Catholic Church in Kyle has slowly become an amalgamation. If it is to survive—which is by no means certain as younger people disdain the missionaries—it must become ever more Lakota and less European. Father Rick, the first to speak during Chief White Thunder's service, has gotten this message. Every time he mentions God or Jesus or the Holy Spirit, it is followed by Tunkashila, which means grandfather, great spirit. In the name of the Father, Tunkashila, and of the Son, Tunkashila, and the Holy Spirit, Tunkashila, amen. No one seems to listen to Father Rick; mercifully, he keeps his presentation short.

All during the day, before and after the service at various intervals, and at the burial that comes later, a group of Lakota singers beat the powwow drum and sing high-pitched, soul-stirring songs. There are other speakers. Ellen is the most passionate. People listen and empathize with her, and this is good, but Vernell's talk is the most riveting. When he speaks, the room is completely quiet; even the children are silent. He thanks people for coming and then speaks in Lakota for several minutes. I do not know what he says, but the sentences are short with halting pauses, emotional; they clearly resonate with his people. A flood of feelings passes through me as I realize for the first time that Vernell will likely take his father's place as chief of the Elder Council. While it is not automatic, the chances are good that he too will be the Chief of the Chiefs. Should this come to pass, Vernell will focus his immense energies on Pine Ridge, and with his law degree, his resources, and his passion for always doing the right thing, who knows what changes may occur. I can only hope to be around to see his dreams come true. Near the end of this talk, Vernell reverts to English. He says, "The one thing I will never forget about my dad is how he loved the children. He always smiled when they were around, took time to play with them and to teach them; more than others, he realized they are our future. To honor him, all you have to do is take care of and love your children."

Father Rick says a closing prayer, one Tunkashila for every Jesus.

People line up, file by the front of the hall, and look again at the photographs and other objects on the tables. At the casket, they stop to bid Chief White Thunder farewell on his journey to the Happy Hunting Grounds, and then move on to the front row of chairs to commiserate with Vernell and Suzy. Once everyone has made this journey, it is time for the feast. Within minutes, the room is reconfigured; long tables are set up, with chairs positioned around them. Another line forms, this time at a table in the back—everyone gets a bowl of buffalo stew, a plate of potato salad, and fry bread. As always, there are big pots of freshly brewed coffee, Kool-Aid for the kids. The donated cakes are for dessert. As people eat, the mood in the hall lightens, and there is much talking and laughter.

With my help and help from Chris and Ellen, Vernell and Suzy take down all the star quilts, fold them, and pile them in front of the casket, which is now closed. From outside, they bring in new pillows wrapped in plastic and dozens of plastic baskets and laundry tubs spilling over with household items—dish towels, hairbrushes, travel mugs, food storage containers, stuffed toys, children's books, crayons, and many other things.

Vernell asks for everyone's attention. It's time for the giving of the gifts. First, he calls up the singers and gives them money and small gifts, then he calls people one by one. The elder women and some elder men receive star quilts and pillows. Younger adults get baskets; some get blankets. The more needy you are, the better your gift. People are very happy. Some skip back to their chairs; some cry.

Gift giving is a Lakota tradition, not only after funerals, but also on other occasions. There is even a specific Giving of the Gifts ceremony. It is a method of redistributing wealth, an idealistic socialist concept, for sure, the Lakota way of helping their poor. And it serves another purpose. It might seem counterintuitive, but the more you give, the wealthier you are; you gain stature, people look to you for leadership. Many years ago I was privileged to be at a Giving of the Gifts ceremony in Kyle held in an open field on a sultry summer night, the only light coming from the moon and a large campfire. It began with small things, but as the evening wore on, people gave more and more extravagant gifts, even horses and cars.

Vernell gives and gives until all that remains are the toys and children's books. He calls up the children, tells them to take what they want. They don't run up and grab. They shyly approach the remaining pile, gingerly take one or two things; there are no disputes—they have been taught to share.

Done with the business of eating and giving, reluctantly they must now get on with the business of burying the old chief. It is time to take his casket outside and load it on the horse-drawn wagon for the procession to Vernell's White Thunder Ranch, where it will be transferred to one of his pickup trucks for the long ride to the Inestimable Gift Cemetery outside neighboring Allen, South Dakota, near Bear-in-the-Lodge Creek.

Realizing that once they get going, there will be no way to go around the line of horses, the wagon, and the automobiles, I leave first, drive a mile or two, and find a hill near the roadway that I can climb for taking pictures. It is an inspiring sight. Riding a fine-looking black stallion and leading an equally exquisite black-and-white riderless Indian pony, symbol of the fallen warrior, Vernell is in front, followed by the horse-drawn wagon. The pallbearers, grandchildren of Chief White Thunder, ride along with the casket; behind them are some of Vernell's Big Foot riders, all on horseback. A long line of cars follow, many with their lights on. Vehicles coming from the opposite direction pull over, wait respectfully for the assemblage to pass. A few older people get out of their cars, stand at attention; some even salute. As the riders draw near to where I stand, Chris White Thunder jumps down from the wagon and starts running. Tears flow down his cheeks as he runs the rest of the way to the ranch. Later he tells me his grandfather was a runner; that was Chris's way to honor him.

When we arrive at the cemetery, it is nearly sunset. Along with the others, I park my car on the dirt road out front. The pickup truck carrying the casket goes through an open field on the side of the graveyard to the burial site. Long shadows fall across the wrought-iron gateway entrance, but the sun still brightly lights up the overhead archway; the words INESTIMABLE GIFT shout out in bold black lettering. It is definitely Catholic; just inside the gate is a gigantic concrete Roman cross.

Because most of the people arrived before me, I suppose I should be in a hurry to catch up with them, but the haunting beauty of this strange place has me lingering. There are many wooden crosses, some new, some very old, some falling apart, and among them a few tombstones. The names are not all legible because these graves date back to 1900. The first to catch my eye, past the gate and to the right, is a wooden cross with the name CONQUERING BEAR painted on the crossbar. I wonder if the person buried here is *the* Conquering Bear, who was killed by soldiers near Fort Laramie in retaliation for the unfortunate theft of a Mormon cow, or if it is one of his descendants.

I stumble along the uneven ground. There is a whole section of Bad Wounds: Cecelia Bad Wound, Oliver, Jacob, Mary, three Roberts, Stella, Willie, but thankfully no Elgin Bad Wound. Buried near the Bad Wounds is Daniel Dull Knife, grandson of the great Cheyenne chief who fled the prison barracks at Fort Robinson. Daniel lived in Yellow Bear Canyon, was friends with Vernell's maternal grandfather, Poor Thunder. Vernell called him uncle. I see many Black Bears, Bald Eagles, Whirlwind Horses, Red Shirts, Moccasin Tops, Standing Bears, Prairie Chickens, Bear Killers, Fast Horses, Fire Thunders, Hard Hearts, Last Horses, and Slow Dogs, but only one Runs After Crow. A testament to French trappers marrying Lakota women, there are groupings of Roulards, Shangreaus, and Dubrays.

It seems like a long hike, but I finally reach the White Thunder corner of these burial grounds. Here, most of the graves are marked with wooden crosses, but the inscription on one with a tombstone catches my attention: WHITE THUNDER: SAMUEL AND SALLIE, BORN 1917, DIED 1918. Obviously twins, did they die from the Spanish flu? An accident? At the appropriate time, I must ask Vernell about them.

Chief White Thunder's casket, wrapped now in a splendid red blanket, held up by two logs, hangs above the freshly dug grave. Pallbearers and others stand around it. To one side is a tall pile of dirt. Father Rick says the Lord's Prayer, and a medicine man I don't recognize says a prayer in Lakota. George White Thunder, Vernell's older brother, his head bowed, stands back with his hands in his jean jacket, looking at the ground. I imagine he is wondering what life is going to be like without his dad. Vernell too stands back, hands clasped behind his back holding his cowboy hat, head also bowed. The pallbearers lift the casket up with ropes, remove the logs, and then slowly lower it into the ground. The singers beat their drums, sing an old warrior song. Once the casket is on the bottom and the ropes have been removed, some of the men drop bits of sage into the tomb. One picks up a shovel and motions to George, who walks over, takes a handful of the dirt, holds his hand over the grave, and lets the dirt fall on the top of his father's casket. Vernell follows, and then the others. Women and children quietly watch from the background; a little boy about five years old stands tall on the tailgate of the pickup truck that brought the casket to this place.

The drumming and singing continue. Father Rick is the last one to sprinkle dirt. People stand silently for a few minutes. Directly behind them, a full moon rises; it is the Moon of Shedding Horns, the time when male deer lose their antlers. Suddenly I realize why Vernell has so many shovels in his barn; as I see them laid out on the mound of dirt, I imagine they have been a part of many burials. First the pallbearers and then others start shoveling dirt into the grave. Chris White Thunder, wearing leather gloves, is on top of the pile; furiously he scoops shovelful after shovelful to the bottom, making it easier for everyone else. Ellen White Thunder joins in. All except Vernell and George lend a hand, even Father Rick. After the hole fills up, they keep on shoveling until there is a mound above the grave, carefully sculpted, so the top is perfectly flat. Placed on this surface are the flowers, wreaths, and potted plants from the funeral.

It is getting cold now. In small groups, by ones and twos, people start to leave. I walk back with the singers; tell them I hope they will sing at my funeral. They smile. A young boy asks me about my camera, says he wants to become a photographer. He says he is one of Vernell's nephews; he goes to the Little Wound School.

Vernell stands by himself near the edge of the cemetery. There is one more task for him before the day is done. As a sign of his grief and respect for his father and as a symbol of his willingness to sacrifice for his people, Vernell asks the medicine man to cut off his ponytail.

I stand for the longest time watching Vernell, marveling at him, his sturdiness, his big heart. Finally he slowly turns around, walks back through the melancholic cemetery, says "hau" to his nephew, stops to shake my hand and offer me one of his nonsensical good wishes:

"Before you leave, David, don't you want to know what it is all about?"

"No, but I'll guess it is about money.' "

"No Jack Daniel's for you!"

"What is it about, then?"

"It's about land. All along, you *wasicus* have only cared about land. But this time it will be different. While you are busy stealing our land and as much of our wealth as you can, we'll be building our Sinn Féin, gaining control of our reservation, and bringing back Wovoka. Imagine Indians dancing everywhere! Old blind Indians seeing again. Dead Indians come back to life, strong like young men. Imagine that whites can't hurt Indians. Aromas from cooking pots. Buffalo everywhere. Plenty of grass in the spring.

"Imagine the medicine man saying, " 'Keep on dancing.' "

ACKNOWLEDGMENTS

Thank you to: Don Nace for his encouragement and boundless enthusiasm; Rodnay Zaks for convincing me that I just had to read *Travels with Charley* by John Steinbeck; Ken Kalman for the perfect map—combining the best of the old rez with the best of the new; Eve Kramer for thinking of me as a photographer (not just a writer); Linda Daney for helping me remember the adventures we had together; Jacqueline Poitier for tirelessly reading and rereading my manuscript; and Suzy White Thunder for enriching all my experiences on the rez.

Added thanks to: My Native American daughter, Buffy Daney, and Becky Thomas at the Knight Museum and Sandhills Center, who let me spend many hours in their research room.

In memory of: Guy White Thunder, Hugh Bunnell, Aaron Bunnell, and John Essay.

Note: Most of what I know about the Hare brothers' trial came from reading my dad's Yellow Thunder articles and ninety pages of notes I found years later in a file folder as part of his extensive archive on Nebraska's Native Americans, which he willed to the Alliance Knight Museum.

NOTES

ACT ONE

1 "Memory is like . . .": Joseph M. Marshall III, *The Journey of Crazy Horse: A Lakota History* (New York: Viking Press, 2004), 57.

ALLIANCE

6 Old Man Hayes Chandler: Knight Museum Board and Partners, *Images of America: Alliance Nebraska* (Mt. Pleasant, SC: Arcadia Publishing, 2000), 55.

6 only significant minority: Mark Monroe, *An Indian in White America* (Philadelphia: Temple University Press, 1994).

7 Sioux, slang for "snake": Stacy Makes Good, "Sioux Is Not Even a Word," *Lakota Country Times*, March 12, 2009, http://www.lakotacountrytimes.com/news/2009-03-12/guest/021.html.

9 Arthur Gene Black Horse: Hugh Bunnell, "Citizens Question Indian Jail Suicides," *Kansas City Star*, September 15, 1971, 1. (Hugh Bunnell Archives, Knight Museum, Alliance, NE.)

9 "He may have hidden . . .": Ibid.

10 "The Elks Club has a tendency . . .": Ibid.

11 "Some of our jail guards . . .": Ibid.

11 "those noisy *squaw* . . .": Hugh Bunnell, "More Repercussions from Indian Jail Suicides," *Lincoln Journal Star*, October 24, 1971, 5. (Hugh Bunnell Archives, Knight Museum, Alliance, NE.)

11 "God, we're not doctors!": Hugh Bunnell, "Nebraska Police Chief on the Hot Spot," *Kansas City Times*, September 18, 1971, 7. (Hugh Bunnell Archives, Knight Museum, Alliance, NE.)

12 from 160 acres: Kathy Weiser-Alexander, "American History: The Homestead Act—Creating Prosperity in America," Legends of America, http://www.legendsofamerica.com/ah-homestead.html.

13 Nebraska Sandhills, twenty thousand: "About the Sandhills," West Central Research and Extension Center, http://extension.unl.edu/statewide/westcentral/gudmundsen/sandhills/.

13 Warren Buffett purchased: W. Hanson, "Buffett Buying Burlington Northern Railroad," NBCNews.com, November 3, 2009.

15 "America's Top Roadside Attractions": TripAdvisor, March 3, 2015, http://www.tripadvisor.com/ShowUserReviews-g29693-d209202-r257457838-Carhenge-Alliance_Nebraska.html.

HAY SPRINGS

18 Great Sioux Reservation: "Establishment of the Great Sioux Reservation," the Web site of North Dakota State Government, http://www.ndstudies.org/resources/IndianStudies/standingrock/historical_gs_reservation.html.

18 "the country north of . . .": Transcript of Treaty of Fort Laramie (1868), Our Documents, http://www.ourdocuments.gov/doc.php?flash=true&doc=42&page=transcript.

18 "scientific mapping expedition": Brian Dippie, Beyond Lewis and Clark: A Symposium on Army Exploration and National Expansion, Washing-

ton State History Museum, Tacoma, WA, September 27, 2004, http://www.friendslittlebighorn.com/Georgecuster.htm.

19 GOLD!: T. J. Stiles, *Custer's Trials: A Life on the Frontier of a New America* (New York: Alfred A. Knopf, 2015).

20 Elder warriors from the Lakota: Helen Winter Stauffer, *Mari Sandoz: Story Catcher of the Plains* (Lincoln: University of Nebraska Press, 1982), 25.

21 three-thousand-mile trip: Ibid.

21 Crazy Horse "surrendered": Thomas Powers, *The Killing of Crazy Horse* (New York: Alfred A. Knopf, 2010).

22 damn thing about: George E. Hyde, *Spotted Tail's Folk: A History of the Brulé Sioux* (Norman: University of Oklahoma Press, 1961).

22 American Indian Religious Freedom: L. Irvin, "Freedom, Law, and Prophecy: A Brief History of Native American Religious Resistance," *American Indian Quarterly* 21, no. 1 (1977): 35–55.

23 "Light-in-the-Lodge": Hyde, *Spotted Tail's Folk*, 333–34.

23 hated Spotted Tail: Ibid., 313–15.

23 night of August 5, 1881: Ibid., 332.

24 case against Black Crow: Sidney L. Harring, *Crow Dog's Case: American Indian Sovereignty, Tribal Law and United States Law in the Nineteenth Century* (Cambridge, MA: Cambridge University Press, 1994).

RUSHVILLE

28 "The whole country . . .": *American Civil War: The Shenandoah Valley*, HistoryOfWar.org, http://www.historyofwar.org/articles/wars_american_civil_war04_shenandoah.html#intro.

28 "Find and destroy . . .": Stiles, *Custer's Trials.*

28 "me Tosawi . . . were dead": Dee Brown, *Bury My Heart at Wounded Knee: An Indian History of the American West* (New York: Holt, Rinehart & Winston, 1970).

28 rich ranchers, the Modisett: Katie Gardner, "Extra Innings: The Story of the Modisett Ball Park," Donning Company Publishers, January 27, 2015,

http://www.donning.com/2015/01/27/extra-innings-story-modisett-ball-park/.

30 porcupine quillwork: Royal B. Hassbrick, *The Sioux: Life and Customs of a Warrior Society* (Norman: University of Oklahoma Press, 1964), 223.

31 Edward Curtis's: Gilbert King, "Edward Curtis' Epic Project to Photograph Native Americans," Smithsonian.com, March 21, 2012, http://www.smithsonianmag.com/history/edward-curtis-epic-project-to-photograph-native-americans-162523282/?no-ist.

32 Sitting Bull danced: Ernie LaPointe, *Sitting Bull: His Life and Legacy* (Layton, UT: Gibbs Smith, 2009).

WHITECLAY

37 four liquor stores that sell: Paul Hammel, "Nebraska Governor, Attorney General Turn Their Attention to Whiteclay," *Omaha World-Herald*, October 14, 2015.

37 Whiteclay on-premises: David Kelly, "In Nebraska, Ministry Reaches Out to Lakota on an Alcohol-Ravaged Skid Row," *Los Angeles Times*, September 13, 2015.

38 Lakota Women's Day of Peace: Vincent Schilling, "Whiteclay Fallout: Women's Day of Peace March Ends with Arrests and Youth Being Maced," Indian Country Today Media Network, August 29, 2012.

38 calling the women "white bitches": Debra White Plume, "Solidarity Gathering, Horse Trailers, and the Lakota Women's Day of Peace," *Censored News*, August 29, 2012.

38 pulling a horse trailer: Plume, "Solidarity Gathering."

39 stone monument on the edge: Alan Hafer, *Descendants of Wounded Knee: The Ultimate Sacrifice on the Pine Ridge Reservation* (Boulder: Johnson Books, 2015).

40 Toad Frohman, a solid: "Leo J. 'Toad' Frohman," Scottsbluff StarHerald.com, July 5, 2001.

42 Roosevelt rescinded: *The Battle for Whiteclay* (documentary film), http://battleforwhiteclay.org/?page_id=140.

PINE RIDGE

43 de facto capital: Matthew Williams, "Urban Jungle on the Reservation," *Time*, http://content.time.com/time/photogallery/0,29307,2048598_2235609,00.html.

49 original Big Bat could speak: Hafer, *Descendants of Wounded Knee*, 94–95.

51 In 1964, when he: Roger Robinson, "Billy Mills' Amazing Olympic 10K Win Was 50 Years Ago Today," *Runner's World*, October 14, 2014.

52 "I'm going to burn . . . change the name": Tim Giago, "Billy Mills, the Pride of the Lakota Nation," *The Huffington Post*, accessed November 11, 2001. http://www.huffingtonpost.com/tim-giago/billy-mills-the-pride-of_b_116612.html

55 tribe tried to shut: Daniel Simmons-Richie, "Anger at Tribe's Decision to Close Pine Ridge's Sole Supermarket," *Rapid City Journal*, May 26, 2013.

BIG FOOT TRAIL

95 the great Tatanka Iyotake: LaPointe, *Sitting Bull*.

95 huge nonstop ghost dance: Hafer, *Descendants of Wounded Knee*.

96 "Lock the savages up . . . necessary": Ojibwa, "Before Wounded Knee," Native American Netroots, October 13, 2011.

97 "What is your name . . . shook hands": Richard E. Jensen, ed., *Voices of the American West, Volume 1: The Indian Interviews of Eli S. Ricker, 1903–1919* (Lincoln, University of Nebraska Press, 2005).

97 Forsyth told Whitside: Brown, *Bury My Heart*, 441-42.

98 James Asay: James E. Titsworth, *Wounded Knee: A Lakota Journey from Passive Resistance to a Mass Grave and the Seventh Cavalry's Failure of Command* (master's thesis, University of Nebraska at Kearney, 2008). Google Books: https://books.google.com/books?id=N1h-RNojOoMC&pg=PA83&lpg=PA83&dq=liquor+dealer+at+Wounded+Knee+James+Asay&source=bl&ots=eI-f2uZajv&sig=zaM6WZgch1prtlUa9jiLrwR3Lcw&hl=en&sa=X&ved=0ahUKEwjvpJ_C5fDLAhW1nYMKHTEKAoMQ6AEIHDAA#v=onepage&q=liquor%20dealer%20at%20Wounded%20Knee%20James%20Asay&f=false.

98 One survivor: Charles A. Eastman, *The Soul of the Indian: An Interpretation* (New York: Houghton Mifflin, 1911).

99 As prophesied by: John G. Neihardt, *Black Elk Speaks* (New York: William Morrow, 1932). Black Elk's Vision online: http://www.welcomehome.org/rainbow/prophecy/BlackElk.html.

99 Memorial Ride, seven: Roseanna Renaud, "Big Foot Memorial Ride: 23 Years," *Lakota Country Times*, January 5, 2010.

102 his final interview: SacredScienceDoc, "Russell Means Final Interview—The Sacred Feminine and Gender Roles," https://www.youtube.com/watch?v=eFt6XRyQhD8.

KYLE

108 pole of inaccessibility: Jerry Penry, "Pole of Inaccessibility for North America," 2014, http://www.penryfamily.com/surveying/poleofinaccessibility.html.

ACT THREE

123 "The Great Spirit . . .": Peter Matthiessen, *In the Spirit of Crazy Horse* (New York: Viking Press, 1983), 137.

WHITE THUNDER RANCH

133 move the sacred arrows: Ojibwa, "Cheyenne Medicine Bundles," Native American Netroots, March 6, 2011.

134 medicine man named Bull: Ibid.

134 good day to die: Ibid.

137 Red Cloud was fond: Bon Drury and Tom Clavin, *The Heart of Everything That Is: The Untold Story of Red Cloud, an American Legend* (New York: Simon & Schuster, 2013).

140 "We always had gay . . .": Beatrice Medicine, "Directions in Gender Research in American Indian Societies: Two Spirits and Other Categories," *Online Readers in Psychology and Culture* (2002): Unit 3, Article 2.

BOMBING RANGE

141 Karlene Hunter: For more on Karlene Hunter and Tanka Bars, see http://www.tankabar.com/cgi-bin/nanf/public/main.cvw?sessionid=8288ba4e5864894bd6b43b87615bc0be0f981137e46c

146 they had thirty days: "World War II Comes to the Badlands," the Web site of the National Park Service, http://www.nps.gov/badl/planyourvisit/upload/Badlands-Gunnery-Range-Bulletin.pdf.

145 250 car bodies: Ibid.

YELLOW BEAR CANYON

159 George Poor Thunder lived: Vernell White Thunder, author interviews, October 12–14, 2014.

160 "Grandfather would tell him . . . two hundred and fifty": Ibid.

160 Poor Thunder's arrival: Ibid.

160 "If we lose the . . .": Ibid.

RETURN OF THE BUFFALO

172 most numerous: Shepard Krech III, "Buffalo Tales: The Near-Extermination of the American Bison," National Humanities Center, July 2001, http://nationalhumanitiescenter.org/tserve/nattrans/ntecoindian/essays/buffalod.htm.

172 "I am safe . . . ride through it": Jed Portman, "5 Things You Need to Know About the American Bison," the Web site of PBS, May 3, 2011, http://www.pbs.org/wnet/need-to-know/five-things/the-great-american-bison/8950/.

173 "Buffalo hunters are doing . . .": William T. Hornaday, *The Extermination of the American Bison* (Washington, D.C.: Government Printing Office, 1889), 225.

173 Millions of buffalo robes: Ibid.

174 grand buffalo hunt: Douglas D. Scott, Peter Bleed, and Stephen Damm, *Custer, Cody, and Grand Duke Alexis: Historical Archaeology of the Royal Buffalo Hunt* (Norman: University of Oklahoma Press, 2013), 315.

175 touring train pulled: "Old West Legends: The Plight of the Buffalo," Legends of America, excerpted from *The Old Santa Fe Trail* by Colonel Henry Inman (New York: Macmillan, 1897), http://www.legendsofamerica.com/we-buffaloplight.html

175 most famous match: Scott, Bleed, and Damm, *Custer, Cody*, 320.

176 "For the sake of . . .": David D. Smits, "The Frontier Army and the Destruction of the Buffalo: 1865–1883," *Western Historical Quarterly* 25, no. 3 (Autumn 1994), 313–38.

177 Yellowstone herd: Laura Zuckerman, "Conservationists Demand Halt to Killing of Yellowstone Bison," Reuters, September 15, 2014.

180 "dehumanizing, derogatory . . .": Robert Lipsyte, "Baseball; How Can Jane Fonda Be a Part of the Chop?," *The New York Times*, October 18, 1991.

180 "pure ignorance . . .": Ibid.

180 animal rights protesters: A. Wilson, "Protesters Down on Fonda," *La Crosse Tribune*, July 31, 1993.

HORSE PASTURE

190 Spaniards brought horses: Dave Philipps, "As Wild Horses Overrun the West, Ranchers Fear Land Will Be Gobbled Up," *The New York Times*, September 30, 2014.

191 run wild on: Ibid.

191 traded horses: "Lakota Horses," the Web site of North Dakota State Government, http://ndstudies.gov/gr8/content/unit-ii-time-transformation-1201-1860/lesson-2-making-living/topic-2-horses-return/section-2-lakota-horses.

191 Lakota immediately saw: Elliott West, "The Impact of Horse Culture," *Journal of the Gilder Lehrman Institute*, https://www.gilderlehrman.org/history-by-era/early-settlements/essays/impact-horse-culture.

193 Mackenzie ordered his men: Andy Wilkinson: "Palo Duro Canyon Tragedy," the Web site of Nebraska's PBS and NPR stations, http://netnebraska.org/basic-page/television/wild-horses-palo-duro-canyon-tragedy.

GORDON

197 Raymond Yellow Thunder took: Stew Magnuson, *The Death of Raymond Yellow Thunder: And Other True Stories from the Nebraska–Pine Ridge Border Towns* (Lubbock: Texas Tech University Press, 2008).

198 "If Raymond had . . .": Ibid.

200 Trips to the: Grant K. Anderson, "The Black Hills Exclusion Policy," *Nebraska History* 58 (1977): 1–24.

201 Army had given up trying: Ibid.

202 coyote hunting that day: Hugh Bunnell, "The Yellow Thunder File." (Hugh Bunnell Archives, Knight Museum, Alliance, NE.)

204 still driving around: Ibid.

205 "I got him good!": Ibid.

206 "Come on, Butch . . .": Ibid.

206 "Ain't no way that . . .": Ibid.

207 "You always have been. . . . I don't mind": Ibid.

207 "Hang on, Chief . . .": Ibid.

208 "What the fuck . . . let me go": Ibid.

210 "Jesus Christ, Les . . .": Ibid.

211 last person to see: Magnuson, *Death of Raymond Yellow Thunder.*

213 Arlene hopped in: Ibid.

213 recognized him as Severt: David Melmer, "Wounded Knee '73 Revisited," Indian Country Today Media Network, March 23, 2005.

215 AIM wanted food: Bunnell, "The Yellow Thunder File."

216 "We came today . . .": Magnuson, *Death of Raymond Yellow Thunder.*

AMONG THE DOG EATERS

218 he created a Spade Ranch company town . . . : Ruth VanAckeren and Robert M. Howard, *Lawrence Bixby: Preserver of the Old Spade Ranch* (Lincoln: Nebraska State Historical Society, 1995).

219 "Life was opulent for Richards . . .": Ibid.

222 he-said: Ibid.

222 white boy called him: Ibid.

223 go-to Indian: Ibid.

224 devoured the big platter: Ibid.

224 The city denied: Hugh Bunnell, "City Turns Down AIM Request for Free Food," *Alliance Times-Herald*, May 24, 1972.

225 They began drumming: Bunnell, "The Yellow Thunder File."

227 "Opportunity Room" at Grandview: Monroe, *Indian in White America.*

227 "the most racist town": Hugh Bunnell, "AIM to Convene an 'Indian Grand Jury,'" *Alliance Times-Herald*, May 25, 1972.

227 "Racists don't convict . . .": Ibid.

227 A crowd of: Hugh Bunnell, "Bellecourt Addresses Alliance High School Grads," *Alliance Times-Herald*, May 26, 1972.

229 "You have prospered . . . all we ask": Ibid.

231 "Dennis, cut the . . .": Bunnell, "The Yellow Thunder File."

231 "Bullshit . . . right now": Ibid.

233 "Eyewitnesses will provide . . .": Ibid.

234 Coors brewery right here: Knight Museum, Alliance, NE.

236 "This 'Indian Gentleman' . . .": Bunnell, "The Yellow Thunder File."

236 " 'So you were being . . .' ": Ibid.

237 Each protester had: Ibid.

BIBLIOGRAPHY

Ambrose, Stephen E. *Crazy Horse and Custer: The Parallel Lives of Two American Warriors*. New York: Open Road Media, 2014.

Brown, Curt. *In the Footsteps of Little Crow: 150 Years After the U.S.–Dakota War of 1862*. Minneapolis: Star Tribune, 2012.

Brown, Dee. *Bury My Heart at Wounded Knee: An Indian History of the American West*. New York: Holt, Rinehart & Winston, 1970.

Buck, Rinker. *The Oregon Trail: A New American Journey*. New York: Simon & Schuster, 2015.

Bucko, Raymond A. *The Lakota Ritual of the Sweat Lodge: History and Contemporary Practice*. Lincoln: University of Nebraska Press, 1998.

Drury, Bob, and Tom Clavin. *The Heart of Everything That Is: The Untold Story of Red Cloud, an American Legend*. New York: Simon & Schuster, 2013.

Dunbar-Ortiz, Roxanne. *An Indigenous Peoples' History of the United States*. Boston: Beacon Press, 2015.

Eastman, Charles A. *The Soul of the Indian: An Interpretation*. New York: Houghton Mifflin, 1911.

Flood, Renée Sansom. *Lost Bird of Wounded Knee: Spirit of the Lakota*. New York: Scribner, 1995.

Frazier, Ian. *Great Plains*. New York: Farrar, Straus and Giroux, 1989.

———. *On the Rez*. New York: Farrar, Straus and Giroux, 2000.

Hafer, Alan and Sandy Sauser. *Descendants of Wounded Knee: The Ultimate Sacrifice on the Pine Ridge Reservation*. Boulder: Johnson Books, 2015.

Hassrick, Royal B. *The Sioux: Life and Customs of a Warrior Society*. Norman: University of Oklahoma Press, 1964.

Hornaday, William T. *The Extermination of the American Bison*. Washington, D.C.: Government Printing Office, 1889.

Hyde, George E. *Spotted Tail's Folk: A History of the Brulé Sioux*. Norman: University of Oklahoma Press, 1961.

Glover, Vic. *Keeping Heart on Pine Ridge: Family Ties, Warrior Culture, Commodity Foods, Rez Dogs and the Sacred*. Summertown, TN: Native Voices, 2004.

LaPointe, Ernie. *Sitting Bull: His Life and Legacy*. Layton, UT: Gibbs Smith, 2009.

Lincoln, Kenneth and Al Logan Slagle. *The Good Red Road: Passages into Native America*. New York: HarperCollins, 1987.

Lone Hill, Dana. *Pointing with Lips: A Week in the Life of a Rez Chick*. Greenfield, MA: Blue Hand Books, 2014.

Maddra, Sam A. *Hostiles? The Lakota Ghost Dance and Buffalo Bill's Wild West*. Norman: University of Oklahoma Press, 2006.

Magnuson, Stew. *The Death of Raymond Yellow Thunder: And Other True Stories from the Nebraska–Pine Ridge Border Towns*. Lubbock: Texas Tech University Press, 2008.

———. *Wounded Knee 1973: Still Bleeding: The American Indian Movement, the FBI, and Their Fight to Bury the Sins of the Past*. Avalon: Now and Then, 2013.

Mails, Thomas E. *Fools Crow: Wisdom and Power*. San Francisco: Council Oak Books, 1991.

Marshall III, Joseph M. *The Journey of Crazy Horse: A Lakota History*. New York: Viking Press, 2004.

———. *The Day the World Ended at Little Bighorn: A Lakota History*. New York: Penguin Books, 2008.

Matthiessen, Peter. *In the Spirit of Crazy Horse*. New York: Viking Press, 1983.

Monroe, Mark. *An Indian in White America*. Philadelphia: Temple University Press, 1994.

Neihardt, John G. *Black Elk Speaks*. New York: William Morrow, 1932.

Nerburn, Kent, ed. *The Wisdom of the Native Americans*. Novato, CA: New World Library, 1999.

Powers, Thomas. *The Killing of Crazy Horse*. New York: Alfred A. Knopf, 2010.

Rinella, Steven. *American Buffalo: In Search of a Lost Icon*. New York: Spiegel & Grau, 2008.

Ross, Gyasi. *Don't Know Much About Indians (but i wrote a book about us anyways)*. Suquamish, WA: Cut Bank Creek Press, 2011.

Ruby, Robert H. *The Oglala Sioux: Warriors in Transition*. New York: Vantage Press, 1955.

Sandoz, Mari. *Old Jules*. Boston: Little, Brown, 1935.

———. *Crazy Horse: The Strange Man of the Oglalas*. New York: Alfred A. Knopf, 1942.

———. *Cheyenne Autumn*. New York: McGraw Hill, 1953.

Scott, Douglas D., Peter Bleed, and Stephen Damm. *Custer, Cody, and Grand Duke Alexis: Historical Archaeology of the Royal Buffalo Hunt*. Norman: University of Oklahoma Press, 2013.

Starita, Joe. *The Dull Knifes of Pine Ridge: A Lakota Odyssey*. Norman, OK: Bison Books, 2002.

Stiles, T. J. *Custer's Trials: A Life on the Frontier of a New America*. New York: Alfred A. Knopf, 2015.

Treuer, David. *Rez Life: An Indian's Journey Through Reservation Life*. New York: Atlantic Monthly Press, 2012.

VanAckeren, Ruth, and Robert M. Howard. *Lawrence Bixby: Preserver of the Old Spade Ranch*. Lincoln: Nebraska State Historical Society, 1995.

Walker, James R. *Lakota Belief and Ritual*. Lincoln: University of Nebraska Press, 1980.

———. *The Sun Dance and Other Ceremonies of the Oglala Division of the Teton Dakota*. New York: The American Museum of Natural History, 1917.